DATE DUE

OC 18 '92			
AP 2 '96			

DEMCO 38-296

STACKED DECK

In the series

America in Transition: Radical Perspectives

edited by Gary L. Francione

R

STACKED DECK

A STORY OF

SELFISHNESS

IN AMERICA

Lawrence E. Mitchell

 Temple University Press
PHILADELPHIA

Temple University Press, Philadelphia 19122
Copyright © 1998 by Temple University

ation Data

America /

p.   cm. — (America in transition: radical perspectives)
Includes bibliographical references and index.
ISBN 1-56639-592-5 (cl. : alk. paper)
1. Fairness.   2. Justice.   3. Law—Philosophy.   I. Title.
II. Series: America in transition (Philadelphia, Pa.)
K247.M58   1998
340'. 1—dc21   97-44347
                                                                CIP

⊗ The paper used in this publication meets the requirements of
American National Standards for Information Sciences—Permanence
of Paper for Printed Library Materials, ANSI Z39.48–1984.

For Alex

"No one acts unless he is aware of the need to help."

Eva Fogelman, *Conscience and Courage*

Contents

Acknowledgments

As with so much else in my life, this book is immeasurably better than it would have been without the help of so many friends and colleagues (none of whom are to be blamed for my mistakes). Two very special people have made this project possible. Without the guidance of my mentor, Bob Tuttle, who forced me to ever-deeper levels of thought and understanding and would not let me rest content with any portion of the manuscript, I simply could not have written this book, and without the friendship, support, and assistance of Theresa Gabaldon, I would never have seen it through to publication. Nor would the book have seen the light of day without my editors, Doris Braendel and Gary Francione, who saw in my original turgid academic prose the possibility for an argument that might have contemporary importance. David Luban, Rick Kahlenberg, and Chip Lupu rose well beyond the call of friendship and duty and carefully and critically read versions of the manuscript, forcing me to sharpen my arguments and confront their relevance. Andrew Altman, Marina Angel, Bill Bratton, Brad Clark, Greg Mark, Susan Mitchell, Jeff Rosen, David Skover, Elizabeth Wolgast, my parents, and participants in works-in-progress colloquia at Washington & Lee University Law School and Rutgers (Newark) Law School read all or parts of the manuscript at various stages and gave me very helpful comments. Jennie Meade and the staff of the Jacob Burns Law Library went well beyond their normal duties to help me with the research. I am also grateful for the research help of several student assistants over the years, including Corby Sturges, Sherri Perlstein, Joshua Henderson, David Levy, John Pollack, and Ian Asch. Dean Jack Friedenthal and The George Washington University Law School provided financial support. Finally, this book is dedicated to my son, Alex, who is why it all matters.

Series Editor's Foreword

This morning, I was watching a news program on one of the many, many channels that I receive courtesy of my satellite dish. During one half-hour period, the same commercial aired three times. It was plugging a financial newspaper aimed, it said, at those "who choose to succeed."

"Choose to succeed"?

Who chooses *not* to succeed?

This simple question may seem simply apparent and wholly rhetorical. Unfortunately, a defining characteristic of modern American life is the myth of autonomy and self-reliance: that people somehow "choose" much of their lot in life in much the same way that one chooses one's clothes in the morning. There are options available and one simply chooses. The people who do not succeed in life have simply chosen badly. The ones who do succeed in life have simply chosen well.

There is no sense that those who fail were somehow made to fail by the system, or that their failure was in any way facilitated by the system. On the contrary, the mythology of autonomy and self-reliance stresses that the "system"—our social institutions—provide the same *opportunity* to all and that discrimination and inequality have largely been eradicated.

Similarly, there is no sense that those who succeed have *their* choices subsidized by the very institutions that supposedly provide equal opportunity to all and that supposedly foster autonomy and self-reliance. On the contrary, the prevailing mythology stresses the image of the successful as those who have achieved success because of *their* initiative and *their* "merit." The successful rarely think of themselves as recipients of subsidies—as beneficiaries of resource distributions that have been made to them not because of their "merit," but because they have had the good luck—and nothing more—to be born with certain characteristics, usually whiteness, maleness, and middle-classness. These resources are favored in so many ways that only a true reactionary would even question the matter.

But these are reactionary times. Witness the current controversy over so-called welfare "reform." Let us put aside the fact that welfare entitlements account for a minuscule fraction of a budget dominated by expenditures designed to facilitate the military-industrial complex. Focus instead on the fact that Republicans and Democrats alike have actually convinced themselves that those who receive public assistance somehow "choose" to be on welfare rather than to have the self-respect and material benefits that come from achieving a greater level of success. There is no sense that the poor remain poor because our social institutions are based on a notion of equal participation that really only allows those with preexisting class or race or sex advantages in the front door. On the contrary, the advocates of welfare "reform" claim that, since our social institutions allow equal participation by all, there is no reason for welfare.

Moreover—and perhaps more astonishingly—the advocates of welfare seem not to recognize that their own lifestyles are subsidized—and heavily so—by public expenditures. We claim to abhor public "handouts" as we buy and sell shares of stock, content in our knowledge that the Securities and Exchange Commission, a publicly funded body, protects us from certain financial vulnerability that would make the risk of such conduct considerably higher. Criminal laws—passed by legislators, enforced by police and prosecutors, and interpreted and applied by judges—all of whom are publicly funded—protect our property from theft by the poor and reduce our vulnerability—all through what can only be described as the same sort of public subsidy that we claim to abhor.

It is precisely that tension between the myth of autonomy and individualism, and the reality of vulnerability, that forms the central focus of Lawrence Mitchell's fascinating book, *Stacked Deck*. Mitchell, a law

professor who teaches corporate law and legal philosophy, argues that
it is our concern for vulnerability—our own and others—that leads us
to be concerned about notions of fairness in the first place. The model
of fairness of our liberal democracy is one that rests on a notion of autonomy and self-reliance and, as such, our social institutions deny in
important ways the very concern about vulnerability that Mitchell argues animated them in the first instance.

On one hand, we fail to recognize the extent to which many of the
vulnerabilities that affect the middle or upper classes are addressed by
our institutions, the extent to which our own lives are subsidized by the
government, and the fact that many of us are just plain lucky. On the
other hand, our notion of fairness based (mistakenly) on autonomy and
self-reliance in a context of formal equality has the effect of ensuring
that the vulnerabilities of the poor are not addressed. Indeed, those vulnerabilities are treated as somehow different from the vulnerabilities
of the rest of us—which most of us are conveniently shielded from in
the first place by a mythology that tells us that we "deserve" to be
successful.

Mitchell argues that if our mythology of self-determination and self-
reliance is to have any meaning beyond its usefulness in deluding ourselves into believing we are somehow "better" than others, it is necessary that we recognize that we are all vulnerable in many similar ways
to many common hazards. We must reshape our social institutions to
ensure that all people are provided with the necessary tools to make
meaningful choices or else the liberal ideology of autonomy and self-
determination *cannot* be realized. In other words, if we are going to believe that people "choose to succeed," we need to have a society in
which we can coherently talk about people having the *ability* to choose.

Stacked Deck is a powerful book that challenges us to examine what
we think about justice and fairness, as well as how we *feel* about them.
Mitchell maintains that we not only long for community with others
but that, as an emotional matter, most of us genuinely do care about
others and about being fair to others. He provides a fascinating—but
devastating—examination of the dissonance between what we say about
fairness, our motivation to help those in distress, and how our resulting
mythology of self-reliance and autonomy ends up treating people in
very unequal and unfair ways. Mitchell develops a prescription for
merging our awareness and concern for vulnerability—that of our-

selves *and* others—with our formal doctrines of fairness in order to obtain a better fit between our motivation to achieve fairness in the first place and our social institutions that presently guarantee only that inequality and unfairness will continue.

Gary L. Francione

Introduction

The other night I told my ten-year-old son, who is an erratic sleeper, that his bedtime would be fixed at 9:30. His response: "That's not fair." So I convened a meeting. My wife, my son, and I sat down to discuss the issue. He argued for a later bedtime, and we listened patiently as he presented his case. We then took a vote. Surprise! The vote was two to one in favor of 9:30, with Alex dissenting.

If we leave aside questions about parental responsibility, juvenile judgment, and the like, we all probably would agree that it was indeed unfair for me to dictate Alex's bedtime. After all, I was imposing my will upon my son, leaving him no opportunity to participate in determining his quality of life and no chance to influence my judgment.

But did the family vote transform the decision from a product of tyranny into one that was fair? Certainly each of the three of us had an equal vote. But the fate of Alex's night-life was in no greater doubt than it had been before. My wife had precisely the same interests as I—having a well-rested child and some time for ourselves. After sixteen years of marriage, and some past discussions about the issue, I had little doubt as to where she stood. And given both our common interests and our desire for marital harmony, the odds that I would be defeated were practically nonexistent.

We had a vote. Each of us had the opportunity to be heard. Nobody could dispute the formal fairness of the process. But it is hard to say that the outcome was fair. The deck, as it were, was stacked. Formal fairness was not enough to offer any meaningful protection for Alex's interests. Nor is it enough in America.

This is a book about fairness. Fairness is an issue that pervades almost every aspect of our lives together. It dominates debates over such major policy issues as welfare reform, income taxation, and health care. It is the core concern in such constitutional issues as the structure of congressional voting districts and a criminal defendant's right to a fair trial. In every workplace, fairness is the touchstone by which we measure our compensation and the demands our employers make upon us. Fairness is the measure of integrity of our commercial and financial marketplaces. In every home, fairness is used to allocate household chores, family activities, and even television time.

You would think that with all this concern about fairness we would have a pretty good idea of what it means. But we don't. My own interest in the subject comes out of my study of corporate law, where fairness provides a legal test to judge corporate directors' conduct. What I found was that, although it is often applied, the concept of fairness is rather ambiguous and courts have a very hard time defining the term even as they use it. This led me to look at the way fairness is used as a measuring device throughout the law, and then to philosophical, sociological, and economic views of the subject.

What I have discovered is that we have, surprisingly, no common way of talking about fairness. Some economists define fairness as reciprocity—that is, exchanging things of like value—and some define it as economic efficiency. Some political theorists understand fairness to mean equality, although they disagree about what equality means. It can, for example, mean equality of opportunity or equality of result, equality of resources, or equality of well-being. Some lawyers and philosophers see fairness simply as justice, by which they also mean different things, such as treating each individual as a person, whatever that means, or giving to each his due, whatever *that* means.

Mostly, though, we don't try to define fairness. Even those thinkers who should be professionally concerned with figuring out what fairness means, such as philosophers, political scientists, lawyers, and economists, have spent astonishingly little time considering this question. They either deal with questions of justice, equality, and efficiency as synonyms for fairness or, like the rest of us, they treat fairness as something intuitive. Fairness either *is*, or it is *not*.

We don't have a language of fairness—or rather we have lots of different languages about fairness. But I am going to present two arguments: first, that we have a dominant political, legal, and economic *model* of fairness that we find in a close examination of our social institutions, and second, that we have very powerful *intuitions* about fairness. The problem is that our institutions and our intuitions are built on two different premises. Our institutions are built on an assumption of individual autonomy derived from liberal political theory. This assumption leads us to construct an abstract notion of fairness as one of free-contracting and equal process that effectively formalizes fairness, much as our family vote did. These formal tools have overpowered our basic intuitions about fairness and, in the process, have created substantial *unfairness* within our society. They have stacked the deck.

Our intuitions about fairness—the *source* of fairness if you will—contrast sharply with the American notion of individual autonomy, which is the idea that each of us is independent, self-reliant, and happy to be let alone. They lie instead in our instinctive understanding that, at some level, each of us is essentially vulnerable, not self-sufficient. On one level we are vulnerable to fate, to the forces of luck and nature—as Florida hurricanes, California brushfires, and catastrophic illnesses regularly demonstrate. But we are also vulnerable to each other.

We do not need to imagine Thomas Hobbes's famous depiction of the state of nature, of the war of all against all, to know that at our jobs, in our consumer consumption, in our financial dealings, and in our political lives we rest on our successes at our peril. Layoffs of blue-collar workers to finance takeovers in the 1980s and the "downsizing" of white-collar workers to increase corporate profits in the 1990s are simply large-scale examples of the rickety bridge between comfort and financial disaster—and all that goes with it. The suffering caused by the failure of such products as the Dalkon shield, or such inherently unsafe products as asbestos, merely underscores the risk we take each time we consume a burger at McDonald's. The massive bank failures of the 1980s, and the dramatic financial frauds like those that helped to cause the collapse of the American stock markets in 1929, highlight the degree of trust we place in the fairness of our financial institutions and the terrible consequences that result when that trust is misplaced. And events such as Watergate, the Iran-Contra scandal, and more recent reports of campaign finance abuse remind us of the ways in which misuses of political power can threaten our common welfare.

On one level, our perception that we ourselves are vulnerable leads us to be concerned with fairness to ourselves. We want to be able to rely upon a measure of job security, including a fair day's pay for a fair day's work. We want to purchase and consume the products of industry confidently, to invest our money and sleep peacefully, and to have faith that the collective power we place in our politicians will be used to help us. But this is merely self-interest. We want to be sure that we get what, in fairness, is due to us.

What gives fairness its essentially moral character is that most of us also worry about our fairness to others. Part of our concern with this fairness to others may originate in self-interest, because we recognize that if we want others to be fair to us we must also be fair to them—hence the idea of fairness as reciprocity. But there is more. As Adam Smith so powerfully argued, our moral sense (which I argue displays itself in fairness) comes from the fact that we see ourselves in others and others in ourselves. We recognize in others the same hopes and joys, the same suffering and pain, that we feel in ourselves. We recognize others as people like ourselves. And this leads us to be concerned with their welfare as well.

Fairness derived from these insights requires us to recognize others' vulnerabilities and to refrain from taking advantage of them. In this sense, I suppose, our family vote was perfectly fair. It transformed a situation in which I was using my greater power to cabin Alex's autonomy into one that appeared to neutralize my advantage.

But surely fairness requires more than this. In a society like ours, based on the rough and tumble of the marketplace and competition for political power, it means ensuring that everybody has not only the chance *but the meaningful ability* to make real choices about how best to live their lives. As with our family vote, American society has done much to achieve this goal by providing formal equality of opportunity, that is, equal access to our institutions and equal process in being considered for the benefits and burdens of society. But if we understand the root of fairness in vulnerability, we will realize that it is not enough that we provide these forms of structural equality. Many vulnerabilities make it difficult, if not impossible, for people to take advantage of these processes. This realization provides the logic, for example, that underlies a law like the Americans with Disabilities Act, which requires a variety of institutions to provide extra resources to enable those who cannot participate to do so. But we need to understand that vulnerability is much more pervasive than one would think merely by looking to physical handicaps. To achieve true fairness, we must, to the extent reasonably practicable, identify and ameliorate those vulnerabilities that effectively preclude so many Americans from participating in our social and political institutions.

As I hope to demonstrate, using examples drawn from history, politics, law, and culture, we have—in our hyper-rational society—lost sight of the relationship between vulnerability and fairness. We have instead replaced it with the formal and structural fairness manifested in ideas of justice, equality, and efficiency. We have lost sight of the extent to which our institutions, created by the least vulnerable among us, eliminate our most common and dramatic vulnerabilities. We disregard, for example, the extent to which food and drug laws, securities regulation, criminal laws, and the like diminish our most obvious vulnerabilities, leaving us with institutions of equal participation modeled on the capabilities of the strongest. It is no accident that those who start out at the top tend to remain on top.

Likewise, it is no accident that the weak tend to remain weak. Our institutions are built on the assumption that those who participate are strong. This is captured in our ur-myth, the doctrines of rugged individualism and self-reliance that form the highest aspirations of liberal society. But the myth is just that. No amount of formal and structural equality will compensate for the vulnerabilities that preclude large numbers of Americans from participating effectively in the system.

As we approach the twenty-first century, we Americans are obsessed with our autonomy—our freedom to choose our own courses of life. Our legal and institutional focus on autonomy directs us inward to ourselves. This obsession with ourselves leads us to reverse the Golden Rule, demanding that others put themselves in our shoes rather than that we put ourselves in theirs. As a result, it leads us, in a very real way, to dehumanize others and thus fail to relate to them. The consequences for American society of this increasing trend are ominous indeed.

The solution I will suggest is nothing less than a reconceptualization of our relations with others. It begins not from the primacy of the individual's right—from the idea of me first—but from the recognition that each of us is vulnerable in many ways to the forces of economics, politics, society, and nature. This implicit appreciation of our own vulnerabilities is, we shall see, at the heart of the trends I mentioned above. And it is, we shall see, at the heart not only of our longing for community but of our motivations to be fair to others as well. Recapturing this deep knowledge of vulnerability at an intellectual level, and understanding its universality, is a necessary first step in restoring our sense of community. It is also, as I shall suggest in a practical way, necessary to ensure that our society in fact operates fairly.

The social consequences of our failure of community are clear. The way in which we privilege individualism leads us to reward talent, skill, and initiative. This may be a good thing—although I will present thoughtful critiques of this reality in Chapter Five. But it rewards something else too. It rewards simple luck. It rewards the advantages of starting out ahead—of starting out with wealth, position, and comfort. And in doing so, it penalizes the bad luck of starting out behind.

I have a name for the rewards that come to the blessed—the selfishness surplus. Although I reserve explanation of the concept until Chapter Eight, the selfishness surplus is a consequence of the way we bury the reality of vulnerability under an artificial and simplistic notion of autonomy. When we think about it—really think about it—we will see that the selfishness surplus and the ethic on which it is based are fundamentally unfair.

I want to be clear from the outset that my purpose is not to defeat the ideals of individual self-determination and self-reliance. In fact, I want to preserve them. But we can do this only if we recognize the extent to which our society—structured upon a mythical form of individualism—subjugates and excludes from vital participation a substantial portion of its population. "All men are created equal"—in the eyes of God and philosophers. The reality on earth is starkly different. It is one of the principal functions of liberal society, and the particular role of the ideal of fairness, to ensure that all persons are equally capable of meaningful participation. This requires that we provide people with meaningful choices and the tools with which to make them.

Some of you will already have dismissed my argument. All I have done, you might say, is substitute an ideal of compassion for the equality or justice that we ordinarily consider to be at the heart of fairness. To level this criticism, however, is to overlook a vital distinction that I will be at pains to maintain throughout this book. This is the distinction between ideas about fairness and the factors that motivate us to be concerned with fairness in the first place. The argument is that unless you understand the motivations—the *reasons* for fairness—your doctrines of fairness will fit those motivations only by accident. Obviously this argument implies that our doctrines ought to be changed to fit our motivations.

But we have to find our motivations. Where do we find them? When we talk about things like fairness, we only *think* about fairness. We tend to intellectualize concerns about fairness with talk of justice, equality, reciprocity, and consent. We treat these as abstract concepts and try to reason them out. But we all know that issues of fairness have deep emotional impact too. We all know the anger or frustration that we feel when we do not think we are being treated fairly, as well as the poignant empathy we have toward others in that position. We can understand Alex's frustration at the unfairness of his bedtime vote yet see how formal argument can continue to drown out his cries of "foul."

That we can and do have emotional reactions to situations of unfairness ought to tell us something. It should, I think, suggest that perhaps we consult our hearts as well as our heads in developing our understanding of fairness and the ways that we implement that understanding in American society. I will, through much of this book, ask you to consult your head. But ultimately I will ask that you join me in consulting our hearts, so that we can complete our intellectual understanding of fairness with our feelings about it.

So I ask you to stay with me. Stay with me, even through the occasional polemical passage, as we take a quick look at the way we perceive individualism in American society and at the way it is firmly embedded in law and philosophy. Stay with me to consult our emotions as we examine together our motivations to help people in distress. And stay with me as I ask you to play out a thought experiment that helps make those motivations more concrete. If you do, I think you will end up agreeing with me that the formal doctrines of fairness in American society today do not fit our motivations. We may disagree on specific proposals to rectify the problem, but I'm willing to bet that we will ultimately agree that our ideas of fairness need to be changed.

The ideal of fairness lies very deep—it is the foundation for more formal ideas of justice and equality. In plumbing these depths, I join a trend toward recapturing the role of the emotions in moral reasoning, a trend that is notable in academic philosophy, law, and sociology, as well as in more general works such as James Q. Wilson's book *The Moral Sense*. The message that emerges from this trend is not only that we feel as well as think but that we should also think about what we feel.

I should be quite clear from the outset that this is emphatically not a book about victimization and victimhood. My argument does not seek to reduce to the status of victims those who are, for whatever reason, more vulnerable than the norm. Nor does it absolve them of responsibility for their fate. Quite the opposite. When we fully understand the implications of our own vulnerabilities, we shall understand our responsibilities to each other as well as our claims on one another. Forgetting the root of fairness in vulnerability has led us to forget those responsibilities as well as those claims. If we understand the fact of universal vulnerability, we will reevaluate the fairness of our institutions in light of the purposes they are to serve. We will see that our contemporary practical application of fairness has resulted in substantial unfairness. It is the purpose of this book to begin the process of remedying this problem by recovering, at an intellectual level, our intuitions about fairness, so that we may ensure that the American goals of individual freedom and responsibility truly are available to all.

The argument proceeds as follows. In Chapter One I briefly give some historical examples of the rise of the myth of individualism in American society and show how our social realities belie that myth. In Chapter Two I explain the ways that our strong belief in the myth of individualism leads us to disregard the reality of universal vulnerability and some of the dangers that it creates. To provide evidence of the ways that a strong ethic of individual autonomy permeates our institutions and thinking, in Chapters Three and Four I explore a variety of legal doctrines that reveal the embeddedness of this idea and in Chapter Five I do the same for several philosophical approaches to the issue of fairness. Chapter Six presents a series of hypotheticals that ask you to imagine your responses to a variety of situations in which you encounter people in distress, and Chapter Seven presents a thought experiment modeled on John Rawls's famous original position—but with a very different twist. In Chapter Eight I present the practical consequence of all of this, the existence of the selfishness surplus, and begin a defense of a more activist legal and social regime. Chapter Nine discusses and dismisses a common metaphor for fairness, that of games, by analyzing the ways in which the metaphor is inappropriate for evaluating social structure. Finally, Chapter Ten concludes with a look at the related notions of trust and responsibility and presents an argument that we all—no matter how vulnerable—ultimately are responsible for one another.

I have tried to keep this book short and reasonably entertaining, in part by limiting the customary scholarly qualifications and explications. I am trying to describe and analyze a way of thinking that is deeply ingrained in American life. Some of you who are fluent in the subtleties of liberal theory, communitarian philosophy, or legal discourse may find my argument overstated or simplistic at times. I hope you will bear with me, for this book is also for those of you who would prefer not to become lost in a sea of academic argumentation and inside debate.

Similarly, I have been deliberately light on endnotes. I have of course acknowledged sources from which I have taken ideas and quotations directly. But I do not want an excess of endnotes to detract from the flow of argument. More important, I have come to many of the ideas I present from years of reading and thinking about the problems of fairness. It would be impossible for endnotes to capture accurately the genesis of these ideas. Interested readers may consult the bibliography for a list of the sources that have most directly contributed to the development of this book.

The Big Myth

"We hold these truths to be self-evident, that all men are created equal, that they are endowed by their Creator with certain unalienable Rights, that among these are Life, Liberty and the pursuit of Happiness."

Declaration of Independence, 1776

"God helps them that help themselves."

Benjamin Franklin, *Poor Richard's Almanac,* June 1736

"Self-reliance, the height and perfection of man, is reliance on God."

Ralph Waldo Emerson, *The Fugitive Slave Law,* 1854

"The first requisite of a good citizen in this Republic of ours is that he shall be able and willing to pull his weight."

Theodore Roosevelt, speech in New York, November 11, 1902

"The new [welfare] bill restores America's basic bargain of providing opportunity and demanding in return responsibility."

William Jefferson Clinton, speech at the White House, August 22, 1996

"I hate quotations. Tell me what you know." So insisted one of the most quotable of all American thinkers, Ralph Waldo Emerson. Despite this admonition, the history of American popular thought shows a progression from knowledge to quotation, from substance to sound bite. My concern in this book is not *why* this may have happened but its effect on our society in general and on our understanding of fairness in particular. For, as I will show, our increasing tendency to elevate rhetoric to the level of thought has profoundly affected our sense of our obligations to each other. The result is a transformation of our understanding of fairness from one of providing *meaningful* equality to one of ensuring formal equality—an equality based on false premises. We talk about ourselves as self-reliant, but we know better.

This is the particular sound bite that interests me—the myth of American individual self-reliance. This myth is built on our dominant— and, for reasons I will discuss, valuable—legal and political ethic of individual autonomy. At the same time, it distills that ethic to a core of self-obsession. Of course, the myth tells us only part of reality, for, as sociologist Robert Wuthnow and countless others remind us, there is a strong caring strain in American society as well. But individualism has taken pride of place in constructing our image of our nation and ourselves with a strength that drowns out our ethic of care.

The pervasiveness of the language and imagery of individualism has important implications for our understanding of fairness. We shall see that our motivation to fairness can be found more in our caring impulse than in our desire for autonomy. We can of course use our individual freedom to express concern for others, so that caring and self-determination are not necessarily inconsistent; indeed, we will see how they can be quite consistent. But the importance we place on our mythology of self-reliance tends to conceal our motivations to fairness and to discourage helping. It leads us to reduce our ideas about fairness to a minimalist regime of formal structures. Ultimately, it reverses the dictum of Louis Sullivan—instead of form following function, the function of fairness follows its form.

The Democratic Faith

Every people needs a justification, a reason for being as a people, that validates its organization into a society. The Bible gives the Jewish people a belief in their chosenness to convey and exemplify to the world the oneness of God. The theocracy of the early Puritan Massachusetts Bay Colony proclaimed its mission to establish a "city on the hill" to model the true path of salvation. The ancient Greek polis took as its purpose the cultivation and modeling of the civic virtues, and the British Empire pursued a mission to civilize the world. Virtually every culture has relied upon a common story, told and retold to each generation and proclaimed to outsiders, as its reason for being.

Our American mission is to model for the world—indeed to bring to the world—freedom, equality, and independence. Our founding during the Enlightenment was based on the Enlightenment principle that the very essence of human fulfillment is to choose for yourself the purposes for which you live and the means to pursue those goals. This individual autonomy is the watchword of our American faith. We believe that our government should exist to sustain that goal and to protect our people in its realization.

The historian Ralph Gabriel observed the source of the American ideal of individualism in our founding. He noted of the framers of the Constitution that, "true to the Enlightenment, of which they were in fact a part, their social philosophy emphasized atomism. They centered their interest on the individual man. Democracy is the appropriate political expression of the atomistic social emphasis."[1] Democratic society—at least in the American version—is like a pointillist painting.

Gabriel traced this ideal of individualism throughout American history and found it to be part of a doctrine he referred to as the "democratic faith." This democratic faith has three major parts. The first part, as I described, is the importance of the individual. But this is coupled with a second part, an American belief in fundamental law—a combination of the natural law of Plato and Judeo-Christian moral law. This fundamental law held that the individual was not only free but responsible as well, and responsible to an authority higher than herself, whether it be nature—in the case of Jefferson's well-known deism—or God. To these two tenets of the democratic faith was added a third, an understanding of the mission of America to bring democracy to the world and in so doing to lift the oppressed everywhere.

Although the democratic faith treated democracy as an "aggregation of discrete individuals,"[2] the American sense of mission helped unify the society and give these individuals a sense of common purpose. But the mission of America was not enough to sustain individuals in their day-to-day lives—to give meaning to daily life. As a supplement, then, to their democratic faith, Americans turned to their smaller communities for aid in their daily survival and to find personal fulfillment.

Alexis de Tocqueville found an American society of joiners—a society of communal organizations that bound subgroups of individuals in common religious, occupational, and civic purposes to help them fulfill their individual goals. More recently, sociologist Frances Fukuyama noted these same strong strains of communalism underlying American individualism, and the philosopher John Rawls described a community of communities, in which the larger community is bound together by the principles of freedom and equality and the component communities are bound by more personal interests and beliefs.

Consistent with our ideal of individualism, you are free to join these communities as you desire—nobody forces you to join. You may, if you like, become a member of the Masons, the country club, the local synagogue, or all three. Or, like Cooper's Natty Bumpo, you may escape to the wilderness to live as a truly free person.

The idea of fundamental law gave individualism pride of place in our philosophies. But it also helped temper the excesses of individualism. Ralph Waldo Emerson, while known to generations of college students as our high priest of radical individualism, also saw the individual as woven in a fabric with nature and God, thus preventing the stark atomism that could tear society apart.[3]

This idea of fundamental law, in a different way, tempered and justified perhaps our most dramatic practical theory of individualism, the Gospel of Wealth, formulated best by Andrew Carnegie during a period (like ours) of increasing inequalities. The Gospel of Wealth had two parts: a belief in the desirability of individual achievement and a doctrine of stewardship. This idea of stewardship qualified the virtue of accumulating wealth by obligating the successful to look after those who had failed. At the same time, more romantic strains of communal solidarity were developing in the labor movement and among adherents of the Social Gospel. But, as Gabriel points out, even these themes were premised on the idea that the purpose of cooperative community was to foster the development of the individual.

Strains of individualism and community have continued to develop throughout our century. From the Progressive movement to the New Deal to the civil rights era and the Great Society, we have seen continued manifestations of the idea that although individualism is our goal, community is our method of achieving it. At the same time, and as we will see in Chapters Three and Four, our laws mostly have developed to protect the individual from the community.

Community is the background. Individualism is our goal. In recent years our concern with our individualism has reached a new level, culminating with the idea of trickle-down economics in the 1980s and beyond. All you now need do to fulfill your obligation to the community is take care of yourself, and the invisible hand of the market will drop the fruits of your success, like table scraps, into the waiting hands of those below. In essence, the Gospel of Reagan, continued by the Republican Party to the present (and aided increasingly by Democrats) has dislodged the Gospel of Wealth from its ideals of stewardship grounded in fundamental law. But more of this later.

Self-reliant individualism and communal participation have always existed together in American society. But this book is not an exercise in descriptive anthropology. It is not about what a dispassionate observer identifies as our practices but what we tell ourselves that we do and value. It is about what the legal philosopher H.L.A. Hart called the internal point of view—what we ourselves take to be legitimate justifications for our actions and inactions. And, ultimately, it is about the ways in which what we say we do shapes what in fact we do. It is a story, to paraphrase Emerson, of how our reliance on quotations leads us to forget what we know.

The essence of my argument is that the privileged position we have given to individualism, and the atomistic form it has taken in our laws and ideals, has doomed community—and thus caring—to failure. As I mentioned earlier, we do engage in communal enterprises, but always from the starting point that it is the individual that matters. By starting with such a premise, it seems almost inevitable that when self and community conflict, the self always wins. The result has been the considerable and well-documented American alienation in modern life. But alienation is only the beginning of the problem. Our emphasis on the self has increasingly made Americans unwilling to help each other out; it has created an increasing tendency for each of us to stand alone. We will see the ways our intellectual expressions of fairness justify this result, as well as the ways that recapturing our intuitive understanding of fairness can begin to reverse it.

A major reason for the failure of community is that a strong ethic of individualism focuses our attention inward upon ourselves. This effect is demonstrated in its extreme form by the rise in our culture of therapy, noted by both Robert Bellah and Alasdaire MacIntyre. This ethic of individualism has led to an increasing culture of victimhood, leading us to blame others for our own failures and to demand compensation from others. It has led to the self-imposed social and political isolation of many Americans manifested in its extreme form by the rise of the militia movement. It has led to the increase in group identification and separatism so prevalent in our universities and evidenced by the demand that we satisfy every ethnic preference, with its extreme form in the black nationalism of Louis Farrakhan. And it has led to increasing class and political warfare, from the backlash of angry white men against any forms of preference for others to the meanness of welfare reform, from the increasing intolerance in social debate to the invective that passes for political discourse.

The Ethic of Individualism

The origins of the ideal of individualism in American social and political thought are murkier than its transformation into the myth that we tell ourselves today. The Puritans who created the Massachusetts Bay Colony in the 1630s brought with them ideals of communal responsibility. But this was grounded in a theology that emphasized individual communion with God and a church organization that abandoned the hierarchical structures of European churches and emphasized congregational independence.[4] In the southern colonies, life was organized around more distant farms instead of villages, which led to the need for greater social as well as economic self-sufficiency. It goes almost without saying that exploration and settlement of the frontier both required and encouraged individualism and self-reliance.

In those days, self-reliance had some meaning. While social and economic intercourse existed among the colonists, and people relied on the help of their families and friends, it is pretty uncontroversial to note that there was no state to speak of and certainly nothing in the way of legalized social welfare protection.

At the same time that the settled colonies were developing into economic and social entities in their own right, the Enlightenment was coming into focus in Europe. Certainly by 1776, theories of the natural rights of man, liberty, and equality under the law had gained currency and, in the view of historian Bernard Bailyn, had helped the revolutionary generation make sense of the colonies' early experiences.[5] The importance both of these Enlightenment ideals and of the actual independence (at least from the state) of most Americans is illustrated by the Constitution's Bill of Rights. The centrality of individual freedom in early American thought is proclaimed in our guarantees of freedom of religion, speech, and association; our right to bear arms; our right to privacy in our homes, reflected in the Third and Fourth Amendments; and the due process clause's respect for the individual and our right to use the processes of justice to protect ourselves from the state's abuse of power.

If these protections reflected the theoretical and actual importance of individualism, they also were superimposed on a nation that prized community. Tocqueville, as I noted, found a land of organizations and joiners. The ideal of community was itself part of Enlightenment thought. John Locke proclaimed the rights of the individual based on self-ownership, and a century later Immanuel Kant reasoned his way to the radical equality and freedom of all. Locke's thought in particular gave us the model of the social contract—based as all contracts are on the self-interest of individuals—as a justification for the continuation of political society. But Adam Smith—the adopted patron saint of laissez-faire capitalism—proclaimed the highest form of social organization to be the one in which people's natural sentimental affiliations with one another led them to be deeply concerned with each other's welfare.

Individualism—not community—ultimately came to dominate American social thought. Community was, after all, neither a new notion nor a very real concern. The European settlers were quite familiar with the old world web of religious, social, and political communities and the ways in which their hierarchies and authorities restricted the life choices of their members. It was liberty that needed to be protected from community, not the other way around. And the settlers' characteristics of individual independence and self-reliance led them to settle the colonies and develop them to the point of revolution. It is no surprise, then, that their critical concern was assuring that this independence was protected.

This concern with the protection of individual independence has become obsessive at the same time that the reality of independence has been virtually eliminated. From the fervor of Jacksonian populism to the civil disobedience of Thoreau, from the social Darwinism of the late nineteenth century to modern notions of trickle-down economics, from Daniel Boone to Natty Bumpo to Theodore Roosevelt to John Wayne to Ronald Reagan, from the transcendentalism of Emerson to the hundreds of self-help and self-actualization movements that fill our society today, our greatest popular ideas and our greatest popular heroes embody the idea of some combination of physical, emotional, and intellectual independence. It may well be that the concept of independence has gone from American ideal to American pathology. What is clear, as we shall see in the rest of this chapter, is that it has become divorced from reality. It is today a myth.

The Myth of Individualism

Who is this American individual? Can we identify examples of the self-reliant person we so idealize? If so, in what respects is he self-reliant? And how, if at all, does he resemble us?

Surely our presidents were largely self-reliant. At least from the candidacy of Andrew Jackson, we have come to accept "as an article of the American faith" that our presidents were generally born into modest, if not downright humble, circumstances.[6] The stories of Jackson's frontier hardships, Lincoln's log cabin origins, and even Ronald Reagan's self-asserted early poverty have served not only to reinforce the myth of the noble, striving individual but to facilitate these presidents' elections by populaces whose belief in, and respect for, the myth of the individual not only was unquestioning but also gave them hope. But reality belies the myth.

Although one of Jackson's biographers described him as "the absolute personification of the self-made man,"[7] and it is true that he suffered the misfortune of his father's death before he was born, Jackson's frontier life was one his contemporaries would have envied. Brought up by his mother and her family, he lived with an uncle who "was a well-to-do land- and slaveholder who owned a fine home, a gristmill, and a still for making whiskey, among other valuable properties," and was described by a contemporary as a "man of considerable substance."[8] Jackson attended a private academy and was raised among horse breeders and local politicians. Though not rich, he clearly enjoyed what we would today consider a middle-class childhood.[9]

Or take Lincoln himself. No president—indeed no American (except perhaps Andrew Carnegie)—so captures our imagination as a rags-to-greatness story. We all know the tales of his mother's early death, of his long walks to school, and of his tireless reading by the light of a fire. But Lincoln's father was in fact a carpenter and a farmer, counting among his assets "two farms of six hundred acres, several town lots, livestock, and horses," which Edward Pessen, in his interesting study *The Log Cabin Myth*, describes as "quite close to the total owned by the wealthiest man in the area."[10] Lincoln was many wonderful things. But poor he wasn't.

What about Ronald Reagan, who perhaps more than any other president preached the gospel of Horatio Alger America and claimed to personify that very ideal? Reagan's father held a series of "excellent jobs" during Reagan's childhood, permitting the family to "live in attractive rented houses on tree-lined streets in scenic areas. When Reagan was a young college graduate, his father was named to head the Works Progress Administration program in Dixon, Illinois. As Pessen put it, "Government programs to help the poor are not normally directed by men themselves poor."[11] According to Pessen, the Reagan family was solidly middle class.

In fact, Pessen's analysis of the childhood circumstances of our presidents (through Reagan) places only one president's family—that of Andrew Johnson—in the lower class compared with the socioeconomic status of their contemporaries and those of Millard Fillmore, James Garfield, and Richard Nixon in the lower middle class. Looking beyond Pessen's research, nobody would claim that George Bush was raised in anything but comfortable circumstances. And Bill Clinton's background was far more middle class than mythology suggests.[12]

So it seems unlikely that we can find the self-reliant, self-made man among our presidents, at least not without searching hard. What about our nation's wealthiest citizens? Can we find the self-reliant, self-made individualist there?

Is it Andrew Carnegie, the high priest of the Gospel of Wealth, whose family arrived in Pittsburgh impoverished and who began factory work at the age of twelve but whose family members were supportive, loving, and closely knit and gave him every advantage they could? Is it billionaire Warren Buffett, whose father was a stockbroker and a congressman and who grew up in middle American middle-class comfort in Omaha and Washington, D.C.? Or Bill Gates, son of a successful Seattle lawyer and graduate of a prestigious prep school, who dropped out of Harvard to pursue his ambition? What about the Forbes listing of the four hundred wealthiest Americans? Are all of these Horatio Alger stories? Are any of them? Do they exemplify what we mean by self-reliance?

Well, some, in a sense, yes. Surely Carnegie created his success from almost nothing. But his is an exceptional case and tends even today to be found more among immigrants (and sometimes sports and entertainment heroes). Much more typical, as the examples I culled from a foray into general periodical literature demonstrate, are people who had an economic head start, an observation that appears to hold true even for all but a small minority of the Forbes 400.[13]

Almost all of my examples are of people who undeniably have worked hard, capitalized on the resources and opportunities available to them, and achieved great success. But they have done so in contexts. It is these contexts we tend to ignore when we see their successes. Like Ben Franklin in his constructed autobiographical self, setting off from home to a distant city to seek his fortune, we tend to look only at the result, not the path, of the successful. When we think of Andrew Carnegie, we tend to focus on his childhood poverty, not on the warm and supportive family environment that enabled him to flourish and make the best use of his talents. When we think of Warren Buffett, we think only of the modest man from Omaha who built his dazzling fortune, not the comfortable middle-class circumstances in which he was raised. And what is true with respect to Warren Buffett is equally true with respect to our own successes.

Bellah and his colleagues noted this tendency in their influential book *Habits of the Heart*: "There are truths we do not see when we adopt the language of radical individualism. . . . And the positive side of our individualism, our sense of the dignity, worth, and moral autonomy of the individual, is dependent in a thousand ways on a social, cultural and institutional context that keeps us afloat even when we cannot very well describe it."[14] It is this tendency to forget, this tendency not only to idealize ourselves as autonomous but truly to think of ourselves as autonomous, that leads us to believe that our successes are due only to ourselves. It is a tendency wonderfully exemplified by the successful car dealer interviewed by Bellah and his colleagues who described himself as self-made—conveniently forgetting that he had inherited the business from his father.[15]

So who is this self-reliant American? Perhaps it is the noble Jeffersonian ideal, the American farmer. Surely the hardworking yeoman, rising early to care for the animals, plow the fields, and plant and reap our food, presents an accurate portrait of American individualism. And despite much talk of corporate farming, the overwhelming number of farms and a substantial majority of their produce continue to be owned by individuals or families.[16]

What of the independent farmer? The O'Brien family of Iowa runs a diversified farm of 187 acres, including an apple orchard, small plots of raspberries, strawberries, corn, and hay, and forty dairy cows. As described in one report, they mostly farm organically, go to church, and pay their taxes. And their three children help out with the chores before and after school—where they participate in the free lunch program because, despite their hard work and Larry O'Brien's full-time construction job, the O'Briens live below the poverty level. Ironically, in light of their food-raising business, the O'Briens can't even afford to feed themselves. They could do better if they took federal farm subsidies. But they refuse to do so, because subsidies encourage the use of chemicals, overproduction, and mono-cropping, which the O'Briens view as destructive.[17] The O'Briens clearly are independent, exercising their autonomy to live in the manner they think best and refusing available government aid.* Yet they can barely survive.

What about other farmers? Like the O'Briens, they may be independent—except of government. Take the farm states of Kansas, Nebraska, and Iowa, for example. In 1995, the federal government spent $12.5 billion in Kansas, or $4,883 for every man, woman, and child.[†] In Nebraska, the like amounts were $7.5 billion and $4,596 respectively; and in Iowa, the amounts were $13 billion and $4,597 respectively.[18] These payments went for a variety of services, including welfare and social security, hiring federal workers and building roads, as well as providing farm subsidies. In contrast, in 1993 (the most recent year for which figures were available), the average Kansan paid $1,873 to the federal government and Nebraskans and Iowans paid $1,745 and $1,648 respectively.[19] Whatever else they may rely on, including themselves, self-reliant American farmers clearly rely heavily on the state.

Perhaps the modern self-reliant American is to be found among the captains of industry. In our modern capitalist era, with the sound of the guns of takeovers in our ears and the sight of corporate titans like Disney's Michael Eisner, surely we can find the self-reliant among those who brave the dangers of the marketplace to enrich stockholders, employ millions, and bring us the goods and services that make our lives so pleasant.

We search again in vain. The federal government alone provides

* Except, that is, for their children's free school lunches.
† Expenditure figures exclude generalized federal expenditures such as interest on the federal debt, expenditures on international affairs, and the budgets of the Central Intelligence Agency and the National Security Agency.

more than $150 billion annually to businesses in the form of direct subsidies and tax breaks (including agricultural subsidies to corporate farmers). In 1996, the *Boston Globe* reported that in the previous year the Walt Disney Corporation, with profits exceeding $1 billion, received a $300,000 federal subsidy to perfect a fireworks display; the McDonald's Corporation received almost $2 million to help market Chicken McNuggets in the Third World; and Lockheed Martin got $20,000 for golf balls as an entertainment expense [20] (not to mention $263,000 to sponsor a Smokey Robinson concert and $7,500 for an office Christmas party that its predecessor, Martin Marietta, had received).[21]

To give some sense of the vastness of these subsidies (as if the numbers alone were not enough), the *Globe* compared them to an annual federal budget deficit of $130 billion and a core welfare bill (excluding social security and medical care) of $145 billion. If American business is self-reliant, it is hard to tell from this level of federal support—at least it seems no more self-reliant than the welfare poor. The average annual cost to each American taxpayer of these corporate subsidies and tax breaks is $1,186 (compared with $415 in overall welfare spending per person).[22]

Moreover, some of this support goes directly into the pockets of industrialists. The *Globe* further reported that Lockheed Martin was scheduled to receive $1 billion in federal assistance to help pay for the costs of its merger, including "more than $16 million in pay and performance bonuses for top executives while nearly 50,000 of the conglomerate's employees have been laid off in the last five years."[23]

Business executives have justified much of this largesse by saying that they need to attain a "level playing field" in world markets, where competition is heavily subsidized. Perhaps so. The point is not that these expenditures are necessarily unjustified (although I suspect that many are, and recent congressional attempts to reduce them support this). It is that even the American businessman, the cream of our capitalist society and the modern market equivalent of the self-reliant individual, feels the need to be sheltered from the rough-and-tumble competition of world markets—and I've said nothing yet of tariffs and trade protection.

What about our modern-day Andrew Carnegies, those entrepreneurs like Hewlett and Packard, who provide us with an image of the market adventurer working in a garage to develop products that bring him billions and better lives and jobs to countless Americans? In 1989,

INC. magazine conducted a survey of the chief executive officers of the Inc. 500—America's fastest-growing private companies—to determine how they got started. The answer? "Instead of iconoclastic individualists, the cowboy capitalists of America's dreams, we found people enmeshed and embedded in industries, with rich networks of contacts and colleagues they could draw on to help them build a business."[24] There is little question that these people did the best with what they had. But in addition to the contacts, experience, and support with which they began, they also had, if they failed, "jobs [that] would have been waiting for them elsewhere in their industries."[25] Independent self-reliance? Not of the sort of which the myth is made.

Or what about the legal profession? Clarence Thomas is often cited as a model of self-reliance. Born in Pinpoint, Georgia, during an era of unspeakable racism and discrimination to a father who abandoned his family, Thomas was raised by his illiterate grandfather, a small farmer. Hardworking and encouraged by his grandfather, Thomas spent four years in seminary before attending Holy Cross College and Yale Law School. He became chairman of the Equal Employment Opportunity Commission, a federal circuit judge, and finally an associate justice of the Supreme Court. Clearly Thomas is to be commended for his hard work and his ability to take advantage of his opportunities. But how self-reliant is he? As Vernon Jordan put it, "Without affirmative action that seeks out qualified blacks, it is unlikely he would have been educated at Holy Cross and Yale Law School [where he received generous scholarships], headed a government agency, or been appointed to the federal bench. He certainly would not have been nominated for the Supreme Court."[26]

So much for self-reliance among the most elite Americans, the highest achievers. What about the rest of us? How self-reliant are we in our daily lives? How much of our own success is self-made? The answer is probably not much. The vast majority of the readers of this book are likely to have grown up in at least middle-class circumstances and to have had significant educational advantages. Derek Bok, among others, observes that there is substantial sociological evidence to show that starting out middle class is a dramatic advantage indeed.[27] And, according to Albert Szymanski, "One is very likely to be in the same class position as one's parents. Working class children generally become workers, capitalist class children generally become capitalists . . . and middle class children are most likely to become middle class."[28] Common sense leads us to the same conclusion. Safe and secure homes, good nutrition, schools with good facilities and teachers, bright and motivated classmates, and educational enrichment opportunities like dance and music lessons start one off on the right foot.

In addition to the advantages with which our families have provided us, we have been provided with other direct advantages by the state. Excellent public universities have been available to those whose early educational advantage—whether at home or at school—allows them to get that far if their families can't afford the bill at private colleges. Even at private universities there have been benefits, such as the government-guaranteed student loans that put me through law school and my wife through graduate school. And let's not forget the all-important home mortgage deduction, without which many of us would have trouble buying houses—at least houses we like.

There are also less visible protections that undergird these more obvious advantages. For all our talk of the rigors of competitive capitalism and the pride we take in our market successes, we are not really at the mercy of a free-market economy. Nor, despite the rhetoric (and occasional failed attempts) of right-wing politicians, do we really want to be. The stunning failure of the Republican Contract with America (about which more later) is an excellent example of our recognition of our vulnerabilities and our desire for protection. But a brief survey of the laws on which we daily rely makes this point even clearer.

There are, of course, the obvious protections of the social safety net. Although most readers are unlikely to rely on receiving social security, we know it's there—and our fears of its imminent evaporation are driving us to find ways to preserve it. Medicare of course will ensure our ability to receive health care in our old age. But there's more.

Few of us raise our own food. When we go to the local supermarket, we buy a cart full of products, from fresh produce grown by others to uninspectable packaged goods from distant and often anonymous producers that contain a variety of ingredients we would be hard pressed to identify beyond the names on the packages. How is it that we so cavalierly buy and consume these products?

The answer, of course, is that we know they are subject to a variety of government regulations and inspections that insure, for the most part, that they will be wholesome. In the absence of such regulation, how willingly would we eat? Some argue that the free market would take care of us, that producers who sold tainted products would soon be driven out of business. While it may be true that the free market *eventually* would weed out bad producers (although history suggests this is probably not so),[29] it would do so only by poisoning enough of us to enable us to identify the bad producers. I personally would not be willing to volunteer to test the market. And the hew and cry that was raised when the 104th Congress attempted substantially to modify the federal meat inspection laws suggests that most of you wouldn't either.

Food and drug regulation is only a part of the laws we rely on every day. When we buy and sell securities and invest our money in mutual funds, when we rely on employer-provided pensions, and when we deposit our paychecks in the bank, we rationally trust that our assets will not be wasted or stolen. Of course some of this trust derives from the reputations of those with whom we deal and our assumption that their economic incentives are best served by serving us honestly. But the history of each of these regulated markets prior to regulation provides ample evidence that reputation and economic incentive are not enough. The same markets existed before regulation, but the history of these industries is rife with fraud and other abuses. Even if some of these abuses sometimes still occur, our legal infrastructure now gives us remedies to compensate us for them. Without these regulations we would need to be truly self-reliant, investigating in some depth the persons with whom we deal. We would have to examine their characters, their practices, their histories. The simple act of opening a bank account would become a time-consuming and expensive project. Our self-reliance in matters like these would leave us little time to pursue goals of greater interest to us.

Each of us, then, is highly dependent. And our dependence makes us highly vulnerable. Even the smartest, most energetic, and luckiest among us still has to buy food, invest money, and go to the bank. True self-reliance would mean constant investigation, and constant suspicion.

In so many ways, the myth of self-reliance is a lie. Yet for all its unreality, the myth has extraordinary staying power, captured in our attitudes toward the American Dream. Much of the American Dream transcends material concerns, as recent surveys have reported.[30] But material concerns do provide a backdrop to achieving other goals. As defined by one group of interviewees, the American Dream includes financial security (although not necessarily wealth), sending one's children to the colleges of their choice, owning a home, having friends, and being the best at one's job.[31] Seventy-one percent of respondents to a 1996 ABC News poll stated that they believed the American Dream remains achievable, and 76 percent of respondents to a 1995 *Washington Post* poll said that they continued to believe in the American Dream. Substantial numbers of respondents to the Wirthlin Quorum survey said they believed that the American Dream would remain available to their children.[32]

The optimism expressed in these figures is further borne out by the beliefs of substantial numbers of Americans that they are well along their way to fulfilling the dream and that ultimately they shall do so (or come close to doing so). An astonishing 80 percent of 1995 poll respondents stated that they either had achieved (45 percent) or would achieve (35 percent) the American Dream.[33] And 83 percent of respondents to a 1994 Times Mirror poll said they believed that their family's financial situation would stay the same (16 percent) or improve (67 percent) during the coming year.[34] We obviously believe that we live in the land of opportunity.

Similar results were reported for 1980 by sociologist John Kluegel and psychologist Eliot Smith in their book, *Beliefs about Inequality*, an analysis and report of their in-depth survey of 2,212 Americans. They concluded that "while Americans assess favorably the opportunity for advancement in our society in general, they view their personal opportunity even more positively," and 90 percent judge their own opportunities as equal to or better than the average.[35] And although Kluegel and Smith noted that these beliefs were declining, they certainly do not appear to have done so significantly by the time of the later Roper poll.

The dissonance between these figures and reality is deafening. In 1992, John Schwartz and Thomas Volgy published their study, *The Forgotten American*, about the working poor. While noting generally that "Americans have always believed that in a free society people showing individual responsibility and diligence will get ahead,"[36] they also noted that "during favorable economic conditions" almost fifty-six million people from a wide variety of backgrounds and with a wide variety of educational attainments had little hope of seeing this dream realized. These people, living at less than 155 percent of the official poverty level ($19,644, based on the 1989 poverty line of $12,674 for a family of four), and another seven million who would be added by applying the original federal concept of poverty, "cannot afford basic necessities, even at the lowest realistic cost, unless they obtain substantial outside assistance. Even then many will fall short."[37] Among these are 9.3 million workers in full-time jobs, in households totaling twenty-four million people.[38] These are people who are hardworking and who have done what they were supposed to do. Although some of them may have limited talents, it seems likely that most of them have limited luck. Yet, although some of these people despaired of improving their situation, the Roper poll found that many nevertheless believed that they could attain the American Dream.

The cause for this optimism isn't clear. One reason may be the socio-psychological explanations given by Kluegel and Smith, that for a variety of reasons most Americans have internalized the dominant American ideology discussed above, leading them to process dissonant information in ways that adapt it to maintain the truth of the dominant ideology. I will have more to say about this in later chapters. Another reason may be, as Roper noted, that for most Americans the ideal of the dream is rather modest. In fact, most respondents gave rather low income figures as those at which they could be comfortable. But, as the evidence Schwartz and Volgy present suggests, these views do not fit economic reality. They surely do not match the dream of financial security and college for one's children.

So why the optimism? One reason may well be the optimism and hope embodied in the myth of self-reliance itself. If you work hard, you'll get ahead. Perhaps this remains true. It may remain true for the average American, who believes that she can fulfill her dreams on $77,000 a year.[39] But it is certainly the case that she will rely on social security in her old age, federally guaranteed mortgages for her home, state universities or scholarships for her children, and a variety of other government services to support her in realizing her dream. Happy? Perhaps. Self-reliant? No.

In the fall of 1994, the myth was brought to new heights in American politics and public discourse. The Contract with America, put forward by Republican congressional leaders and signed by 367 sitting and hopeful Republican congressional candidates, was one of the most dramatic modern uses of the myth of the rugged American. It led, at least in part, to the overwhelming elections of Republican representatives and senators and to Republican rule over both the House and Senate for the first time since the Truman administration. The story of the Contract, and the Republicans' quick and precipitous fall from grace, help to demonstrate both that the myth of independence is a lie and that we know it is.

The Contract was based on five principles, four of which are relevant here. They are "individual liberty," "economic opportunity," "limited government," and "personal responsibility."[40] These principles, according to the authors of the Contract, set out the Republican vision for America, a vision that "seeks to renew the American Dream by promoting individual liberty, economic opportunity, and personal responsibility, through limited and effective government."[41] The details of the Contract are unimportant, as is the fact that later research showed it to have only minor significance in the Republican victory. What is significant is the extent to which the rhetoric of the Contract and the publicity surrounding it sounded the themes by which Americans identify their national characters as well as the fact that the Republican leadership, after extensive research, determined that the message of the Contract would appeal powerfully to Americans.

It is worth pausing to note that not even the constituents of the Contract's primary author, Newt Gingrich, are very independent of government. The average Georgia taxpayer sent the federal government $1,876 in 1993 according to the most recent figures available. In 1995, two of the counties Gingrich represents, Cobb and Fulton, respectively received $6,861 and $8,230 per person from the federal government, compared with a national average of $5,180.[42] Undoubtedly the citizens of Cobb County could survive without federal largesse. But they would do so with less.

Regardless of ideology and rhetoric, even brief reflection will make it obvious that almost all Americans are highly dependent beings. We are dependent on our families and friends, of course, and that dependency is especially important in helping us recapture our intuitions about fairness, as I will explain in Chapter Six. But we are also highly dependent on our institutional and social structures. In particular, we are highly dependent on the state and its laws.

Conclusion

There is surely no single point, or even identifiable set of points, when the majority of Americans ceased to be independent of government in any meaningful sense. On one level, the very existence of government implies a certain degree of dependence, whether it is the minimalist state envisioned by Hobbes to keep us from killing one another or the omnipresent state envisioned by communism. Certainly by the end of Franklin Roosevelt's administration record numbers of Americans relied on government for more than physical safety. But one need not identify that point to know that today all of us are dependent on the state in ways we hardly even think about. At least as important, and despite the political rhetoric of recent years, I suspect that few of us, if faced with a real choice, would want to forgo that reliance.

Most of you who are reading this book are people who have achieved a measure of success in your chosen enterprises. But only a vanishingly small percentage of you are likely to be self-made in the manner suggested by our mythology. Far more likely, each of you grew up reasonably well educated, in reasonable comfort or at least not in dire poverty, and with a strong and supportive family. Most of you have capitalized on the opportunities you were given and, to your credit, made the most of them. But if Bellah is right, and the evidence strongly suggests that he is, most of you have taken those opportunities for granted, or not really thought of them as significant, perhaps because almost everyone you know had similar opportunities or, like Bellah's car dealer, because you have forgotten about them entirely.

Our forgetfulness is not simply a problem of ingratitude, or lack of perspective. It is a problem far more serious. To the extent that we fail to realize the advantages with which we have begun, we are led to dismiss, or not even to perceive, the extraordinary difficulties of those who do not share those advantages. As I will discuss in more detail later, this failure to understand the plight of others leads us to be considerably less sympathetic than we might. By putting others in our shoes—size self-reliant—instead of putting ourselves in theirs, we tend to believe that if only they worked as hard as we do, or were as virtuous as we are, or as smart as we are, they too would succeed. But of course we did not forge our work ethic, our virtues, and our intellects by ourselves alone but with the help of others, and in very different circumstances from those of the disadvantaged. As Bellah described the results of hundreds of interviews, "Most of those we talked to emphasized that they attained their present status in life through their own hard work, seldom mentioning the part played by their family, schooling, or the advantages that came to them from being middle class to start with."[43]

2

The Myth's Dark Underside

What's wrong with our mythology? In the first place, as we have seen, it's not entirely false. After all, hard work, talent, and discipline make a difference to those who start out with advantages. And they sometimes even make a difference to those who start with very little.

More important, perhaps, is the way that the myth of American individualism and self-reliance creates a climate of hope. It provides us with goals to aim for and a sense that we can achieve them. We want to believe that if only we work hard, if we apply ourselves and make the most of our abilities, we *will* get ahead. Whether we aspire to wealth, personal satisfaction, or a variety of other goals, our mythology encourages us—as the army recruitment ad says—to "be all that we can be." Our belief in the myth helps us not only to better our situations but also to maintain the stability of the social order. For in a society with inequalities as dramatic as ours, the disadvantaged *must* believe that their situations are not permanent or they would revolt—or simply give up. As columnist Richard Cohen suggested, Walter Mondale may have lost to Ronald Reagan in 1984 because he told the truth about the need to raise taxes and the limits to the American economy and in doing so destroyed hope.[1] We want to believe in the myth and seem to need to believe in it.

Finally, and as I noted in Chapter One, there is a strong strain of social responsibility in American morality. This observation is supported by a 1995 *New York Times*/CBS poll that revealed that almost two-thirds of Americans believe that government should take care of those who cannot take care of themselves.[2] If this is true, then fairness is unlikely to be a problem. We want to be fair to others despite the strength of the myth. If it gives us hope at the same time, what can be the harm?

The harm is substantial. Our conception of "those who cannot take care of themselves" is always of an other, and a rather narrowly conceived other at that—it is never of ourselves. We attribute vulnerability only to a very narrow class of people, just as the way we phrase this ethic suggests. Few people appear to us to be completely unable to care for themselves, and usually they are either children, the elderly, or the mentally or physically disabled.[3] Because we link vulnerability with these apparent differences, we do not think of those who are disadvantaged as being in any material way like ourselves. After all, we do not have the disabling physical or mental disabilities that make them different and unable to care for themselves. Because they are not like us, they comprise a special class of people, and that leads us to treat our obligation to help as somehow special.

The corollary is that we owe no particular duties to those who outwardly appear to be able to care for themselves. Their failings, we say, must be moral. After all, these people look like us and so they must be like us except for the fact that *they* are lazy—as some two-thirds of Americans consistently seem to believe.[4] By viewing the vulnerable as different, we undermine the normal moral response that leads us to care about them. They do not look like us; therefore, they are not like us. From this perspective, it is hard to empathize with them, leaving us resenting any help we give them.

Support for this view is found in polling data that conflict somewhat with the data in the *New York Times*. In 1994, the Times Mirror Center for the People and the Press reported a 12 percent decline to 57 percent in the number of Americans who believe that the government should take care of needy people. And 74 percent of respondents to a 1996 ABC News/*Washington Post* poll supported the Welfare Reform Act of 1996.[5] Although the polling data also suggest increasing distrust of government—so that we could attribute these results to attitudes regarding government inefficiency rather than attitudes toward the poor—additional data suggest that attitudes toward the poor are indeed changing. The Times Mirror report noted "increased indifference to the problems of the poor and minorities" as well as "resentment towards immigrants."[6] All of this is accompanied by Americans' "strong and growing support for the principles of self-reliance."[7] These facts suggest that our helping impulse is becoming weaker as our attitudes toward the disadvantaged are becoming more negative.

It is, of course, dangerous to rely too heavily on polling data, and it is fair to say that the survey evidence as to our attitudes toward the poor is somewhat conflicting. But two conclusions are clear. While we may have a general sense that we ought to help others, that sense is tempered by a deep (and sometimes decisive) ambivalence about their deservedness.[8] And our general belief is that people should—and can—go out and work, even when we doubt that work is available or at least available at a living wage.[9] One suspects that much of the ambivalence is caused by the conflict between our appreciation of the need to help and the ethic of self-reliance, the conflict at the heart of this book.

Besides leading to an "us" and "them" attitude, the disjunction between the myth and the reality has the potential to lead to deeper social conflict, some of which we can see developing today. If we assume that everyone except the radically disadvantaged is independent and autonomous, we resent the failures of others that require us to care for them. We come to believe that it is unfair for our tax dollars to support people who are just like us except for the fact that they have worked less hard or are less talented than we are, and we despise the use of government compulsion to achieve this result. Finally, to the extent that we believe that resources are being taken from us to support the unworthy, we ourselves begin to feel increasingly vulnerable to forces over which we have little control.[10]

Although I will discuss both harms here, I will wait to develop the moral relevance of the first harm (or set of harms) until Chapter Seven. For now, I will simply lay out the factual argument as I understand it. The relevance of the second, purely instrumental harm should be immediately obvious, and I will illustrate its importance with examples. At the same time, I will also treat its moral significance later in this book.

We Have Met the Vulnerable and They Are Us

Meet the Lamberts, introduced to us by John Schwartz and Thomas Volgy.[11] Paul is thirty-nine. His wife, Jane, is thirty-seven. They live with their three children, ages six to sixteen, in a mobile home in the exurbs of Cleveland, Ohio. Paul began working in 1982 at Doby's, a chain drugstore, and became manager of its liquor department (after starting as an assistant manager) before leaving in 1990 to join Andrews Electronics as the supervisor of the shipping and receiving department. As we can see, Paul advanced in his position at Doby's, and he received an excellent work evaluation at Andrews. In 1991, Jane was the full-time manager of a warehouse, a job she also held during at least part of the time Paul worked at Doby's.

During 1988, Paul's last full year at Doby's, he made $5.50 an hour and worked approximately forty-four hours a week. During the time Paul worked at Doby's, Jane's full-time salary was $10,000. Their combined 1988 income was $22,300, well above the official poverty line of $12,092 for a family of four.

On this income, they had the following necessary expenses (which I suspect most readers would judge as modest):

Mobile home	$470 (monthly)
Utilities and phone	$150 (monthly)
Food	$90-$100 (weekly)*
Car expenses	$3,000 (annually)†
Medical insurance	$800 (annually)
Unreimbursed medical	$600 (annually)
Clothes	$400 (annually)
Taxes	$2,800 (annually)

That left $2,000 for other expenses "including the purchase of school supplies for the children, replacing an old mattress, fixing a broken washing machine, repairing a vacuum cleaner, getting a daily newspaper, buying postage to pay the bills, and purchasing nonfood items like sheets and towels, paper products, cleaning supplies, shaving cream, shampoo, soap, toothbrushes, toothpaste, and light bulbs." [12] And this without confronting an emergency.

When interviewed by Schwartz and Volgy, the Lamberts could not remember the last time they had gone out to dinner—not even to McDonald's. They had not gone to movies or even taken day trips on weekends because they could not afford gas for the car. Because the Lamberts had no dental insurance, their daughters had never seen a dentist, Paul and Jane hadn't seen a dentist in years, and their son had

* Schwartz and Volgy report that Jane clipped coupons and looked assiduously for bargains and sales.

† 1988 insurance, gas, repairs, and license fees for a 1974 Oldsmobile and a 1965 Ford, each with more than 300,000 miles.

gone only when his grandmother had paid. Jane reported that the only reason she always had money for food was that she was able to borrow from her parents when the financial situation got desperate. * The Lamberts frequently relied on help from family.

Paul was laid off in 1990 when Andrews went into bankruptcy. Since then, he had been unable to find a full-time job and was working at two part-time jobs for a total of forty-five hours a week. He was earning only $155 a week but refused to go on welfare, which would have paid $123 a week. He had been diligently looking for a full-time job.

Both Paul and Jane had completed high school. Both were working as hard as they could to support their family. But imagine what life must be like for the Lamberts, even in those months when they are able to pay all their bills. And the Lamberts have company. As I reported in Chapter One, at least nine million working Americans are in a similar predicament, supporting families of twenty-four million people (including themselves).

The Lamberts work hard and apparently do well in their jobs. They have gotten as much free education as our country allows. They are careful, even frugal, with their money. And yet they seem not to have enough to lead what most of us would consider a decent life. They are poor by any standard except the official standard of the U.S. government.

David Gordon, in *Fat and Mean*, his indictment of American corporate behavior, updates and extrapolates from the story of the Lamberts. He notes that in 1993 the median family income of Americans in the bottom 80 percent of income distribution (excluding single individual households) was $24,730 *before taxes*,[13] only $2,400 more than the Lamberts earned in 1988. People in this range normally spend about $2,000 more than they earn and so are "net borrowers." On what do they spend this money?

Gordon answers this question by hypothesizing a relatively well-to-do family, one that has annual gross earnings of $30,037, consisting of one member working full time at $11.13 per hour and another half time at that wage (representing the 1994 average nonfarm production worker's wage in the private sector). The couple has two children. Their combined taxes come in at $5,076, at average rates. Their housing expenses total $10,182, which includes rent or mortgage payments of

---

* Jane's parents ran a bakery shop, and although Schwartz and Volgy do not provide their income, one suspects that they are not particularly wealthy.

$468 and the balance for repairs, utilities, and the like. Of the remaining $14,779, they spend $3,300 for food (at about $2.28 per person daily), "$1,952 on health care, $3,394 on transportation, and $1,862 on clothing."[14] This leaves a balance of $4,776 for everything else, from life insurance to nonfood supplies to books and entertainment, vacations, and supplemental education for their kids. Needless to say, this *average* income for the lower 80 percent of American families does not go a long way, and it certainly doesn't provide much, if anything, for general expenses or retirement or college savings. Yet, as it should be clear, this average family is far from poor—its gross income is $14,896 above the 1994 official poverty line of $15,141 for a family of four.

Okay, so much for the working poor. Perhaps many of them do the best they can and still can't quite make it, and perhaps we ought to help them out. But what about welfare recipients? Surely theirs is a world of absentee fathers off loitering on street corners, mothers who have children in order to increase their welfare payments and then sit at home watching television and buying lottery tickets or expensive trinkets. If these people would stop having children and start finding work, they would remove themselves from the public dole and better themselves in the process.[15] Why should they bother working?

One answer, which is not the one I shall rely on, is that they shouldn't. Indeed, some of them may have friends or relatives like the Lamberts. Paul Lambert earns only a little more than he could if he were on welfare—and he works awfully hard to do it. So why make the effort?

Of course this isn't an answer. There are many reasons we should make the effort, but the most significant answer for my purpose is that our common portrayal of welfare recipients is deeply flawed. Take the case of the popularly maligned welfare mother. In general, welfare mothers both work and look for work. A 1995 study by the Institute for Women's Policy Research (IWPR) found that 43 percent of welfare mothers worked for pay at least three hundred hours during a two-year period and an additional 30 percent spent between twenty-two and twenty-eight weeks looking for work. During the 77 percent of that two-year period when they were receiving welfare, these mothers spent more than 30 percent of their time working or seeking work. Finally, fully 75 percent of persons receiving welfare also receive some compensation from work and other sources such as family members and the like.[16] Whatever else appears to be clear, "most studies show little, if any, effect of welfare assistance on willingness to work."[17] In fact, the

U.S. government reports that 70 percent of welfare recipients stop receiving welfare within two years, and 90 percent do so within five years.[18] Although 75 percent return to welfare, these figures seem more consistent with a desire to work than with enjoyment of life on the dole.

The fact that large numbers of recipients return to welfare suggests that something troubling is going on. Some of it may be the poor education and undeveloped work habits of those who have been raised or spend a substantial portion of their lives in poverty. But the story of the Lamberts may suggest another reason as well.

It's Their Own Fault

Who is to blame for the Lamberts' fate? Sociological and psychological evidence suggests that we believe it is primarily themselves. The evidence suggests that Americans tend to blame the poor for their failings and that those who fail to succeed tend to blame themselves as well. Why? The answer lies in the myth of American individualism.[19]

The corollary to our strongly held belief that hard work and diligence leads to success is that those who have failed have only themselves to blame. Those who succeed tend to attribute success to their own efforts; those who fail blame themselves (and are blamed by others).

Kluegel and Smith have provided empirical evidence to show that those who succeed tend to credit themselves with their own success—empirical evidence that supports the conclusions I drew from the anecdotal evidence in Chapter One. By itself this is harmless. But it leads people who have succeeded to extrapolate from their own circumstances to those of everyone else, leaving the likely reason for the failure of the poor to be their own lack of industry and thrift.

Kluegel and Smith found that the higher your socioeconomic status, the more you believe that all Americans have equal opportunities to succeed. In general, Americans believe that the top five causes of poverty (in order) are "lack of thrift and proper money management skills; lack of effort; lack of ability and talent; attitudes that prevent advancement; and failure of society to provide good schools for many Americans."[20]

Which of these failings apply to the Lamberts? Clearly they spend their money carefully, and they manage it quite carefully. They certainly work hard (at least by my standards). As far as ability and talent go, Paul always got excellent job ratings and advanced at an appropriate rate, so they aren't lacking in talent and ability unless we define these as the qualities necessary to be a high-powered lawyer or doctor or business executive (or sports or entertainment star). And surely we don't mean to limit the opportunities for a decent livelihood to those relatively few (nor would our country function well if that was all we encouraged people to do).

Nor is there evidence in Schwartz and Volgy's rather lengthy report on the Lamberts to suggest that their work attitudes are bad. In fact, Paul refused to go on welfare because of his pride and desire for independence, even though welfare would have paid him almost as much each week as his forty-five hours of unsatisfying work. What about education? We have no evidence on the quality of high schools that Paul and Jane attended, but since their parents were middle class (although seemingly on the lower end), it seems fair to assume that their schools were adequate (at least by contemporary American standards).[21]

Interestingly, only 44 percent of the people Schwartz and Volgy surveyed believed that luck was a factor of any importance in consigning people to poverty.* A 1996 Public Agenda Foundation survey found that 63 percent of those surveyed believed that there was no real difference in luck between welfare recipients and others, and only 25 percent thought that welfare recipients were more likely to have suffered hard luck than other Americans.[22] These data are corroborated by several other studies that find that Americans generally attribute to the poor responsibility for their own failures. But what seems flawed about the Lamberts *except* their luck? Paul had looked hard for work and seems to have taken the best jobs he could find. Yet the best jobs for a high school graduate paid him a salary that put him practically at the official poverty line and in practical conditions of poverty, even with his wife's full-time salary. What else could the Lamberts do?

I work about as many hours as Paul, yet I earn a substantial multiple of what he does and my job is, I suspect, considerably more rewarding. And I know people, as you must, who work only a few more hours than Paul yet earn fifty and even one hundred times as much as he does. Why? Well, one reason may be that we had more schooling. But how much of that is luck, and how much is attributable to our own initiative?

---

* Sixty-nine percent believed luck to be a factor of some importance in achieving wealth, although a whopping 95 percent said personal drive and inherited wealth were significant in achieving this end and 92 percent ranked hard work and initiative as important. James R. Kluegel and Eliot R. Smith, *Beliefs about Inequality: Americans' Views of What Is and What Ought to Be* (Hawthorne, N.Y.: De Gruyter, 1986), p. 77.

I was raised in an atmosphere in which the only decision was *where* to go to college, not *whether* to go—and you probably were too. This is traceable to the fact that my parents had both the resources to make my decision to go to college (and my choice of college) a nonfinancial issue and the sociological and educational status to take the importance of college for granted. In short, I was luckier than Paul.

If we have only limited sympathy for the Lamberts and the rest of the working poor, how do we feel about the welfare poor? Not very warmly. A 1994 Roper survey, conducted among residents of New York State (which roughly correlated with national trends, except more liberal according to the survey's authors), found that New Yorkers believed welfare to foster irresponsibility in its recipients. Fifty-nine percent believed that welfare encouraged teenagers to have babies (an impression quite at odds with the IWPR survey discussed above), half thought that the existence of welfare increased the number of poor, 60 percent saw welfare as "fostering dependency," and 78 percent believed that welfare led to "a spiritual and moral disintegration."[23] And this is in a decidedly liberal state. The Roper Center report described New Yorkers' attitudes toward welfare recipients as one of "tough love."

Political scientist Theda Skocpol sees the matter differently, and in a way that conforms with Kluegel and Smith's sociopsychological research: "Some voters feel better about punishing the underclass than about helping it. More broadly, and especially in America, the poor serve as a negative example against which those who 'make it on their own' and 'earn their own way' can define themselves."[24] This attitude also permits us to be freed "from feelings of guilt or indirect responsibility for the plight of the poor in society."[25]

This perspective is corroborated by evidence that shows that members of the working class are themselves willing to blame the poor for their own fate, evidence that is particularly striking in light of the plight of the Lamberts and the working poor in general. One reason for this negativism is that "living close to the poor (both in the sense of average income and in the likelihood of falling into poverty due to unemployment or disability), working-class people need to distance themselves psychologically from the poor in order to maintain a favorable social identity and self-esteem," a function that blaming the poor serves well.[26]

As important as these explanations are, it seems that another vitally important explanation for the tenacity of our negative attitudes toward the poor—despite substantial evidence that these views are unjustified—

is that these beliefs help to remove poverty as a counterexample of our American myth of success for the self-reliant. If people like the Lamberts have done the best they can, what does this tell us about the veracity of the ideals by which our society is governed? If the deeply poor who receive public assistance make regular and concerted efforts to work their way out of welfare—as the myth tells them they can and must—and nonetheless find themselves unable to escape, perhaps this suggests a deep pathology in the economic structure of our society, a fundamental unfairness that we would rather not face. And if we admit that such unfairness does exist and that those who live by the American creed are not thereby rewarded, what portent does this hold for the ultimate stability of our society?

If, instead, we see the poor (even the working poor) as in fundamental ways just like us, we need not worry. They *could* have better lives if only they *chose* to. That they have not chosen to do so, whether out of perverse desire or moral failing, limits our responsibility to take care of them. After all, we have made the effort to take care of ourselves, an effort the American myth tells us will be rewarding for them (as it has been for us) if only they would undertake it. To admit otherwise is to confront our own, uncomfortable vulnerabilities.

Vulnerability and Public Policy

The prevalent belief that the poor are just like us (except in their sloth and indifference) appears to have had a significant effect on American public policy in ways that support my thesis that our attitudes of public and private charity are reserved only for the radically disadvantaged. Recounting the development of the welfare state during the Johnson administration's Great Society era, Harvard professor Paul Peterson writes: "Although the 'deserving' poor—the blind, deaf and disabled— were placed within a new, nationally funded program that materially improved their welfare, the government was still reluctant to address the needs of the 'undeserving' poor—those who many people thought could and should earn a living for themselves."[27]

The truth of this assertion is made clear when one examines the major social welfare programs that have been in effect in this country during the last several decades. One obvious example is social security, which, coupled with Medicare, has been enormously successful in eradicating poverty among the elderly. Of course the elderly are deserving candidates—in my terminology, among the radically disadvantaged—because they are, in many cases, unable to continue to work or to provide fully for themselves.[28] In this way they are fundamentally unlike us and therefore acceptable as cases of need. Their deservedness is compounded by our general belief that the elderly have made a contribution to our society during their lives and should be supported when they can no longer help themselves.

The principal and original welfare program, Aid to Families with Dependent Children, provides an additional example at the other end of the chronological spectrum. If the elderly are highly vulnerable despite the fact that they at least had the chance to accumulate some wealth during their working years and may have successful children to help support them, how much more vulnerable are children, especially those born into poor families? Our understanding of childhood throughout most of this century—and certainly during the second half—has viewed children as more or less totally dependent on the support of others, at least until their early teens. Because we do not believe that children are capable of caring for themselves, they are, like the elderly, a species of "other" whose need for support gives us no particular cause for offense. In fact, like the elderly whom we view as having made their contribution, we anticipate that the children we support will also grow to be contributing members of our society (and perhaps support us in our old age), and so we have a self-interested reason for looking after their welfare, as well as moral reasons to do so.

Look at the other principal programs that comprise the welfare state. Medicaid is provided to care for the poor at their most vulnerable—when they are sick and otherwise unable to care for themselves. Social security disability payments are made available to those who are not able-bodied and therefore, unlike us, are unable to work. It is worth noting, in considering these programs, that Americans have an almost pathological tendency to distance themselves from the sick and the infirm, viewing them, for a variety of reasons, as both distinctly other and distinctly threatening, arousing our own sense of vulnerability.[29] But however uncomfortable the disabled and the sick make us, we also know, for the moment at least, that they are not like us and are worthy of support.

In this same line of social support programs, although relying heavily on the federally compelled use of private funds rather than public funds, is the Americans with Disabilities Act. This statute, whatever its abuses may be, is an explicit recognition that when others are distinctly unlike us—in this case because of their physical or mental disabilities—they may need additional assistance to achieve the American goal of self-reliance. Thus, we are expected to devote our resources to ensuring that people with disabilities have what we insist in our mythology all Americans have—equal opportunity.

There is a final category of federally compelled programs that I shall mention that is, in some ways, distinctly unlike the others but like them in relevant respects. That is affirmative action and laws generally prohibiting discrimination. As our laws stand, and as the U.S. Supreme Court has fashioned its doctrine, the most stringent antidiscrimination rules and the most defensible forms of affirmative action are provided for those who are demonstrably disadvantaged because they are identifiably different. Nobody in our society can seriously question the reality that people whose skin is black have historically been treated as other in ways that worked to their severe disadvantage. Because they are visibly unlike us, they are easily identifiable and therefore highly vulnerable.*

Our response has been twofold. On the one hand, antidiscrimination measures prohibit us from treating such people as other, at least without punishing consequences. On the other hand, programs such as affirmative action acknowledge the reality of otherness and use it as a means of ensuring compensating advantages for those who are so identified.

All of these examples of instances in which we as a society are willing to help have two related features in common. The first feature is that those we are helping are, in one or more ways, decidedly different from us. They are too old, or too young; they are sick or disabled; or they are identifiable victims of historical discrimination. The second feature they have in common is that all of these people are, *precisely because of their differentness*, highly vulnerable in ways we are not. It is this vulnerability, caused by their difference, that moves us to help. But, at the same time, it leads us to identify vulnerability with difference in ways that lead us to deny vulnerability in ourselves and others. This is, ultimately, the reason that we fail to see the devastating structural disadvan-

---

*Obviously some of you will be African American, or disabled, or otherwise in the groups that I characterize as other and my use of the inclusive "us," as will undoubtedly be painfully apparent to you, is not meant to include you. This only reinforces my point in the text concerning the extent to which differentness helps identify vulnerability.

tages of the poor and the working poor. This is why our public policies and our charity overlook the Lamberts and those like them. Because we do not see them as different—because outwardly they look just like us—we fail to see them as vulnerable. And we fail to see them as vulnerable because we do not see ourselves as vulnerable.

Social Dependency, Modern Society, and Vulnerability

We do not see ourselves as vulnerable, but in fact we are. And in many ways each of us is as vulnerable to the forces of markets, nature, society, and politics as any of those we see as different. We fail to realize our vulnerability at our peril, because our invulnerability is simply contingent.

Vulnerability is universal. If nothing else, the vulnerability that is common to all of us at all times derives from the simple fact of human inequality. By using the phrase *human inequality* I do not mean to make a metaphysical observation or to contend that Locke or Kant or our founding fathers were wrong to hold that all people, in some fundamental way, are created equal. All I mean is that people *in fact* are unequal because people in fact are different. To make this assertion I need not draw upon the radical differences I have previously discussed. Nor do I need to talk much (at least not yet) about talents, or ambitions, or bad luck in terms of the ways they reward or punish people. All that I need to support this statement is the modest observation that people live together in society.

Even in a simple society people will have very different roles and abilities.[30] Imagine, for example, a group of six castaways on a desert island. One, perhaps, has physical strength and mechanical ability and would naturally be the person to build shelter, dig a well, and the like. Another has cunning and good aim and would likely be the hunter and fisher. Another has intellectual powers and so will design tools and devices to make life more comfortable and ease the tasks of the others.

However reasonable it would be to expect these people to divide their responsibilities in a way that suited their talents, it is dramatically more so when our focus of attention shifts to modern industrial society. The division of labor in modern industrial society clearly demonstrates the reality of our mutual dependencies. And these dependencies do not necessarily relate, at least directly, to physical or mental strength. Instead, they are based on the intricacies of society itself, on the complexity of social, economic, and political relations and functions. For it is obvious that, unless we remove ourselves from that society, we cannot function—economically or otherwise—without the help of others.*

Recognizing this character of social interaction broadens our understanding of the causes of vulnerability from the more obvious forms I discussed earlier to those created by divided responsibility and training and ability. In our modern society the butcher, the brewer, and the baker have their own specific functions, but so does the union official, the bank trust officer, the stockbroker, the government bureaucrat, and the corporate director. The corporate director would be no more able to slaughter and butcher his own meat than the butcher would be to determine the amount of corporate funds that should be devoted to ensuring the safety and effectiveness of antibiotics. The butcher and the corporate director depend on one another's training and skill to make their lives together possible, and this makes them vulnerable to one another. In light of this, it should not be surprising to see that we have laws that govern their relationships with one another.

Our willingness to help others is, as I demonstrated above, based on their vulnerability. But acknowledging that reality is only the start of a meaningful understanding of fairness. We are led to help the vulnerable at least in part because we all are vulnerable. And this more universal understanding of vulnerability is one that is based on a social reality here and now. It is a reality that has probably existed in one form or another since primitive society but that has attained its greatest realization in our contemporary social structure: vulnerability based on social complexity.[31]

I shall, from this point on, use the concept of vulnerability in this broader sense. By making this understanding of vulnerability the central focus, I do not mean to dismiss the seriousness of the other, more obvious, forms of vulnerability I have already discussed. Physical, mental, and emotional disabilities create significant vulnerabilities, as do disabilities based on social status. But the proliferation of vulnerability in complex society may diminish the importance of these examples as model cases for a complete theory of fairness.

---

* Even the independent Larry O'Brien, introduced in Chapter One, needed to take a full-time construction job to supplement his family's income from its farm.

It is possible, however, to see even cases of physical, mental, and emotional disabilities as having social causes, for it is beyond question that the development of modern society has dramatically increased the incidence of each, at least in part by creating causes unknown in primitive society. People are maimed by the vehicles of modern transportation and manufacture. People are sickened by pollution. People are injured by dangerous or defective products. People become emotionally disabled by the stresses of tedious and unrewarding jobs and by the increasing anonymity and complexity of social interaction. Each of these vulnerabilities is inherent in modern society.[32]

There is also a different sort of vulnerability that isn't caused by industrial complexity but by the pluralistic nature of our society. This is vulnerability based on social status, which includes race, religion, ethnic origin, and gender. The way in which we deal with this type of vulnerability presents a nice test for my theory, in that it partakes of both modern and traditional forms of vulnerability. Like traditional vulnerabilities based on physical characteristics, these vulnerabilities are largely immutable.[33] You cannot change your race or ethnic origins. But, like socially caused vulnerabilities, these characteristics become *vulnerabilities* only in a social context where they identify their bearer as somehow different from the other members of society.

All of this makes it clear that my argument uses the idea of vulnerability in a special way. All of us are vulnerable in this sense, because all of us are mutually dependent. We are not all vulnerable in the same ways or to the same extent, and this has consequences for how we conceive of fairness. But vulnerability is an intrinsically social condition, because inequality is a social condition.[34] It is the fact of such universal vulnerability that leads to our intuitions about fairness, that causes our concern with fairness.

The Denial of Vulnerability

If vulnerability is our normal condition, if it is as pervasive a reality as I have claimed it is, then why have we not recognized it? Why do we treat the obviously vulnerable as different and vulnerability as pathological? Why is our political discourse so lacking in an appreciation of vulnerability? Why have we failed to structure our institutions around the reality of its existence? These are critically important questions for my argument, and their answers show that the way we conceive of and react to vulnerabilities has important implications for the way we conceive of fairness.

Masking Vulnerability: The Law

The simple answer is that we have, in fact, structured many of our institutions around the fact of vulnerability. They have performed so well, however, that over time they have come to mask the reality of vulnerability, at least for the better-off members of society (who are our intellectuals and policy makers). The effectiveness of many of our laws and institutions conceals their origin in this mutual dependency.

An excellent example of this effect is the recent flap over Congress's attempt to reduce meat inspection resources substantially. When I walk into the local supermarket to buy my family's meat, I generally do not stop to worry that the meat may be tainted or that I am vulnerable to the negligence or greed of meatpackers. I know, at least subconsciously, that the meat I am buying has been inspected by agents of the federal government and so have reason to trust that it will be safe. When Congress attempted to reduce funding for this activity, however, I, and apparently millions of others,[35] were made aware of our vulnerability. We recognized that without trustworthy inspection, our every grocery purchase would put us at risk of sickness or worse. The threat of repealing regulation was the threat of restoring vulnerability.

Similarly, I do not feel particularly vulnerable to crippling medical expenses. I have a good job (thankfully with tenure), and my employer provides me with adequate medical coverage. When I invest my retirement savings in mutual funds, I am not particularly worried that the fund managers will walk away with my money. I know that there are laws and regulatory mechanisms to ensure that I am reasonably safe. I don't worry that my doctor is incompetent—his state-granted license hangs on his office wall. Again, modern social devices mask our vulnerabilities, which, until they are unmasked by law or circumstances, can be comfortably ignored. A few moments' reflection will undoubtedly reveal many other ways in which you might be vulnerable to a variety of bad consequences without protective laws and devices to shield you.[36]

The most common social vulnerabilities, then, appear to be those that are most easily eliminated. As the examples above suggest, many of the dependencies that are created by the social division of labor can be relieved (and largely disguised) by laws and regulations that permit us to go about our business without even recognizing that we *are* dependent and vulnerable. These laws ensure that we are provided with accurate and complete information, they require licenses and permits for conducting business, and they demand that those on whom we depend treat us as equals.

A similar set of solutions presents itself with respect to the other broad category of vulnerabilities I mentioned, those based on minority status within our society. We can and do take legal steps to ensure that no member of society is discriminated against because of minority status.[37] My bank advertises itself as an equal opportunity lender. The university where I am employed discloses that it is an equal opportunity employer. If these institutions violate these precepts, I know that I have legal redress.

We can and do use our laws to reduce the effects of these vulnerabilities even if it is impossible to eliminate them. Sometimes, especially in the areas of commerce and business, laws are successful in making these dependencies appear to fade away. Once they do so, we tend not to think of them as part of the universal condition of social life.[38]

Masking Vulnerability: Circumstances

It's easier to see how the circumstances of the powerful help to hide the reality of vulnerability. By the powerful, I don't mean simply politicians and the wealthy. Rather, I mean to include the upper middle class, if not much of the middle class. I mean, in short, people like you (and me). These people are our policy makers, our voters, our intellectuals, and our tax base. It is from these ranks that the American mythology is sustained and reinforced,[39] and it is in these ranks that it most resonates, as the statistics I discussed earlier suggest.

You need not rely on statistics to prove this point, however, for it is supported by common sense. People who are comfortably well off, who have good jobs and a good education, are people for whom our society is designed. They are people who, in the main, can compete in our markets and in our business, educational, and government institutions. They are people who generally live at some distance from our direst poverty and the conditions of our greatest despair. They are people who can, for the most part, anticipate decent lives for themselves and their children, who have options as to how to live their lives, and opportunities to succeed. Psychological evidence supports the observation that people tend to extrapolate from their own circumstances to a broader world view.[40] It is easy to see how such people can favor a social and institutional structure that appears to leave them on their own (disregarding, of course, the effect of the laws I wrote of above) to pursue those lives.

The fact that these circumstances can mask vulnerabilities is demonstrated by recent social trends. The popular media have made much of the backlash by white middle-class men over affirmative action and women's rights.[41] Preferential treatment for those who historically have been oppressed, particularly in a contracting economy, means discrimination against others. Thus, such treatment creates vulnerability that previously did not exist and a diminution of such people's ability to compete as well as they might have. The backlash, in short, is a cry for the social elimination of these new vulnerabilities.

We no longer acknowledge our own vulnerabilities. In the language of the American myth, we do not see that in fact we are neither independent nor self-reliant. This produces two significant effects. First, by overlooking reality, we are able to continue to perpetuate the myth, to continue to believe that our prosperity and security are largely a function of our own efforts. Second, and perhaps more important, our lack of perspective permits us to overlook the needs of those, like the Lamberts, whose vulnerabilities our system has not as well ameliorated.

We limit our options: either people are different from us in ways that we can directly observe and that produce vulnerabilities we can identify, or they are like us and therefore are no more vulnerable than we are. In the first case, we are moved by their vulnerability to help. In the second case, because we do not see the vulnerability, we do not see a reason to help. I will revisit this argument later when I examine in detail the moral relevance of vulnerability, the mechanism by which vulnerability motivates us to help.

Contempt and Conflict

I have now dealt with the first sort of harm that the American myth creates, its tendency to blind us to the reality of universal vulnerability and its related tendency to lead us to blame the poor for their own failings and to absolve ourselves of responsibility for assisting them. There is a second harm as well. That is the potential of the myth to lead to dramatically increased social conflicts. These conflicts have become more pronounced in recent years, as a brief discussion will show.

Pleasanton, U.S.A.

Let's start at the top. Katherine Newman, in her recent study of the increasing economic and social intergenerational divides in America, *Declining Fortunes*, examined the growing anxiety of both the postwar generation and their children in a comfortable—indeed affluent—New Jersey suburban community she calls Pleasanton. The older residents of Pleasanton are among the vanguard of the great American middle class, people who raised their families in the '50s and '60s on one good salary, living comfortably and providing their children with the good schooling and other advantages of affluence that would enable them to succeed and replicate, if not exceed, their parents' standard of living.

While not rich, the residents of Pleasanton live far different lives from the Lamberts. And they know it. For all their concerns, and the concerns of their children, Newman is careful to note that the people of Pleasanton recognize their relative affluence and feel undeserving of sympathy. She also notes, however, their deep sense of anxiety as they see their (largely college-educated) children fail to achieve home ownership in their own community (and often in *any* community), the parents' concern as they see their children head families in which both mother and father work simply to afford a decent standard of living (and are unable to save for their future on it), and the prospect of an increasingly declining American economy with an eroding economic infrastructure.

These are people deeply worried about the future, and with good reason. Their concern leads them (and especially their children) to a sense of vulnerability that they have not previously known. While they continue to work hard and try to improve their economic well-being, "they live with a vague sense of dissatisfaction and an underlying desire to blame someone for their grief. They are especially perplexed by the arbitrary character of the trends that have had such a profound influence over their standard of living." [42]

While Newman allows that some of the causes of baby boomers' anxiety may be of their own doing, she believes that structural forces within the economy are much more to blame. The reason for their emotional discomfort is not, however, what is primarily of interest to me. Rather, it is the fact of the anxiety itself, an anxiety born of an increasing sense of vulnerability to forces beyond their control, and it is because of this anxiety that they have increasingly developed negative attitudes toward those whom Americans traditionally have helped. Newman notes a marked decline in sympathy for "the down and out"[43] as middle-class baby boomers find it increasingly difficult to make ends meet. As she puts it, "The squeeze on the middle class creates political agitation for tax cuts: the more Americans need their income to pay for essentials, the less generous they feel toward Uncle Sam."[44] This anxiety and increasing lack of sympathy and generosity are reflected in the attitudes of the baby boomers' parents, who see their children unable to come close to replicating the quality of lives they led.

Part of this increased sense of vulnerability is due to actual economic conditions. But part of it, as Newman recognizes, is driven by the way in which a declining economy has instilled within the people of Pleasanton a feeling of lost control. The baby boomers of Pleasanton came from comfortable families, were well educated, worked hard, and did pretty much everything the myth tells them they must. Instead of success, their reward is economic stagnation. And, like the Lamberts, they feel subject to forces beyond their control and do not know what to do about it. As Newman puts it, "The role of a puppet on someone else's string is not a happy one."[45]

The upshot of all of this is a search for causes and, primarily, a search for places to lay the blame. Given their circumstances, the desire to attribute blame to others is understandable. I have already noted the American tendency to blame the unsuccessful for their own failings and the corollary tendency of the unsuccessful to assimilate that blame. But if the children of Pleasanton have done everything right, everything the American myth tells them they should, they might reasonably conclude that their failures cannot be attributable to themselves.

Newman finds plenty of evidence of denial and blame in her interviews with the people of Pleasanton and their progeny and notes that they look both above and below them to assign blame in ways that are consistent with the survey data I reported earlier. Further, it is readily apparent how, in a blaming society, new problems without apparent causes go in search of scapegoats. The coexistence of the lie with this new reality breeds cognitive dissonance. And that has the potential to lead to increased conflict between the newly vulnerable and those whom they find to blame for their misfortunes.

If the disjunction between lie and reality has this effect on the relatively sophisticated and well-educated citizens of an affluent New York suburb, what effect must it have on those less fortunate?

Some evidence is provided by a recent phenomenon, the rise of the militia movement. The story is complex and has many causes. But central to it is a strong sense of vulnerability.

The Militias

The militia movement gained national prominence after the 1995 bombing of the Alfred P. Murrah Federal Building in Oklahoma City. Federal officials arrested Timothy McVeigh and Terry Nichols, men who were identified with an organization called the Michigan Militia. This and other so-called militia became the focus of widespread news reports in an attempt to identify these organizations and what they stood for. Although various right-wing extremist agendas have been attributed to these militia, including the eventual overthrow of the U.S. government, and though it is clear that they hold a wide range of beliefs and goals, one unifying factor is that all of them are motivated by fear, specifically fear of the federal government. And fear, of course, is an emotion caused in large part by feelings of vulnerability.

Where does the fear begin? According to one unsympathetic report, it begins on the economic margins: "Pick just about any pocket of economic and social distress . . . and you will find thousands of Americans who spent part of last year dressing up in camouflage, undergoing automatic weapons training and preparing for final battle with what they consider to be an enemy federal government."[46] As one observer describes a segment of militia that also engage in tax protests, "They all have the same MO (modus operandi). They are white, high school graduates who are the working poor and they can't figure out why their world is falling apart. Two generations ago, they would have had good jobs."[47] And as one unsympathetic sociologist describes it, "There's just a feeling of alienation and complete detachment from the political system."[48] These attitudes are confirmed in other reports, both sympathetic and not.[49]

Economic fear is one motivating factor, but there are other fears that become evident when one looks at the militias: "First and foremost, the militias are a movement that for some time has been waiting to happen, born in the backlashes against civil rights, environmentalism, gay rights, the pro-choice movement and gun control."[50] These various movements, of course, have the effect of shifting the balance of power in America toward minorities and the disempowered and from traditional "mainstream" Americans. With this shift comes not only increased feelings of vulnerability but increased vulnerability in fact. Affirmative action places whites at some disadvantage in job and educational opportunities with respect to various minority groups. Environmentalism arguably threatens jobs in already precarious economic communities, and gay rights and pro-choice movements threaten the fundamentalist Christian values that most of the movement's participants hold. As they see these and other usurpations of what they perceive as their "rights" being acceded to by the federal government, that government has become the focal point of their discontent.

Economic dislocation, conflicting values, and increasing rights of access to scarce resources by previously disadvantaged groups breed feelings of vulnerability. This is not the place to analyze the militia movement and the legitimacy of its claims and tactics. For my purposes, the only relevant point is their grounding in vulnerability, and the tendencies toward extremism, social strife, and rebellion that the militias engender. We ignore this vulnerability at our peril.

The Power of the Myth

While I have spent the first two chapters of this book attempting to explode the American myth and expose its dangers, there is no question in my mind that the myth rests on an admirable ethical foundation, one that is well suited to a pluralistic society like our own. That ethical foundation, tracing back to the philosophy of Immanuel Kant and beyond, is the moral significance of each individual and the relevance of exercising free will not only to morality but to the project of pursuing a life of one's own choosing. To this end, an ethic of individualism is valuable and probably essential. The problem is that it is just that—an ethical foundation. Yet we have turned it into an empirical assertion.

In brief here (but more later), we assert not only that the individual's rational pursuit of her own good is desirable (with the corollary that she must live with the consequences of her choices) but that each of us is, in fact, capable of doing precisely this. Thus, we have structured our laws and institutions on the assumption that all we need is to provide equal procedures and equal opportunities and fairness and harmony will result. All we need is to be free to choose.

The Lamberts tell us otherwise. It would be a cold, if not cynical, person indeed who would tell us that each of the Lamberts is pursuing a rational life plan in accordance with his or her respective visions of the good. The Lamberts are just trying to survive. The choices they make are restricted by that need and are directed solely toward it. And in a state of bare survival, they are unlikely to be able to take advantage of the formal mechanisms we expect them to use to fulfill their life plans.

In introducing his commendable Points of Light Initiative, George Bush claimed, "What millions of Americans need is not another government program, but a set of meaningful relationships that results in the conviction that their future is not limited by their present circumstances." [51] In so doing he was, of course, attempting to tap into the American strain of communitarianism through private organization observed at least as far back as Tocqueville. And perhaps Bush was right that government programs per se are not needed. But the story I have told in this chapter is one that suggests that present circumstances do indeed limit the futures of millions of Americans. And these circumstances have structural causes that run deep throughout our society.

Government programs, in the sense in which that term is taken in contemporary political discourse, might not be the answer, although I will discuss this later. It is clear, however, that the American myth is embedded deeply in our laws in ways that ensure that the vulnerable remain in that condition. Even when our laws are expressly designed to address vulnerabilities, they are applied in ways that deny vulnerability and assume autonomy. It is to an analysis of this assertion that I now turn.

3

The Myth Lives in the Law

Private Law

The Purposes of Law

aw has many functions in our society. At its most basic, it
helps to maintain order and keep the peace. Thomas Hobbes
thought that in a lawless state of nature the rough physical
and mental equality of most people would lead to a war of all
against all. We would spend our short, miserable lives protecting ourselves and our property from everybody else and
this would give us no time or incentive to improve upon the
natural conditions of life—to create industry and comfort,
arts and culture, or any of the other conditions we think
make our lives worth living. To escape that state of perpetual
fear and turmoil and to enable us to build a civilized society,
we put ourselves under the authority of a lawgiver with the
power to maintain the peace through rules and punishment.
A law professor's favorite example of this purpose of law is
our obligation to stop at red lights.

Classical liberal theory accepts the need for law to maintain order. But it also gives law a higher purpose. John Locke
saw law as permitting us to pursue our lives, our liberties,
and, most of all, the development of our property. It is this
last goal that Jefferson transformed into his felicitous phrase
"the pursuit of happiness." Law's main function in this view
is to keep each of us out of the way of the others, so that each
of us is equally able to pursue his goals. Our liberties are

constrained, but only by so much as is necessary to enable everyone to have equal freedom. This liberal ideal is embodied in our great constitutional doctrines of due process and equal protection.

This liberal conception of law is the one that most influenced our founding fathers and the one that most clearly persists in our laws today. It is the foundational conception of law necessary to sustain the myth, the idea that each person should have the freedom to choose his life course. If we have fulfilled our public responsibility to ensure this goal, to provide each person with an equal opportunity to exercise his own autonomy, then we have fulfilled our obligations to him and his life becomes his own responsibility.

Modern liberal thinkers have created a number of variations on this basic conception in ways that appear starkly different but that, upon examination, converge at the same endpoint. I will later have occasion to discuss three of the most prominent liberal paradigms as reflected in the thoughts of three philosophers. These paradigms present a variety of ways of realizing the liberal ideal, from support for the modern welfare state to a radical free-market economy. Although they present visions of society that appear to be dramatically different, these paradigms ultimately all rely on the liberal vision on which America was founded.

There is another purpose of law that is grounded in what I shall call, for want of a better term, the romantic vision of law. By so naming it, I should be clear that in no way do I mean to disparage it. Indeed, it is— more or less—the approach to law that I take in this book. I use the term both because it captures a distinct vision of society through law and because it has taken such different forms throughout history that a more precise phrase is hard to find.

The romantic vision of law has, in some ways, its historical antecedents in idealist philosophies as different as those of Plato and Rousseau and, in its extreme form, Marx. These ideals see law as a tool to be used in building a good society. This phrase—"good society"—requires a moment of explanation. Philosophically, a good society is one that aims for some goal that, by common agreement of its members, is the goal that makes life worthwhile. While philosophers like William Galston and Will Kymlicka have argued that a liberal society can be a good society in just this sense, the romantic view tends to hold a richer conception of the good. The good can be, as Alasdaire MacIntyre has argued, the heroic society of the ancient Greeks, or a theocratic state, or even a state based on secular communism. The idea that ties all of these societies together is the idea of a common purpose, with the related notion that every member of the society has her particular role, or place, in accomplishing that end.

In America this strain is grounded in part on the Puritan ideal of the city on the hill, creating an example for the rest of the world as to how we should live, although as a society we no longer agree on the Puritan goal of salvation. The persistence of this ideal is reflected to varying degrees in such diverse notions as Madisonian manifest destiny, the Social Gospel of the late nineteenth century (and the succeeding progressive movements of the early twentieth century), Roosevelt's New Deal, the civil rights movement, and the Great Society programs, as well as in more extreme movements, such as that of the contemporary religious right. In almost every case, however, American romanticism—unlike many European versions—remains tempered by our acceptance of the value of a degree of individual independence, and so shall my ideas.

Despite its ubiquity, the romantic vision has always been subordinated to the liberal ideal. A major reason for this is our fear that, in its more extreme forms, the romantic vision robs people of their liberties, forcing them to conform to a regime of values with which they may disagree and compelling them to live lives not of their own choosing. Look again at the way I described romantic law—as aiming toward a common goal and a role for each person. It doesn't take an ardent feminist or the descendant of slaves to realize that such roles can force some into lives of subjugation and unhappiness. Greek and American slaves, Russian serfs, Jewish merchants, Indian untouchables, the English lower classes, and countless other oppressed people might be forgiven for questioning social structures that have prevented them from rising above their imposed stations.

In light of this fear, it is no wonder that cries of fascism and communism often confront modern attempts to foster community through law. When different manifestations of the romantic vision seem to have become too powerful, this fear has led us to suppress them by emphasizing our liberal rights. Abortion rights, school prayer, flag burning, and similar issues provide the most obvious contemporary context in which these battles are fought.

I will use this and the two following chapters to show the ways in which the liberal ideal invariably defeats the romantic strain, although

I shall later argue that this result is not inevitable. An easy way to do this would simply be to present an analysis of general laws assuring liberty, such as those reflecting freedom of contract and business association, constitutional protections of free speech and freedom of religion, and the like. Instead, I will take a more difficult route, because by so doing I hope to be more persuasive in arguing that the liberal ideal has become pathological in our society, privileging liberty even when we say we mean to privilege community. I want to show that even when our laws confront people at their most vulnerable—when their opportunities, and often their abilities, to embrace their liberties through the exercise of their personal autonomy is most compromised—the law in fact demands that they do so. And this at the same time that the rhetoric of the law asserts our intent to help them.

This phenomenon is pervasive throughout our legal doctrines, but limitations of space preclude me from examining all of them. To make my point, then, I will draw upon doctrines of law that expressly, or by clear implication, embody a notion of fairness. This fairness ideal is perhaps most explicitly reflected in laws of fiduciary obligation, which we will examine in this chapter. We shall do this through a look at marital law—specifically the laws governing marital contracts—and corporate law. We shall see that in these areas the law abandons us to our own devices after promising to help at precisely those times that we most need help. It disregards our vulnerability and pretends instead that we are fully autonomous.

While the fairness ideal is clearly compromised in our laws governing these essentially private relationships, the same problems exist in our fundamental constitutive laws. Thus, in the next chapter we will look at the constitutional doctrines of due process and equal protection to see how the goal of liberty overrides the ideal of fairness even in the basic structures of our society. Finally, in contrast, we will take a brief look at the Americans with Disabilities Act as a case in which we actually use the law to provide fairness by ameliorating vulnerabilities—but only in situations in which those we help are obviously and sometimes dramatically vulnerable.

We shall see that our laws and institutions leave us on our own at the very times that they claim most to help, at the times we most need their help. In doing so, they compound the dangers of the myth. In doing so, they maintain the status quo.

The Laws of Fairness

I begin with laws that express a very special ideal of fairness that we say we apply under very special circumstances. These are the laws of fiduciary obligation. In its purest doctrinal expression, fiduciary obligation requires one person to look after the best interests of another. This is not a request for us to act upon feelings of charity or benevolence. It is *law*, and thus it uses the compelling power of the state to force us to fulfill this obligation. Further, it is law that appears to conflict sharply with our dominant liberal ideal of individual autonomy and with the fundamental American myth of self-reliant individualism.

The circumstances in which we apply fiduciary law are those in which one person has given power to another to look after his interests. The classic example is the law of trusts. In a trust relationship, one person (Charlie) gives his assets to another (Susie), and Charlie charges Susie to hold and develop those assets either for Charlie's benefit or for the benefit of somebody else he identifies. Why does Charlie do this? Because Charlie (or his designated beneficiary) lacks the ability to manage the assets himself, an ability Susie presumably has.

Susie's obligation as trustee to act as a fiduciary, to act in the best interests of Charlie or his designee, is based on two factors. One is the simple fact that Charlie asked her to do so and that she accepted. This provides a contractual basis for the relationship and to some extent determines Susie's obligations. Through the creation of this contractual relationship, Charlie can make specific demands of Susie—for example, that she invest the assets so as to provide him with income.

The other factor is the power that Susie acquires over the assets (and thereby Charlie's welfare) by virtue of the relationship. Once the trust instrument is signed and Susie takes control (indeed legal ownership) of the assets, Charlie becomes entirely dependent on Susie for the management of those assets. Susie may be guided by the contract, but the contract is embodied in language, typically written language. Circumstances may arise that make the language ambiguous or its applicability uncertain. More commonly, matters may come up that the contract does not cover, since these relationships are often long term and the unforeseeable can occur. Finally, Charlie is not likely to have provided much detail in the contract. After all, if he had wanted to, or could, manage the assets, presumably he would have done so himself. He therefore expects Susie to use her discretion in managing the assets during the life of the trust.

The relationship this transaction creates is one of power and dependency. Susie has assumed power (typically absolute power) over some aspect of Charlie's life. And to the extent that Susie has assumed this power, Charlie has become entirely dependent on her for his well-being.

What compels Susie to act in Charlie's interest? After all, she now has the assets. She could abscond with them entirely, or pay herself well, or invest the assets in projects from which her friends would benefit. We hope that she will be restrained by her good faith and Charlie's trust in her to use the assets in his best interests. But we are not entirely content to leave it to trust. Even the best-intentioned people face conflicts between their personal interests and their duty, and human weakness sometimes leads to a favoring of self over other. We back up Charlie's trust in Susie with the power of the law.

The law we use is that of fiduciary obligation. Broadly put, it tells the fiduciary to act in the best interest of the beneficiary. In its original formulation, this law was strict. Any time Susie even appeared to act in her own interests, the law demanded that she return any benefit she received to Charlie—regardless of whether her actions harmed him, helped him, or had no effect on him at all. Over time, courts began to question the efficiency of this rule. After all, the Susies of the world argued, if I truly and reasonably believe that my husband is the best stockbroker around, it's in Charlie's interest to invest with him. Why should I be forced to rebate the commissions to Charlie just because I also happen to benefit from them too? If the assets include a piece of real estate that I'd like to own and I am willing to pay the best price, why shouldn't I be permitted to buy it?

Courts began to see some merit in this argument. Not every conflict of interest meant that Charlie would suffer. Sometimes he might do better if Susie acted in these conflict situations. But how could we distinguish cases in which Charlie benefited from such actions from those in which he was hurt? The law's answer was that Susie could do personal business with Charlie's assets as long as she could prove that the result was fair to Charlie.

Thus, the law of fiduciary obligation moved from one that strictly prohibited Susie from acting in her own self-interest to one that acknowledged the potential benefit of this action as long as it was fair. But, as we will see, in the process of reaching this result, the laws that developed to define fairness have come to disregard Charlie's vulnerability to Susie. In fact, they have come to treat him largely as independent and autonomous in his relations with her. And underlying this transformation is the power of the American myth.

Fiduciary Law in Marital Contracts: Love and the Myth

Marriage presents the classic fiduciary relationship (or so at least thought Benjamin Cardozo).[1] In many ways it puts us in our most vulnerable state. In marriage we are emotionally vulnerable, as we place our happiness and well-being and pledge our loyalty entirely to another. In the ideal marriage, we expose our deepest selves and partly constitute our deepest identities to and through another and in so doing make ourselves emotionally vulnerable to that other.[2]

For those of you of a less romantic bent, marriage also creates financial vulnerability, as two people mingle together their assets and rely on one another to provide the necessities and luxuries of life, now and for the future. If the marriage produces children, each partner leaves the children vulnerable at least in part to the skill, love, and compassion of the other. Ultimately, we subordinate a portion of our autonomy, and merge a portion of our identity, to and with that of another.

It is no surprise that the marriage relationship is considered a fiduciary one. But the ongoing state of a healthy marriage is not my concern here. Instead, I will look at the marriage in formation, a situation in which the vulnerabilities created by marriage are rawly exposed. These are the circumstances surrounding antenuptial agreements.

Two kinds of contracts—antenuptial and separation—govern the division of marital assets. Antenuptial agreements establish, in advance of the marriage, the type and quantity of assets each partner will receive if the marriage ends. Separation agreements are entered into by married persons whose marriages have failed and are in the process of dissolving the marriage.* Courts often apply fiduciary law, using a test of fairness, to each of these contractual relationships, because they recog-

---

* I will not analyze the legal doctrines governing separation agreements because of limitations of space. Often—but not always—they are treated as similar to antenuptial agreements.

nize that these contracts are entered into under conditions of vulnerability and dependency similar to those of marriage.[3]

The law presumes that parties entering into a contract do so rationally; for present purposes this means coldly, calculatingly, and looking
out for themselves. This presumption is reflected in the legal ideal of
freedom of contract—courts generally will not interfere with bargains
that people have freely entered into because the parties are presumed to
know and to have bargained for their own interests. But two people contemplating marriage may be different. They have—we hope—developed strong emotional ties.

Most people think that emotions differ from reason (although, according to the philosopher Robert Solomon in his book, *The Passions*,
they are in fact the ultimate form of reason). While emotional involvement may not cause the parties to behave entirely irrationally, it surely
alters the range of what they consider reasonable. As William Blake
wrote, "Love to faults is always blind,/Always is to joy inclined,/Law-
less, winged, and unconfined,/And breaks all chains from every mind."
The partners' developing emotional sense of shared interests, including
trust and emotional dependency, is likely to limit the extent to which
they coldly pursue their individual self-interests. The circumstances
that surround the negotiation of an antenuptial agreement, then, differ
dramatically from those of the paradigm arm's-length commercial contract. In short, the partners love each other and, as poets and novelists
throughout history tell us, love doesn't always make for clear, self-
interested thought.

What is true at the premarital stage often is also true, although in
different ways, at the time a marriage is dissolving. The partners already
have commingled their assets and financial well-being, and frequently
one partner is financially dependent on the other—as evidenced by the
fact that women typically suffer dramatic financial declines following
divorce.[4] While the fact of marital dissolution signals the end of love, it
hardly is evidence of the end of reason-impeding emotions—it's just that
the emotions are different. We have all witnessed bitter divorces that
rival Italian opera for dramatic impact. Feelings of betrayal, breached
trust, disappointment, faded love, and sometimes bitter hatred and a
desire for revenge replace the rosy glow of love's true bloom. To paraphrase Ira Gershwin, the song has ended but the melody lingers on—
cacophonously.

Love may have died, but its demise does not necessarily make the partners more rational. They no longer see their interests in common, and this removes an impediment to clear reason that existed at the premarital stage. But love is replaced with negative emotions that can create different kinds of vulnerabilities and impair clear thought. The process can also be complicated by reason-blinding issues, such as child custody, which can empower the financially stronger partner to hold the other hostage and thus lead the weaker partner's love for the children to overcome financial self-interest.

Courts in these circumstances often say that they will examine the contracts to evaluate their fairness. They recognize the context of dependency sufficiently to identify the relationships as fiduciary, for all the reasons I gave above. The striking thing is that in each context courts in fact almost always disregard the real and obvious emotional and financial dependencies that can result in grossly unequal bargaining advantages. Instead, they treat each party as rational, independent, and able to take care of herself. In other words, they treat each party as the myth says they should. Not surprisingly, the stronger party almost always comes out on top. The status quo is maintained. *

John and Cristina DeLorean were married on May 8, 1973. She was twenty-three years old, a model who had once before been married. John DeLorean was forty-eight, twice married, and a "high powered senior executive with General Motors Corporation"[5] who would go on to form the DeLorean Motor Company (which would lead to his own dramatic travails of bankruptcy and accusations of drug dealing). Only hours before the wedding, John presented Cristina with an antenuptial agreement and demanded that she sign it—if not, he would refuse to go through with the wedding. At the same time, he supplied her with an attorney to advise her. The attorney recommended that she not sign the agreement. "Yet, for whatever reasons," in the words of the court, she signed.[6] The agreement provided that she would receive only a modest share of her husband's assets if the parties divorced.

Thirteen years later, and with two children, John and Cristina obtained a divorce. John's assets were worth at least $20 million. Cristina would receive half of that under New Jersey divorce law; under the

---

* Not surprisingly, too, the woman is almost always the weaker party. Gail Frommer Brod, "Premarital Agreements and Gender Justice," *Yale Journal of Law and Feminism* 6 (1994): 229–95.

agreement, almost nothing. She sued to invalidate the agreement, arguing that she did not sign it voluntarily.

It is crucially important for our discussion to understand the court's idea of voluntary action. It reveals a strong assumption that a person's choices almost always are voluntary, regardless of individual characteristics or circumstances. The court here noted that Cristina had been divorced before and knew the problems that one could encounter in a marriage. Moreover, while "it may have been embarrassing to cancel the wedding only a few hours before it was to take place,"[7] nobody (literally) held a gun to her head. Finally, although her husband had provided the lawyer (which might cause us—but not the court—to have a slight question about the lawyer's independence), she did at least have a lawyer whose advice she chose not to follow. The court therefore concluded that Cristina had signed the agreement voluntarily.

Did Cristina sign the agreement voluntarily? Or perhaps a better question is, On the facts the court reported, could it be reasonably confident that she signed the agreement voluntarily? Consider this. The court noted that Cristina's prior marital experience gave her some degree of sophistication about these matters. Presumably the court meant to suggest that Cristina's prior experience should have prevented her from—starry-eyed—imagining an ideal relationship with John that would last until death parted them. Undoubtedly some people are hardened to the wiles of romance by prior bad experience. But an empirical study by two law professors shows that this typically is not the case.

Lynn Baker and Robert Emery studied the perceptions both of marriage applicants and of law students who had completed a course on family law (and thus had been exposed to case after case of failed relationships). They found that the first group's median response to a question about the American divorce rate was accurate in estimating that on average roughly 50 percent of Americans divorce. *Yet every single one estimated that her own chances of divorce were 0.* Perhaps most surprising, the hardened and cynical law students (who should have shared Cristina's presumed perspective) gave similar responses[8]—and nobody I know has accused law students of being hopeless romantics. Professor Baker tells me that there is no similar study of people who have been divorced, but her strong impressions are that the results wouldn't vary much. And common sense, I suspect, would tell us the same (it's those irrational emotions again).

Another issue is raised if we look at the characteristics of people who typically remarry. Statistics tend to show significant age disparities among many couples who are remarrying, with the men generally older than the women. Law professor Gail Brod reports evidence that this age disparity creates a power imbalance that may favor the older partner in negotiating issues regarding the marriage, an observation compounded by the fact that men who remarry tend to be wealthier than their spouses.[9] None of this appears to have occurred to the court.

What does this tell us about Cristina DeLorean? It tells us that if she was normal, she probably did not expect that she and John would get divorced and that she was taking little risk by signing the agreement in order to marry the man she loved. (It also suggests that John was in a superior bargaining position—and we know he was wealthier.) Sure, it was creepy of him to spring the agreement on her at the last minute. But nobody's perfect.

The rest of the court's reasoning raises questions too. The court makes nothing of the difference in John and Cristina's ages. But those of us who once were twenty-three (and now are rather older) don't need statistics to tell us how significant that difference can be.

What of the court's apparent belief that the only consequence to Cristina of canceling the wedding would have been some embarrassment? Here the court appears to have no appreciation of the context of this decision. Certainly the imminence of the wedding ceremony, including invited guests and a caterer who presumably wanted to be paid, suggests that cancellation would have been inconvenient and embarrassing. But the wedding ceremony is symbolic—John and Cristina were about to enter into a most serious relationship. Presumably she loved him and wanted very much to marry him, not simply to ensure that the ceremony occurred. By all accounts, John DeLorean is a very attractive and charismatic man.[10] Perhaps Cristina was afraid that if she canceled the wedding to contemplate the agreement, he would not have married her. And compounding the ordinary pressures of a twenty-three year old about to marry, she was forced to make this analysis in the whirlwind of wedding preparations.

Or perhaps she was cool and calculating and made a rational assessment of the costs and benefits to her of entering into the agreement. Perhaps she calculated the odds of divorce and assessed the probable value of marriage with the agreement versus spinsterhood without it. Perhaps. But the court didn't know, because the court didn't ask. Instead, it *assumed* that this was her thought process, because that is the thought process that a normal rational person would undertake under such circumstances. It assumed that this was her thought process, because the law suggests that it *should* have been her thought process. The normative perspective of the law is one of self-protection and rational calculation, even in circumstances of extreme vulnerability.

Perhaps you don't cry for Cristina. After all, she was attractive—indeed glamorous—and had other career and probably marriage possibilities. Consider then the case of Belinda Williams. Although Belinda was ultimately rescued by the Alabama Supreme Court (over a dissenting opinion), the actions of the two lower courts and the opinion of the dissenting Supreme Court judge testify to the strength of this normative stance.

Belinda Culp was a twenty-four-year-old interior decorator in a small Alabama town. In September 1983, she began dating William Thomas Williams, a thirty-year-old businessman and livestock farmer. Six months later, Belinda discovered she was pregnant and told William. She had moral objections to abortion, but William would not talk about marriage with her until June. He told her then, with his lawyer present, that he would not marry her unless she signed an antenuptial agreement.

The agreement provided that if the parties divorced, Belinda would receive $1,000 a year for each year of the marriage, up to a total of $10,000, and no more. The court reports that Belinda took the agreement to a lawyer who William recommended but who did not discuss it with her. According to her testimony, "she was too upset to ask questions and cried throughout the time that she was in the attorney's office."[11] She signed the agreement, and they married. Seven years and two children later, William divorced Belinda. He argued that the agreement provided for all of Belinda's rights to the marital property and that he would give her no more.

The trial court and the intermediate appeals court agreed with William as a matter of law. They decided that Belinda had signed the agreement voluntarily. The Alabama Supreme Court disagreed and demanded a retrial.

Perhaps it is not as obvious as I think it is that the facts of this case raise a very substantial question about what it means to do something voluntarily. True, Belinda signed the agreement voluntarily, in the sense that nobody physically forced her to sign it. True, she had no right to demand that William marry her. And it may even be true that she understood that divorce under the agreement would leave her in a precarious financial position. Assume all of this. And then ask whether, if you were Belinda, under the circumstances she faced, you would have felt that you had any meaningful option but to sign the agreement. And if you had no meaningful option, what is the relevance of a theoretical option?

The relevance is that the law treats theoretical (if unrealistic) options as real choices. It does so because it values the ethic of individual self-reliance over all contenders. Because it starts with this value, the law attempts to fit all situations upon the matrix of this value and to assume that the normal starting point is free choice. In so doing, it discourages courts from asking serious questions about Belinda's subjective beliefs—about what Belinda thought was really happening—and, for that matter, about what William thought was happening too. After all, if nothing else is obvious, it is clear that William was using Belinda's pregnancy and strong desire for marriage as a tool to compel her to sign the agreement; he (unlike the court) realized that she would have no choice.

What of all this? Even taking a more nuanced and, frankly, realistic analysis of the facts into account, the courts may well come out the same way. But if they did, they would do so having been forced to confront the reality that the assumption of free choice is *not* in fact a statement about reality but a statement about values. They would have to admit that the right normative approach is to treat people *as if* they chose freely and then to justify that standard in cases in which free choice was absent. By treating Belinda's actions as voluntary, the courts are hiding the strong normative grounding of free choice in a questionable assertion about reality.

The Laws of Corporations

Euphemia Donahue was a widow. Lest you think that I am about to tell a heartbreaking tale, rest assured—she was not an impoverished widow. In fact, her late husband, Joseph Donahue, had, through hard work and some luck, parlayed his trade as a finisher of electrotype plates into 20 percent ownership of his employer, Rodd Electrotype. The only other shareholder was his friend and coworker, Harry Rodd, who became the controlling stockholder (owning all the stock that Donahue didn't). As time went on, Harry Rodd brought his sons into the business and began to distribute his shares to his children, although he retained a controlling interest.

By the time Harry was an old man, his sons were firmly in control of the business. But as long as their father held his stock, the boys' independence was constrained. Perhaps like Regan and Goneril, perhaps for more noble reasons, they persuaded their father to retire. He agreed to do so on the condition that he be paid for his shares. He agreed to sell most of his shares to the corporation for $800 each and distributed the rest among his children.

By selling his shares to the corporation, Harry received a distribution of corporate cash that was not available to the other shareholder, Mrs. Donahue.[12] For some years prior to this, the corporation had offered to buy Mrs. Donahue's stock at prices ranging from $40 to $200 per share, considerably less than it eventually paid for Harry's stock. Mrs. Donahue now asked the corporation to repurchase her stock for the same price it paid Harry. The corporation said no. Mrs. Donahue sued.

The court ruled in her favor, recognizing that the Rodd family, taken together, owned a majority of the stock and, in the typical corporation (of which Rodd Electrotype was one), the majority rules. For this reason, Mrs. Donahue was completely vulnerable to the Rodds. There was no market for the stock, because the corporation was privately held. If she chose to sell her stock, her only choice was the Rodds or the corporation, and she would be stuck with whatever price they chose to pay. She had no prospect of receiving dividends—that decision would be made by the Rodds as directors, and they had no need for dividends themselves because they could pay themselves salaries as employees of the corporation. The court recognized that the shares likely represented Mrs. Donahue's major asset—her principal source of income—which, as I have noted, the Rodds were in a position to cut off. Moreover, they had an incentive to cut off this income stream, because she might then feel forced to sell her stock to them at whatever price they asked in order to realize some return. They could then be rid of her and keep all the goodies for themselves.

In short, like the fiduciary situation in which our marital partners found themselves, the court recognized that Mrs. Donahue was entirely dependent on Rodd Electrotype for her welfare. She had no power, no control, of her own. And so the court ruled that the corporation had to buy back her shares at the same price it paid Harry Rodd.[13]

Thus was the rule of equal opportunity established for closely held corporations like Rodd Electrotype. The peculiar vulnerability of minority shareholders led the court to apply an understanding of fairness that attempted to redress the gross imbalance of power by providing a legal means for such a shareholder to obtain some leverage. Fairness in this respect is like the fairness that courts claim to apply in marital contracts, a standard that attempts to restore some power to a vulnerable party. And like the standard applied to marital contracts, it looks a lot better than it is.

The *Donahue* rule was widely cited, but it didn't last long. In short order, courts, including the Massachusetts court that created the rule, became troubled because the rule seemed to constrain the autonomy of the controlling party. Of course, this was its purpose. But such a purpose was not in keeping with our fundamental ethic. As a result, courts began to take account of the *motives* of the controlling party. As long as he could show a business reason (including his own advantage) for favoring himself, the courts would let his action stand. Only if his only possible motive was to inflict damage on the weaker party would the controlling party be required to equalize advantages. Not surprisingly, it is pretty easy to come up with business reasons to justify almost any transaction, especially when you include—as courts do—personal advantage within the idea of business reasons. And, not surprisingly, an exhaustive review of the cases reveals that the controlling party almost always wins. In short, the law preserves the status quo.

This might be troubling enough by itself. But at least the rule, even in its diluted form, leaves open the possibility that a Euphemia Donahue will occasionally win. It establishes a baseline, a ground rule if you will, that, while perhaps quite low, nonetheless demands at least a minimal standard of conduct by power holders to those who are vulnerable to them. The trouble is that some states, led by New York, have kicked out the props from under the rule entirely.

The cases are not hugely sympathetic on their face. We are, after all, dealing with relatively wealthy people. But we are dealing with them in situations of great vulnerability. The point is not that we should weep for well-heeled business executives. It is that we should see in the stories of Phillip Ingle and James Gallagher a tale of how American law leaves people at their most vulnerable to take care of themselves.

Phillip Ingle was a car salesman for Glamore Motor Sales. He initially offered to buy an interest in the dealership, but James Glamore, its only stockholder, decided to offer him a job first. Two years later, James agreed to sell Phillip slightly more than 20 percent of the company, with an option for him to purchase 18 percent more over five years. As part of the deal, James agreed to make Phillip a director and secretary of the company. The agreement provided that James could repurchase all of Phillip's stock if for any reason Phillip ceased to be employed by the company.

Phillip was successful and dedicated. He was named a codealer with James and personally guaranteed up to $1 million of corporate debt. Sometimes when the business needed money, he lent it some of his own. Seventeen years after Phillip first became a stockholder, James unceremoniously kicked him out to make room in the business for James's sons. Under the terms of the contract, Phillip was obligated to sell his stock to James for a total of $96,000; since Phillip had paid $75,000 for it seventeen years earlier, it was a modest rate of return at best.

Phillip sued.[14] He did not complain about the price for his stock but argued instead that he wanted to keep the stock and participate in the company's business. The court said no. The problem, it held, was that Phillip was an *at-will* employee. This meant that Glamore Motor Sales, which James controlled, could fire him at any time, for any reason, and so it said that Phillip should have realized that his ownership and role in the business was precarious. Had he wanted greater security, the court said, he should have bargained for it.

In so noting, the court made an argument with some superficial appeal. After all, nobody forced Phillip to work for Glamore or buy its stock. It was his idea to purchase Glamore stock, and the buy-back provision was part of the deal.

The trouble with this reasoning is that it misses one small reality. That reality is the seventeen-year relationship that developed between Phillip and James. During that time Phillip became more than an employee—he became a partner, a partner who invested his own funds in the business and who bailed it out when it needed extra money, a partner who guaranteed the company's debt, a partner who had an executive voice in the business. Presumably there were many times during the course of this relationship when Phillip could have walked. He did not, presumably, because his loyalty to James, and James's presumed loyalty to him, added value and meaning (not to mention stability) to the business relationship. Throughout the course of their seventeen years together, while the agreement was lurking in the background, Phillip placed his trust in James, trust that James would repay his loyalty and not take advantage of his vulnerability as an employee at will and as a minority stockholder.

Phillip was a sap. Or so it turned out. And this is one of the major problems with a decision like *Ingle*, a problem I identified in the last chapter (and will take up again later). If we tell the Phillip Ingles of the world that they ought not to make themselves vulnerable, that they ought not to place reasonable trust in others, because we will leave them hanging if they trust wrong, we breed a society of conflict, division, and suspicion. In this particular context of corporate law, we can imagine business partners spending much of their time protecting themselves from each other, much of their time guarding their flanks. As a result, far less business will get done. It will also send the message that even if you do all the things that we consider good and praiseworthy, you will find no protection in our laws when you are taken advantage of. What incentive does this give people to act in ways we consider good and praiseworthy?

Phillip's case is bad. But it can, perhaps, be justified on the ground that courts should not force a business to continue to employ a person it would prefer not to. In some ways, James Gallagher's case is worse. James Gallagher was a real estate broker who was employed by Eastdil Realty, serving also as a director and officer and president of a subsidiary company. He did quite well for himself; at one point his commissions reached $1 million. James, along with other Eastdil executives, was offered the opportunity to buy Eastdil stock, under a plan that was later modified in favor of the executives to discourage them from leaving the company. As a result, James eventually acquired 8.5 percent of Eastdil's stock, making him its third-largest stockholder. As part of the deal, each executive was required to sign an agreement providing that if his employment was terminated within twenty-four months, the company had the right to buy back the stock at book value. Thereafter, if employment was terminated, the repurchase right continued but the price would be set according to a formula.

On January 10, twenty-*three* months after James signed the agreement, Eastdil fired him and demanded that he sell back his stock. The book value price, which was then in effect under the agreement, was $89,000. If James had remained employed for one more month, until February 1, the price would have been $3 million under the formula. The only reason that James was fired was that Eastdil's other executives wanted to buy back his stock at the low price and distribute the extra wealth among themselves.[15]

James sued. Too bad, said the court. James had signed the contract and that was that. If he had wanted greater protection, he should have bargained for it. Failing that, he should have realized that Eastdil could take advantage of him at any time during the two-year period of the agreement.

Of course what the court was telling James Gallagher, as it told Phillip Ingle, was that his loyalty was foolish. James, who evidently was quite a successful broker, should have left the company instead of taking the stock offer. He should have disregarded the company's needs, because he should have realized that his "partners" could not be trusted. The decision to trust them, to remain loyal, and to work for the good of Eastdil Realty was his choice. If he chose wrong, he bore the consequences of that mistake alone.

James Gallagher's situation is a far cry from that of Euphemia Donahue's. After all, he had acquired significant wealth and was easily able to support himself. But he was like Euphemia Donahue in more ways than he was different. He too was in a powerless minority position within a corporate structure, in a situation in which his control was severely limited. He too put his financial well-being and his trust in others, and nothing in the facts suggests that at the time he did so that decision was unreasonable. People in James Gallagher's situation have limited information at the time they make such decisions. In particular, they cannot foretell the future. Future Gallaghers, at least those who are well counseled, will not make the same mistake. They will not give their talents and certainly not their loyalties to others. And to the extent they need to sell their talents, they will do so with extreme caution, self-protection, and distrust. They will rely entirely on themselves. And in relying on themselves, they will be strongly disinclined to care about the interests of others.

The story of James Gallagher is instructive, for it exposes the strength of the myth in the law. It tells us that when we join together to accomplish a common purpose, we do not really join together at all. Instead, we retain our separateness dramatically and completely. Our common purposes are transitory, lasting only so long as they suit our interests. Our organizational commitments are ephemeral, because they really are commitments only to ourselves. Our communal life is promiscuous.

One might respond by noting that these cases involve business and, after all, business is business and therefore different from the rest of our lives. But this observation is specious. In the first place, not even Adam Smith accepted this argument, grounding *The Wealth of Nations* in the broader moral universe he envisioned in his *Theory of Moral Sentiments*.[16] Besides, if we think that business is different, we must ask *why* business is different. Is it because we think that it is acceptable for people to be predatory in acquiring wealth but not in acquiring love, or power, or fame? If so, why? All of these are scarce resources. And presumably (at least according to most theorists) our minimal purpose in banding together socially is to regulate the distribution of scarce resources, or at least (in the Hobbesian world) to keep us from killing each other in the process of acquiring them. If we disavow that purpose, what hope do we have of pursuing any higher purpose? It is a question I will not answer here, for I think it is obvious that the objector herself has the burden of providing the answer. "Business is different" is no answer at all.

The abandonment of the vulnerable that I have demonstrated to exist in corporate law is pervasive in that field. Take the example of publicly held corporations. In these organizations, stock is widely held, sometimes among millions of people, and the personal corporate relationships I described in the other cases do not exist among co-owners. Instead, the business is managed remotely, by its board of directors and executives.

In this context, as one might imagine, directors and managers face the temptation to help themselves to a portion of the corporation's assets. Of course, they rarely give in to this temptation directly. Most people, after all, would draw the line at embezzlement and theft, either because of moral strictures or for fear of being caught and the destruction that it would bring to their reputations and careers. Instead, they yield to temptation more subtly. *

Here's an example. Let's say that you are a director of Software Corp., a publicly held developer and manufacturer of computer games. And assume that your spouse is the president and sole stockholder of an advertising agency, AdCo, that specializes in computer products. You go to a board meeting one day, and the president announces that Software is not happy with its current advertising campaign and needs to

---

* I hasten to point out that most corporate directors and managers are decent, well-intentioned people who would not (at least knowingly) steal from the corporation. My point is to illustrate the ethic embodied in the law that transforms what might ordinarily be thought of as theft into fairness.

find a new agency. You go home and tell your spouse, who presents a proposal to Software's board and gets the job.

Conflict of interest? You bet. The possibility of a sweetheart deal (quite literally) lurks in the background. You, of course, receive a benefit from that deal. But even if Software pays a competitive market price, the possibility still remains that AdCo was chosen, regardless of whether it was the best agency, because your spouse owns and runs it. You still receive a benefit, and AdCo is enriched by the new job.

How does corporate law deal with the problem? It says that you (and the other directors) have a fiduciary duty to look out for the interests of Software and nobody else. But this fiduciary duty is applied in an interesting way, a way that at bottom is consistent with the myth.

The law says that if you told your fellow directors that your spouse owned AdCo and that you obviously had a conflicting interest and if you didn't vote on the deal and it was approved by the other directors, that is good enough. It assumes that your personal conflict of interest did not affect the rest of the board. In short, and consistent with the assumptions underlying the myth, it assumes that the board's actions are independent and autonomous.

Maybe they are. But maybe the rest of the board members have spouses in business too. And maybe someday they would like to arrange for their spouses to do business with Software. And maybe—just maybe—they think that if they turn your spouse down, you will reciprocate.

We don't really have to get that personal. The most recent data I have show that 93 percent of the directors of Fortune 1000 corporations are men, most of whom are over fifty-five years old and the chief executive officers of other corporations.[17] It seems obvious that these people will have rather similar interests (remember our family vote?), including a desire not to be challenged on their own boards, and will often find themselves in positions in which they can do favors for other board members. While the law leaves open the possibility that in extreme cases a court might actually examine the substance of a conflict of interest deal, it is a possibility reserved only for extreme cases. Ordinarily, as long as boards follow the general procedure I outlined above, their decisions are beyond challenge. And they are beyond challenge because courts fail to recognize the vulnerability of the corporation to conflict of interest transactions.

I don't want to overstate the point. If a board were grossly to abuse its power, it would be stopped under law, and perhaps even by the discipline of the securities markets. But it is not the gross overreaching that concerns me. Rather, it is the observation that on a day-to-day basis law assumes the self-reliant independence of people who exist in an interdependent web that makes such independence illusory. It is a premise that is based on our myth. And, in making such an assumption, the law disregards the vulnerability of the corporation and its stockholders to the power held by these directors.

4

The Myth Lives in the Law
Public Law

We have thus far focused on what has traditionally been called private law.[1] There are two principal reasons we have done so. The first is that our general philosophy governing personal relationships is one of free association. We develop relationships with those people with whom we choose to do so and on terms of our mutual agreement. The areas of the law we have examined involve these freely chosen relationships. When the law imposes obligations of fairness on such relationships, the contrast of that obligation with our normal freedom is likely to throw our ideas of fairness into high relief.

A second—and more important—reason we have focused on private law simply is that many of these laws developed for (and to a large extent continue to develop and be applied to) personal relationships. This context provides the best testing ground, in Humean terms, for our understanding of moral concepts in general, for, according to Hume, our moral ideals develop precisely in the crucible of such relationships. To the extent that laws are responsive to human needs and expectations, laws deriving from the expectations of persons actually engaged in such relationships undoubtedly will be revealing of our ideas of fairness. We will explore the implications of this point thoroughly in later chapters.

As important as these areas of private law are to fairness, however, our story would be incomplete if we failed to look at the understanding of fairness embodied in those laws generally considered to be our public laws. These are the laws that deal with the structure and functioning of our government and our obligations to our government generally (ranging from tax laws to environmental and occupational safety regulations). We will focus, in particular, on two of the great constitutional doctrines that provide a strong moral under-girding for our entire political structure and that consequently permeate our public laws. The doctrine of due process, located in the Fifth and Fourteenth Amendments to the Constitution, seeks to ensure that the awesome compulsory power of the state is applied consistently, dispassionately, and impartially and in a context in which the persons subject to that power have an opportunity to question its use. The equal protection clause seeks to ensure that minority groups are treated equally with the dominant groups in our society.

We have thus far seen that our political, economic, and social lives are predicated on the ideal of individual autonomy. We have seen that even in our most intimate relations, our laws privilege autonomy over other values. It should not be surprising, then, to find that the public laws that constitute our social structure also are based on the value of autonomy. In addition, abstracted as they are from particular human relationships, and broad and general as they are in application, it should not be surprising to see that they are not particularly sensitive to human relations values. In fact, we will find that when our laws have attempted to account for those values, they have failed.

Due Process: Fundamental Fairness

"The essential guarantee of the due process clause is that of fairness."[2] This striking statement, echoed throughout the leading cases,[3] demands that we look at the conception of fairness underlying the due process clause, for surely it expresses our core ideal of fairness, embodied as it is in our constitutive law.

The due process clause applies to many of our dealings with the state—its courts and its agencies. It doesn't take much to reflect upon how much due process means to us. Suppose, for example, that the IRS audits your tax returns and, despite your honesty and care in preparing them, sends you a deficiency notice telling you to pony up another $10,000 (or more if you consider $10,000 to be mere pocket change). You take the notice to your accountant, who carefully reviews the materials and decides that the IRS is just plain wrong. If there were no procedures that permitted you to challenge the IRS, you would pretty much be left at its mercy. Your situation wouldn't be a lot better if the IRS were allowed to provide whatever procedures it felt like—say a hearing before the examiner who audited you in the first place.

Think about how much more terrifying your situation would be if you were entirely dependent on the state—say a welfare recipient faced with the termination of your benefits or a defendant in a criminal trial. The constitutional guarantee of due process is an assurance that your dealings with the state involving your life, liberty, and property will be regularized through fair procedures that give you a fighting chance.

The typical study of the due process clause concerns the question of what process is due—what are the particular procedures to which a person is entitled? Our concern is similar but perhaps deeper. Why is it accepted wisdom that the due process clause is about fairness? Why is it that we seek to ensure fairness, at least at the constitutional level, through procedural devices? What does this tell us about our understanding of fairness?

It may be that we think that the due process clause provides a concrete political expression of our intuitions about fairness in the form of its requirement of mandatory procedures. This reading would be plausible (if not indisputable) if the Constitution specified certain procedures that were fair by definition. We could then conclude that the due process clause is about fairness because it tells us the requirements of fairness. But it does not. Instead, the measure of fairness to be applied to our procedures must come from a different source. Our attempt to identify the process that is due is an attempt to determine the meaning of fairness in this context. We will find, as we have before, that fairness is keyed to a person's ability to exercise autonomy at the same time that it generally presumes that she is able to do so.

On the one hand, the scope of the due process clause is huge. Because it applies to state interference with life, liberty, and property, it goes directly to the heart of the individual's concern with state coercion. Our understanding of fairness in this context, then, ought to be pretty good evidence of our understanding of fairness generally.

On the other hand, due process provides a somewhat limited understanding of fairness. It is concerned exclusively with fair *process* and thus expressly excludes concerns of substantive fairness that may exist at a deeper level;[4] therefore, broader issues of social justice—wealth distribution, for example—are outside the scope of its concern. But these broader issues of substantive fairness are largely, if not entirely, absent from our Constitution (at least as generally interpreted by the Supreme Court). So when we examine our understanding of fairness from the perspective of due process—and indeed from the perspective of the Constitution as a whole—we must remain aware that due process requirements, despite their grounding in fairness, do not exhaust our field of fairness concerns.

While this observation is true, however, it is not entirely complete. For, as we shall see in the leading cases, our understanding of fair process is very much related to the substantive interests at stake. In *Arnett v. Kennedy*,[5] for example, a plurality of the Supreme Court held that a public employee could not separate his right of employment from the narrow procedures provided to enable him to challenge his termination. The process itself, in other words, limited the property right he had in his job tenure.

Although a majority of the Court rejected this approach in a later case, it continues to have its adherents, as does the broader view that substance and process are difficult to separate. Thus, in examining the requirements of due process, we will pay attention to the way in which the substantive interests at stake influence the determination of the process that is fair, as well as the extent to which the process affects the value of those interests. At the same time, we will see that these substantive concerns tend to be reflected in an abstract and arbitrary manner that divorces them from the realities of the world.

Due process analysis ultimately is concerned with individual autonomy. Vulnerability is a given, as the state threatens to take the life, liberty, or property of the individual. The question is whether this vulnerability impairs the individual's autonomy. The answer clearly is yes. The very fact that we require certain procedures before the government may take life, liberty, or property recognizes that the individual cannot, without help, overcome her vulnerability to the state and challenge its actions. At the same time, the due process clause also seems to suggest that, by providing some procedure to permit the individual to protect herself, the individual's autonomy can be restored. The question thus becomes what procedural protections are necessary to enable the individual to act autonomously in defending her life, liberty, or property from being taken by the state.

To talk about autonomy in this context may seem somewhat forced and peculiar. Due process casts us in a narrow and particular circumstance, in which the goal of the state is to deprive the individual of something that she has. The "good" of the individual in this context is therefore a given—to prevent the state from doing this. Autonomy in this context is far from the founding liberal vision permitting every individual to define and pursue her own conception of the good. The scope of autonomy is thus severely constricted to begin with.

But autonomy is at issue in two ways. First, the individual will always be arguing that her use of her life, liberty, or property in pursuit of her own ends is a use with which the state cannot interfere. Second, and more important, the individual's opportunity to participate in a process with the government on equal terms recognizes her autonomy both in determining the way in which she will go about formulating and conducting her defense and in her right to participate as an equal.

My purpose here is not to critique the Supreme Court's development of due process doctrine as a legal matter or even its efficacy. My only goal is to show the strong grounding of the doctrine of fairness as autonomy and, in a related way, to demonstrate the pull of that doctrine to abstraction from reality.

Autonomy concerns are central to our understanding of fairness as it underlies due process.[6] I begin my analysis with a leading case, one that shows the Supreme Court in its most ardent (if short-lived) attempt to tailor process to the real autonomy needs of human beings. This is the famous case of *Goldberg v. Kelly*,[7] which, perhaps more than any other, proclaims that the importance of individual dignity and autonomy lies at the root of due process.

The question in the case was whether a state could terminate a person's welfare benefits before holding an evidentiary hearing—in the nature of a trial—to determine whether she was in fact eligible to receive the benefits. New York, which administered the welfare program at issue, did provide certain procedural protections to a welfare recipient threatened with termination. These included an opportunity for the recipient to discuss the matter with a caseworker and to respond in writing in several stages before the welfare benefits were stopped. A personal hearing for the recipient was provided only after benefits were terminated.

The Supreme Court's opinion is rather dry and technical, giving no sense of the human drama underlying the issue. Before discussing the opinion, it might be valuable to have a look at the situation of the plaintiffs involved in the case. Between the time that Angela Velez's benefits were (wrongfully) stopped and the time they were restored, she and her four small children were evicted from their apartment. They then lived with Mrs. Velez's sister and her nine children, who themselves were on welfare. The entire Velez family slept in one room in the apartment, sharing two single beds and a crib, and were poorly fed. It was in such circumstances that Mrs. Velez was required under New York procedures to challenge the termination of her welfare benefits—to find a lawyer, participate in constructing her case, and persuade the bureaucracy that it was wrong.

The welfare benefits of Esther Lett and her four minor children also were wrongfully terminated. The Lett family then lived solely on food given to them by their neighbors, which in one case resulted in the entire family being food poisoned. Yet it took weeks, during which there was no scheduled hearing, and the initiation of a lawsuit before her family received temporary benefits.[8]

The Supreme Court reviewed the facts in light of the due process clause and held that welfare benefits could not be terminated before the recipient had been given an opportunity to have a personal hearing. The paper processes New York provided were inadequate. Welfare, obviously, is a critically important benefit, one that is as essential to our "nation's basic commitment . . . to foster the dignity and well-being of all persons within its borders"—in other words, to our national concern with individual autonomy—as it is to the individual's well-being.[9]

There must then be a hearing. And the hearing must have value. The individual must be given an opportunity to participate meaningfully in the decision to terminate this essential benefit. "The opportunity to be heard must be tailored to the capacities and circumstances of those who are to be heard."[10] Many welfare recipients are functionally illiterate and certainly unable to present a coherent written case on their own behalf. Not only did the Court find that written submissions were inadequate, it also rejected the practice of having the caseworker present the welfare recipient's case. The caseworker has conflicting interests; after all, it is he who has the task of assembling the facts that prove his client's ineligibility. Besides, this deprives the recipient of the opportunity to put the case in her own words and to demonstrate her credibility. The Court's reasoning seems largely directed to its concern with accuracy in decision making, but it is clear that tailoring the process to facilitate the individual's participation is grounded in concerns of human autonomy as well.

The Court's sensitivity to the need to respect human dignity and its appreciation of the limits on a person's abilities to exercise autonomy are pretty much limited to the welfare context. George Eldridge received a different form of state assistance—disability benefits under the Social Security Act.[11] After four years of receiving benefits, he was informed by the state agency responsible for monitoring his condition that it had tentatively decided that his disability had ended and therefore to stop his benefits. The agency provided information to Eldridge and offered him the opportunity to submit written evidence of his own. The procedures provided that Eldridge could challenge the termination in an evidentiary hearing after his benefits had ceased. At the time his case arose, there was a delay of more than a year between the request for such a hearing and the final decision.

Eldridge decided to challenge the procedures as constitutionally inadequate. His family had suffered because his disability benefits were terminated. The Eldridges' mortgage was foreclosed, and they lost their home. In addition, their furniture was repossessed, reducing the entire family to sleeping in one bed.[12]

These facts, noted by Justice Brennan, were disregarded by a majority of the Court, which held that Eldridge—unlike Ms. Velez and Ms. Lett—was not entitled to a pretermination hearing. Although it recognized that a disabled worker may suffer hardship because of wrongful termination, "still, the disabled worker's need is likely to be less than that of a welfare recipient. In addition to the possibility of access to private resources, other forms of government assistance will become available where the termination of disability benefits places a worker or his family below the subsistence level."[13] In other words, either the Eldridges had independent means or could go on welfare, which, as we have seen, cannot be terminated without a prior hearing. The Court noted evidence suggesting that the mean income of a disabled worker's family was rather low (and that the median income was even lower) but dismissed this evidence because the figures did not take account of other assets available to these families—disregarding the obvious fact that the Eldridge family at least seemed to have no other resources. * In

* Nor does it seem likely—even in 1965 dollars—that a family with an income of $3,803 (the mean) or $2,836 (the median) was likely to have substantial resources. Statistics also showed that the mean liquid assets of these families was $4,826 and that the median was $940. While a family with the mean liquid assets probably could survive the year prior to the hearing (although it would end the year with very little liquid wealth), obviously—and more significant—a family at the median could not.

other words, the Court assumed that most disability claimants would manage once their source of income was cut off—that they could rely on themselves—for surely the opinion makes no sense if the Court thought that it would swell the welfare rolls.

The Court's opinion recites a phrase that has become a mantra of sorts in due process cases: "Due process, unlike some legal rules, is not a technical conception with a fixed content unrelated to time, place and circumstances."[14] Instead, it is flexible, taking account of all of these factors. But these are just words. In fact, the Court ignored the Eldridges' situation. Instead, it treated disability payments—the abstract interest at stake rather than the Eldridges' lives—as the relevant circumstance and, in so doing, rendered a formal opinion in which it assumed autonomy in the face of obvious vulnerability.

This approach is striking for several reasons. First, it demonstrates the clear tendency on the part of the Court to categorize vulnerabilities in a context where it has asserted the need for more subtle judgments. In terms of my analysis thus far, the Court acknowledged the contextual nature of fairness—and its relationship to vulnerability—but proceeded to disregard both that context and relationship. More striking, it was willing to engage in these abstractions in the face of facts that demonstrated extraordinary vulnerability and need. The Court's refusal to deal with the reality before it at least suggests that a strong—indeed irrebuttable—presumption of autonomy may underlie due process.

The critical question for examination in due process analysis after *Matthews v. Eldridge* is the extent of the individual's vulnerability. It should therefore not be surprising to see a great deal of attention paid to the question of whether the "property"[15] in question is in fact property and its importance to the individual. In *Matthews*, the Court found that, despite the Eldridges' poverty and the family's dependence on Mr. Eldridge's disability benefits, this entitlement was less important to him than welfare was to Ms. Velez and Ms. Lett. Not surprisingly, the Court has taken the same position with respect to public employment—no matter how dependent a person is on receiving her salary.[16] Thus, identification of the degree of vulnerability at issue is a critical focus of our inquiry into fairness. The Court limits its gaze to the vulnerability of a class of people and a class of interests—that is, to their common characteristics—without focusing on the reality of individuals with differing situations and dependence on their interests.

In examining vulnerability in the due process context, courts look at the nature of the life, liberty, or property of which the individual is to be deprived. Since life and liberty are obvious when they are involved, the issues more commonly focus on whether a person has a constitutionally relevant property interest at stake and the process that the nature of that interest demands. The nature of the interest thus drives the analysis. This reasoning leads to an understanding of vulnerability that, because it is generalized to the interest rather than the person, is abstract, categorical, and formal.

Even when the Court looks at due process protections of liberty—which, of course, is the heart of autonomy—it engages in the same kinds of abstractions. Take the case of *Ingraham v. Wright.*[17] James Ingraham was a somewhat rambunctious eighth grader who sometimes disrupted class and posed a disciplinary problem for his teachers. It was his bad luck to attend school in Florida, a state that permitted a teacher to administer corporal punishment. The legally accepted disciplinary practice was for the teacher to deliver several blows to the buttocks with a paddle. Ingraham had received paddlings before, but on one occasion his teacher hit him so severely that he missed several days of school because of the resulting injury. He alleged that he was denied due process because the teacher punished him before he had an opportunity for a hearing to determine his guilt or innocence. The Supreme Court held that the due process clause did not require a formal hearing—only that prior to such a beating, the accusing teacher and student had to engage in an informal give and take to permit the student to defend himself, after which the teacher could administer the beating.

Is this fair? Is it consistent with the fundamental guarantee of fairness implicit in the due process clause? Or should Ingraham have been entitled to at least an informal hearing with an impartial arbiter before he was subjected to such punishment? The law now presumes that the demand of fairness is satisfied by the informal give and take, as well as the possibility that Ingraham could sue the teacher after the beating on the ground that it was excessive. Thus, Ingraham—the child—is presumed to be able to exercise sufficient autonomy to provide a meaningful defense by sitting down with his teacher—his accuser and executioner and, in this process, judge as well—and having a conversation about the matter.

This is ridiculous on its face. Imagine your own child in Ingraham's position. How comfortable are you with that child's ability to defend himself? First, most schools are hierarchical institutions in which the lines of authority, and the vulnerability of students to teachers, are clear. Second, your daughter or son is a child and thus likely to be less developed emotionally and intellectually than the teacher. The circumstances of these vulnerabilities are exacerbated by the exclusive role of the teacher in the beating proceedings. Finally, tort litigation after the fact is unlikely to provide relief. The beating may not be sufficiently severe to sustain a claim for personal injury, but the punishment may still have been unwarranted. And even if a personal injury action is available, the fact remains that Ingraham's autonomy was already impaired and he was physically injured. Thus, he was left without any meaningful remedy. Moreover, the authority structure within the school might lead a child and his parents to fear retaliation by his teacher and others were he actually to sue. In this situation, Ingraham lacked any meaningful autonomy, under circumstances of domination by his teacher supported by the school system, yet the Court treated the due process requirement as having satisfactorily protected his autonomy.

To what extent do our ideas about due process help to define our notions of fairness in law and society? The predominance of process-based fairness in the law is, as we have seen even in private law, indeed quite striking. It may be that we intuitively think of fairness in terms of process, but I doubt it. More likely, the centrality of law in our society, the centrality of due process to our law, and the importance of fairness to due process have led us to conflate fairness and process to the disadvantage of the former. And to the extent that process assumes autonomy—that people are able to take advantage of the relevant process to make a meaningful case—that process disserves the goal of fairness.

Equal Protection: The Foundation of Equal Autonomy?

The Constitution promises to all persons the equal protection of our laws. This doctrine not only is embodied in the Fourteenth Amendment, it also pervades constitutional jurisprudence generally as an independent constitutional value.[18] It is a legal value that seems even to predate its inclusion in the Constitution.[19] It hardly seems a stretch to suggest that equal protection serves as an important conceptual foundation for our understanding of fairness.

How would you feel, for example, if you wanted to enter a local restaurant and encountered a sign proclaiming "No [Blacks] [Jews] [Women] [Gays] [WASPS] [Asians] [etc.] Allowed." It is stating the obvious to suggest that you would be pretty unhappy for a variety of reasons. One reason, which is central to our discussion, is that the restriction would impair your autonomy—it would preclude you from making a choice you wanted to make. It is in this sense that equal protection law aims at ensuring that all people have equal rights to exercise their autonomy.

Although equal protection law is historically grounded in the desire to protect an extremely vulnerable class of persons—liberated American blacks—equal protection has become a more general manifestation of fairness as equal autonomy. Constitutional scholar Laurence Tribe makes this point. Distinguishing between the concepts of equal treatment and treatment as equals, Tribe suggests that the latter more accurately expresses the equal protection mandate, which "holds with regard to all interests and requires government to treat each individual with equal regard as a person." [20] He goes on to note: "The core ideal of equal protection strict scrutiny . . . is to subject governmental choices to close inspection in order to preserve substantive values of equality and autonomy." [21]

The expression of equal protection as a fundamental value gives the Supreme Court license to veto legislation that violates this principle. To balance the ideal of equality with the competing political value of legislative supremacy in lawmaking, the Court has adopted a policy of deference. Thus, when the Court reviews legislation under an equal protection challenge, it initially presumes that the statute is valid. In practice, this means that the Court will examine the statute to determine whether it is rationally related to a legitimate government interest. Government powers are broad; this test almost always will be satisfied. So, for example, the Supreme Court upheld California's Proposition 13, which created a dramatic inequality in property taxes between new and existing homeowners, on the basis of "plausible policy reasons" having to do with neighborhood stability and financial predictability. [22]

If, however, the legislation limits the ability of a person or group of persons to exercise a fundamental interest (the right to travel interstate, to vote, or to marry, for example) or makes distinctions among persons or groups based on criteria determined to be "suspect" (race, alien status, or national origin), the presumption of validity is defeated. In these cases, the Court requires the state to demonstrate that the legislation either is narrowly tailored to advance a compelling state interest or bears a substantial relationship to a legitimate state interest.[23] A Virginia law prohibiting interracial marriage was struck down on the ground that it had no legitimate state purpose other than its obvious discriminatory aim.[24] The relationship of this inquiry to the value of equal autonomy is clear: to oversimplify somewhat, judicial scrutiny is heightened when state classifications either affect important means of exercising one's autonomy or when they deny one full personhood because of legally irrelevant characteristics.

The way in which legislation manifests this discrimination is significant, relating to the likelihood of its invalidation as well as to the fairness concerns we have been addressing. Some statutes expressly discriminate among persons or groups on their face. Courts, historically, are more likely to invalidate these examples of *de jure* discrimination than statutes that discriminate only *de facto*—that is, by failing to create classifications that are necessary to ensure treatment as equals.[25] As an example of the latter, Tribe recalls Anatole France's famous description of the equality of French law that prohibited rich and poor alike from sleeping beneath the bridges of Paris.[26] According to Tribe, one reason for the "relatively more immune position of *de facto* discriminations" is "traceable, at bottom, to a reluctance—diminishing over the long run but still very much a reality—to recognize and especially to enforce affirmative governmental duties to redress disadvantages or injuries not thought to be actively engineered by government itself."[27]

The way this observation relates to our discussion of fairness is by suggesting that the Court has had a tendency to perceive only some types of vulnerabilities to be worthy of judicial redress—that is, those created by government itself. * The critical question, then, is what vulnerabilities count for serious equal protection scrutiny and what are the remedies for these vulnerabilities?

One type of vulnerability is inherent in the constitutional system. This is the vulnerability of any political minority—the American Communist Party, for example—to any political majority (principally Democrats and Republicans). There is nothing intrinsically wrong with the existence of political minorities in a democratic system and nothing inherently wrongful in their minority status. As legal scholar Bruce Ackerman writes, "Minorities are supposed to lose in a democratic

---

* As we shall see later, however, almost all the vulnerabilities with which we are concerned in this book are created by the structure of our society, if not directly by the government.

system—even when they want very much to win and even when they think (as they often will) that the majority is deeply wrong in ignoring their just complaints."[28] Such vulnerability results from a system of government to which all, hypothetically at least, agree.[29] Moreover, the system is grounded in the opportunity for each citizen to have an equal opportunity to participate in the political process. Consequently, only certain types of minority status—those that have historically been used to preclude their bearers from meaningful political participation—have been found to deserve remediation under equal protection analysis.[30] The appropriate remedy, therefore, has been to restore the opportunity of these minority groups to participate in the process, or at least to ensure that their interests are accounted for.[31]

The determination of which individuals or groups need protection from the majority focuses on the nature of the vulnerabilities at stake. Those, like race, that mark their bearers as a "discrete and insular" minority[32] (and therefore presumably powerless) result in the application of the highest level of equal protection scrutiny. Some other types of vulnerability do not necessarily imply powerlessness. For example, members of one of our two major political parties are not vulnerable in a sensible way when they have failed to elect a presidential candidate or have only a minority in Congress. In addition to the fact that their legislative representatives have devices by which they can demand majority attention to their interests, they are freely, and, generally, practically, able to pursue legislative majorities or executive dominance in the future.[33] Thus, the Supreme Court refused to strike down Indiana's reapportionment of its state legislative voting districts in a manner that disadvantaged Democrats.[34]

Other vulnerabilities result from historical stigmatization and discrimination. Race is the most obvious example of such a vulnerability, and it is therefore no surprise that race is the classic case of suspect classification.[35] Although characterization of a group classification as suspect and thus deserving of judicial protection can pose problems, including the more or less permanent stigmatization of the group as a class in need of special help,[36] it nevertheless is closely linked to fundamental rights and thus the equal ability to exercise autonomy.[37]

Although determining which classes of person are vulnerable (in the way recognized by the Constitution) and which rights are fundamental (and thus necessary to the exercise of free autonomy) are the central points of equal protection inquiry, only the former is directly relevant for our purposes. The Supreme Court identifies a very narrow range of classifications as suspect. In their entirety, these are race, alienage, and national origin.[38] They are, centrally (and perhaps consistently with their constitutional context), identified largely as political vulnerabilities rather than social or economic vulnerabilities. Poverty, for example, is not a suspect classification, although as we have seen (and shall see further) it creates almost insurmountable vulnerabilities. Moreover, as one can see from the nature of the categories considered suspect, the vulnerabilities that raise them to that level are ones that can fairly easily be ameliorated, at least through political participation. To put it differently, they are not vulnerabilities that alone would, in the absence of discrimination, keep their bearers from acting autonomously.

The Court's limited recognition of suspect status raises two important observations. One relates to vulnerabilities that are like those that are considered suspect in that they do not intrinsically preclude autonomous action. The other concerns vulnerabilities that do intrinsically preclude such action.

The first model of vulnerability is exemplified by the case of gender, which currently receives heightened but not strict scrutiny.[39] The Court's most recent statement on the issue—the famous VMI case—holds that gender classifications are acceptable only if the state provides an "exceedingly persuasive justification" for them.[40] Yet, in our society, gender has a long history of being a basis for institutionalized and persistent discrimination. As recent feminist scholarship has shown, much of that discrimination has been so systemic as to be invisible[41] and thus has not been adequately recognized as imposing vulnerability. An example is the Supreme Court's opinion in *Geduldig v. Aiello*, which held that it was not unlawful discrimination for California's state disability insurance program to refuse to treat pregnancy as a disability: "Absent a showing that distinctions involving pregnancy are mere pretexts designed to effect an invidious discrimination against the members of one sex or the other, lawmakers are constitutionally free to include or exclude pregnancy from the coverage of legislation such as this on any reasonable basis, just as with respect to any other physical condition."[42] It just so happens that pregnancy is a physical condition affecting only women.

Sexual preference presents another category of vulnerability that has not been constitutionally identified as such and that does not therefore receive equal protection examination beyond the rational relationship test.[43] Sexual preference cases may present a slightly different type of case than discrimination cases against women on the basis of gender, for there is little evidence to suggest that homosexuals as a class are relatively powerless in the political process. Their powerlessness is different. It derives not from the sustained, historical, and institutionalized deprivation of equal rights but from the fact that their ability to participate in public processes has historically depended on a denial of their full autonomy—that is, concealment of their homosexuality.

Homosexuality has long been the basis for discrimination in the workplace, alienation from family, and physical violence, among other obvious disadvantages. Thus, one who chooses to have a complete and open life otherwise may well be led to suppress or conceal his or her homosexuality. This results both in self-denial of a truly complete and autonomous existence and in the practical inability to fight the untoward social and political consequences of homosexuality in the public arena. The application of rigorous equal protection analysis would not eliminate all of these consequences but it would go some way toward a public recognition of their illegitimacy.[44] The very vulnerability that ought to receive protection, however, is precisely the cause of its remaining relatively invisible as such.

While gender and homosexuality may not constitute vulnerabilities that interfere with autonomous action, there is a second model of vulnerability that has this effect. Mental illness, physical disability, and poverty are examples of this type of vulnerability. Although laws do not generally discriminate against people bearing these vulnerabilities, the simple and obvious fact is that these vulnerabilities can preclude people from full and autonomous existence. Those who are mentally handicapped often cannot fully participate in the political and legal processes that are supposed to protect them, let alone fully compete in our market society. Those with physical handicaps may also be limited in their access to public and commercial facilities. Extreme poverty may also constitute a significant handicap in this way, as the *Goldberg* court recognized and as John Rawls acknowledges in requiring that certain basic goods, including at least minimal food, clothing, and shelter, be available to each member of society, for without these necessities no person can live a meaningful autonomous existence. Yet, despite this effect, the Court does not apply heightened scrutiny to classifications based on mental illness,[45] physical disability, or the possession of property.

Constitutional equal protection presents a powerful foundation for fairness as equal autonomy. At the same time, its limitations, whether intrinsic or merely contingent, in adequately identifying vulnerability may carry over into other legal analyses of fairness. As a consequence, vulnerabilities giving rise to fairness concerns in nonconstitutional legal contexts may not be properly identified, while other vulnerabilities may not be considered as worthy of legal amelioration at all.

The Americans with Disabilities Act: Fairness as Ameliorating Vulnerability

The Americans with Disabilities Act (ADA), which became law in 1990, provides an example of legislation that suggests an attempt to deal with fairness in a manner that transcends the typically formal and procedural approaches of legal fairness that I have discussed thus far. While the idea of fairness that undergirds the statute very much remains a notion of fairness as equal autonomy, the ADA recognizes that substantive approaches to fairness sometimes are required to make this equal autonomy a reality. In other words, the ADA suggests that it is not simply enough to prohibit discrimination against the disabled or to provide suitable processes for them to follow. The act recognizes that sometimes the disabled also need to be provided with special material resources in order to take advantage of formally equal opportunities and processes. Thus, the central provision of the ADA prohibits discrimination against individuals on the basis of their disabilities (as defined in the statute).[46] But it goes on to define discrimination as failing to make "reasonable accommodations to the known physical or mental limitations of an otherwise qualified individual with a disability."[47]

In terms of the analyses we have seen courts apply to fairness, then, Congress, in enacting the ADA, understood that certain disabilities do indeed prevent individuals from exercising equal autonomy and that those disabilities might well be ameliorated through law. The difference between the ADA and the other areas of law we have examined lies in how these disabilities are ameliorated. In the case of the ADA, Congress decided that formal methods were insufficient.

This is an important point. In the other legal areas we have examined, we have seen the tools of liberalism, mainly contract and process, used to attempt to cure problems that belied the assumed condition that makes liberalism work—in other words, autonomy. The ADA expressly recognizes that sometimes those tools are insufficient, that the means of liberalism must be abandoned to achieve liberal goals.

There is little doubt that a notion of fairness as equal autonomy undergirds the ADA: "The continuing existence of unfair and unnecessary discrimination and prejudice denies people with disabilities the opportunity to compete on an equal basis and to pursue those opportunities for which our free society is justifiably famous."[48] In enacting this view of equal autonomy, the ADA transcends any distinction between the public and the private sphere, for this public legislation not only makes private discrimination illegal, at least within the broad parameters of its covered areas, but it also requires private employers to use their own funds to ensure that the formal requirement of nondiscrimination is practically realized.[49] Thus, in its conception and scope, the idea of fairness that not only motivated but is mandated by the ADA is a more sophisticated notion of fairness than that which appears in other areas of the law and more closely resembles a complete instantiation of the moral concept of fairness.

This approach has obvious costs. The fundamental assumption on which the ADA is based is that disabled persons are vulnerable. The act recites that: "Individuals with disabilities are a discrete and insular minority who have been . . . subjected to a history of purposeful unequal treatment, and relegated to a position of political powerlessness in our society."[50] A great deal depends, therefore, on how we determine who is in fact disabled under the act and therefore entitled to its benefits. The act sweeps rather broadly and therefore has the potential to be expensive.[51] In the first year that the ADA was in effect, 12,670 charges alleging violation of the act were filed with the Equal Employment Opportunity Commission. The range of disabilities involved was broad, leading to legitimate questions about whether every disability results in vulnerability that needs to be relieved by the force of the state.[52]

The important fact about the ADA for our purposes, however, is that it explicitly acknowledges the concept of vulnerability that lies at the heart of fairness, as well as its understanding that ameliorating vulnerability sometimes requires extraordinary measures. Like other forms of vulnerability we examined in Chapter Two, though, the ADA has the characteristic of being focused only on an "other" and of using that otherness to identify vulnerability. In so doing, the ADA is predicated on at least an implicit understanding of the denial of vulnerability that, as we will now see, leads us to a narrow notion of fairness.

5

Liberal Philosophy's Fundamental Mistake

Where you come out depends on where you start. As computer programmers know so well, "Garbage in, garbage out." And pollsters (and law professors) know that the way you ask a question strongly influences, if it does not determine, the answer you get. To assess our understanding of fairness, we must first isolate our starting point.

We saw in our examination of legal doctrine that the dominant value of autonomy strongly influences even those rules that are expressly designed to govern relationships in which at least one person's autonomy is compromised. Even where the relationship, like marriage, is itself an inseparable aspect of the problem to be resolved, courts have trouble getting beyond the individuality and autonomy of the parties to the dispute. Because they start with autonomy, they end with autonomy. The dominant value of autonomy blinds courts to the reality of vulnerability.

The same problem exists in our leading philosophical approaches to fairness, those based on classic liberalism. Liberal philosophy is, by definition, concerned with autonomy. As we saw earlier, the Enlightenment vision on which our nation was founded professes the value of every individual. This is perhaps best captured in Kant's formulation of the categorical imperative, which tells us, in one important version, to treat each individual as an end in himself, not merely as a means to achieving other goals. The liberal ideal seeks to protect the individual in his pursuit of his own vision of the good life in a manner that does not interfere with the ability of other individuals to do the same. The task of modern liberal philosophy has been to explore the appropriate limits of individual autonomy and to distinguish legitimate and illegitimate means of achieving its fulfillment.[1]

This notion of autonomy includes both an ideal of freedom and an ideal of equality. Freedom needs little explanation. The best way to be sure it exists is to limit our use of the coercive power of the state. Equality, by contrast, implies more active state involvement in the initial distribution or redistribution of whatever it is that we use to measure equality—money, power, well-being, and the like.

Versions of liberal philosophy on the right side of the spectrum—those tending more toward libertarianism—emphasize the value of freedom. The more left-leaning theories, those tending toward socialism, emphasize the importance of equality. For most thinkers, however, achieving a balance between freedom and equality is an important goal. Those who favor freedom recognize that if inequalities become too severe, if our inner cities boil over, freedom may be threatened by violence, uprisings, and, in extreme cases, revolution. Those whose greater concern is with equality nevertheless embrace the values of self-determination that are at the heart of individual autonomy and thus seek to use the power of the state only to the extent necessary to ensure equal autonomy for all. The leading theory of fairness may therefore be described as "fairness as equal autonomy." Although the variations of the theory have different emphases, they all center on this same goal.

All of these theories start with the ideal of autonomy and do not question its fundamental value.[2] That is not to say that the value of autonomy has gone unquestioned. Certainly such organicist theories as communism have provided a serious critique of autonomy. More significantly for contemporary debate, during the last several decades a group of philosophers in America, known broadly as communitarians—some of them liberal in their basic orientation, some of them not—have questioned both the value of the autonomy norm and its philosophical validity. While some communitarians, such as Harvard philosopher Michael Sandel, argue that a strong notion of autonomy is inconsistent with the way we conceive of ourselves, others, such as philosopher and political adviser Bill Galston and sociologist Amitai Etzioni, try to reconcile the autonomy values of liberalism with a strong concept of community.

Liberal theory is our dominant theory. And autonomy lies at the heart of liberal theory. The principal debate centers, then, not on the value of autonomy but on the question of whether autonomy is best achieved with or without the help of the state. There is another common element to liberal theories, and it is this element that is at the heart of the problem of fairness. The theories not only begin by accepting the *ideal* of autonomy, but, like the legal doctrines we have examined, they also start with the *presumption* that autonomy is the normal human state of affairs. As we will see, even the most egalitarian liberal theories assume, at least implicitly, that generally people are *in fact* autonomous and self-determining.

Without the underlying assumption that people are in fact autonomous, these theories would make little sense. If autonomy were not the reality, the theories would work for the people we would like to be—not for the people who we are. They might express lovely aspirations. But they would not be theories that we could use to build a society, because society is composed of real people, not ideals.

This in fact is the failing of all of these theories. As we shall see, each of them necessarily assumes that the people for whom the theory is designed are able to behave in a self-determining manner and that adjustments are needed only at the margins. Autonomy is the central case; vulnerability is the exception. If the reverse is true, however—if vulnerability is a better expression of the central human reality than is autonomy—the theories all miss the mark. Autonomy may well be a value worth pursuing (I think it is). But for most people to achieve their fair measure of autonomy, they need to come to the starting line properly equipped. We can create a world in which it is fair to privilege autonomy and its consequences only if we help them reduce or eliminate the vulnerabilities that inhibit their autonomy. *

By starting with a presumption of autonomy in fact, our leading theories miss the condition of vulnerability that I shall argue is at the heart of our concern with fairness. As a consequence, these theories tend to reinforce the positions of those who are most able to exercise their autonomy—those who already are our elites and in positions of

---

* I don't want to overstate the distinction between autonomy and vulnerability. As I see it, they are end points on a spectrum over which the American population (indeed the world population) ranges. My critique goes to the question of which end of the spectrum we focus on—which more accurately describes reality.

power. They therefore more or less justify the social and political arrangements we now have.

If the predominant human condition is really vulnerability, not autonomy, then vulnerability must be the starting point for a persuasive theory of fairness. If we need to make exceptions to the theory, these must be exceptions for people who do *not* need help, not for those who do. If we start with vulnerability as the baseline assumption, we can be more confident that those who need help will get it. In contrast, theories of fairness that start with a presumption of autonomy in fact will either tolerate some measure of despair or make arbitrary determinations as to those vulnerabilities for which it will provide help. John Rawls, whose work I shall discuss below, himself admits that "it seems impossible to avoid a certain arbitrariness" in drawing this line.[3]

A fair question you might ask before engaging in this analysis is, If liberal theory is so centrally flawed, why not abandon liberal theory? Why not develop a new structure for society based on socialist or communist principles that give little or no regard to human autonomy?

The reasons go well beyond the scope of my project in this book, but I will suggest three brief answers. First, purely as a practical matter, the values of individualism and autonomy are so deeply ingrained in American society that any attempt to destroy those values will not be taken seriously by policy makers. I hope that my ideas will have some impact on public policy. I therefore wish to make them palatable by showing their consistency with our professed values (and indeed that they lie at the core of our professed values).

Second, autonomy is indeed a noble ideal. Few of us believe that we have the knowledge to instruct, much less compel, others as to how best to live their lives. Moreover, much of what gives our lives purpose and meaning is the search for meaning itself. To limit this process too severely is to take away much of what we think makes us human.

Third, and finally, much of what makes our lives richer—technology, the arts, the humanities—is the result of individuals exercising their autonomy. If we were to restrict individual autonomy unduly, we would greatly impoverish our lives, as the bleak experience of the communist east may demonstrate. So autonomy is a worthwhile value. My project is to make that value meaningful for everybody in the world in which we actually live—not in the ivory tower world of philosophers.

Before we look at the failings of liberal theory generally, however, we need to establish the common underpinnings of the theories in which it is expressed. * Let us consider three distinct variations on liberal theory—social democracy, resource equality, and wealth maximization—to see how important autonomy is to each and also whether each necessarily assumes real-world autonomy. If these theories are inconsistent with our basic intuitions about fairness, it may be that vulnerability provides a better starting point for explaining both liberal theory and our motivations to fairness.

Model I: Social Democracy

Fairness and Justice

One of the most famous and beautiful expressions of the Enlightenment ideal of the equality and value of all humanity is John Donne's "Devotion No. 17": "No man is an island, entire of itself; every man is a piece of the continent, a part of the main; if a clod be washed away by the sea, Europe is the less, as well as if a promontory were." Donne proclaims that although each person is an individual, he is also very much a necessary and equal part of the aggregate of humanity. Modern liberal philosophy has no better-known expression of this ideal than the work of John Rawls. Model I is based on Rawls's ideas. It provides a theory of justice, based on fairness, that might best be described as a form of democratic socialism.

Rawls is the Harvard philosopher who is often credited with reviving political philosophy generally and liberal philosophy in particular in an era in which utilitarianism had seemed to become the accepted theory. His 1971 book, *A Theory of Justice,* and his subsequent articles clarifying and defending that book (which are the basis of his 1993 book, *Political Liberalism*) set forth an ideal that attempts to reconcile the goals of lib-

---

* I should note at the outset that the particular theories I will be examining, especially those of Rawls and Posner, have evolved since these authors wrote the particular works I will be discussing. To some extent, therefore, I have (and necessarily so) caricatured their positions, for no work of this type could (pardon the expression) be fair to the subtleties and nuances of each of their arguments. I have chosen the works that I have, however, because they each capture strong arguments of a particular type that is prominent in American political and legal thought and that has been the widespread legacy to date of each of these thinkers. So, although it would be a mistake to attribute these views in the precise forms they are presented here to the authors as they are writing today, they present important approaches to the problem of fairness.

eral autonomy with the activist state associated with welfarism and distributive justice.

My ideas, which I will present more fully in Chapters Seven and Eight, share some important similarities with Rawls's work, and indeed Rawls is the liberal philosopher with whose work I feel the most affinity. In particular, in his concept of the contingencies of merit and the notion of primary goods (both of which I will discuss below), he reveals an appreciation for the ways in which vulnerability can severely limit a person's ability to exercise autonomy. But, like the other theorists I will discuss, I think that even Rawls falls short of the mark because, like the other liberal philosophers, he begins with an assumption of autonomy that limits the extent to which he really is willing to redress the vulnerabilities of others.

Rawls's theory is importantly based on consent, which, in political and legal theory, is the way we express our autonomous choices. We generally agree that the American form of government is based on our initial and, in some abstract way, continuing consent to the Constitution itself. This is social contract theory, and, like such theories, Rawls's theory asks us (hypothetically) to agree on the principles that we will use to govern ourselves.

Sharing: The Difference Principle

Rawls comes up with two governing principles (or rather suggests that we would come up with two such principles) that work together. As Rawls presents them, these principles themselves are not laws. Rather, they establish standards of justice that provide a test for the legitimacy of our laws—we can consider our laws just only if they are consistent with these broad principles.

The first principle says that we all are to enjoy equal liberty. The traditional liberal emphasis on individual autonomy obviously lies at the heart of this principle.

The second principle, called the difference principle, is a little more complicated. It permits us to tolerate inequalities but only to the extent that they work to the advantage of everybody. Rawls suggests that we evaluate the effects of inequalities by looking at whether they work to the benefit of society's least advantaged people. This works as a sort of "trickle-up" process—if inequalities improve the situation of the worst off, they will work to the advantage of the rest of us too. So, for example, we could tolerate a world containing Bill Gates and the homeless only if it meant that the homeless would have better lives than if we prevented Bill Gates from acquiring his breathtaking wealth.[4]

Notice that the way this principle works effectively makes Bill Gates share his talents with the rest of us. This reflects Rawls's belief in the contingency of merit that I noted earlier. The idea is that the distribution of talents, skills, and even ambition is pretty much a matter of luck, so that as a moral matter, nobody deserves his special attributes. If you do not deserve your talents, you have no special claim to deserve the rewards that come from exercising those talents. And since society provides those rewards, it does so legitimately only if the rewards benefit all of society.

This seems like pretty radical stuff. The difference principle obviously implies an activist state and potentially massive redistribution. But don't worry. Rawls shows that the principle, in application, works less radically than an upper-middle-class American might fear. (I haven't the space to go through this, but you can read Chapter 5 of Rawls's *A Theory of Justice*.) More important, as I will show, not only is this principle actually rooted in individual autonomy but Rawls subordinates it to the first principle, which is all about autonomy.

Modeling Fairness

Rawls calls his theory justice as fairness. What makes the two principles of justice fair is that we would agree to them under fair conditions.[5] To show this, Rawls invents a mind game he calls the original position. The original position is an imaginary debate among imaginary persons who are equally autonomous and rational.

Rawls defines *autonomy* as existing when a person is free and independent—that is, free to choose. You are *rational* if you know your own interest, can pursue a chosen course of action and understand its consequences, can put off immediate gratification for long-term gain, and are not especially jealous of others.[6] Most of us probably fit this description, more or less, and so we can put ourselves in the posture of the participants. Rawls also tells us that rational persons are indifferent to the interests of other people. In short, they are basically self-interested. I will argue that this assumption is wrong, or at least not inevitable, and that it is what dooms Rawls's theory to failure as a model of social justice. Finally, and perhaps most important for Rawls's notion of fairness, these imaginary persons deliberate behind a "veil of ignorance"—they have no idea who they are (or will be) in the real world.

According to Rawls, these people will come up with principles in the original position that will be fair *by definition*, because the participants are equal in all morally relevant respects—they are equally autonomous and capable of rationally exercising that autonomy—in circumstances in which no one can take advantage of anyone else. The circumstances are fair; therefore the principles will be fair. These principles express the idea of justice as fairness.

The Importance of Motive

Why do the people in the original position adopt the principles of justice? To understand the limitations of Rawls's theory, it is important to understand their motivation. We can begin to do so by looking at what Rawls has done in creating his veil of ignorance: he has made each participant in the deliberations equally vulnerable. Each knows that there will be a real world in which he will live and that will be governed by the principles he and the other participants develop. But none of them knows who he will be in that world; will he be Bill Gates or Jane Lambert? He doesn't know whose shoes he will fill and so he is forced to put himself in everybody's shoes. Rawls assumes that because each person will see himself in the shoes of the least-advantaged member of society, he will be afraid to take much risk. Thus, the persons in the original position will come up with a principle of sharing to temper the principle of equal liberty (which Rawls assumes they will all desire). They will thus agree on the second principle of justice, the difference principle.

Recall that the difference principle holds that social inequalities are legitimate only if they work to the advantage of the worst off. Bill Gates is entitled to his billions only if it makes Jane Lambert (or really someone entirely destitute) better off. In effect, the difference principle treats almost all of our natural endowments as matters of luck and so requires that we share them. Gates is not really entitled to his business brilliance and the lucky circumstances that put him in a position to create Microsoft—they must therefore be harnessed for all to share. Michael Jordan's basketball talent is mostly a matter of luck—he must therefore share the benefits of that talent with the rest of us.

At first blush, this difference principle recalls Donne with a vengeance or, to wax poetic for another moment, Whitman's opening stanza in *Song of Myself*: "I celebrate myself, and sing myself,/And what I assume you shall assume,/For every atom belonging to me as good belongs to you." But not quite. Recall that I emphasized the importance of Rawls's explanation of our deliberators' motives. They came up with a principle of sharing. But why? For *selfish* reasons. They came up with the difference principle because they were afraid that *they* would be left behind in the world of radical autonomy expressed in the first principle. But this pursuit of self-interest is just another way of describing rational autonomy as Rawls defines it. And so, somewhat paradoxically, the difference principle, which reflects an ethic of caring, is really grounded in self-interest.

Who cares? As long as we wind up with an ideal that protects the vulnerable, why do the reasons matter? This is a familiar argument and one that is especially attractive to die-hard individualists and many economists, as we shall see in discussing Model III. Well, the reasons matter a lot—in a sense, that's the whole point of this book. If the reason you are willing to share is to protect yourself, then you will share only up to the point that the cost of sharing equals the risk that you will be harmed by not sharing. It's sort of like buying a car. You will pay only what the car is worth *to you*. If the dealer won't sell at your price, you won't buy the car. You surely won't pay more because you want to make the dealer happy. So with the difference principle. If the motivation behind the principle is to protect yourself, then you will not share any more than you need to in order to protect yourself.

Rawls might respond by telling me that I'm wrong—that although the development of the principle is motivated by self-interest, once you've agreed on it, you're bound by its terms, even if you have to pay more than you'd like.[7] But this answer would fail, because it is based on an important but demonstrably untrue underlying assumption. The answer assumes that the difference principle is clear, unambiguous, and self-executing.

Many critics of Rawls have focused on the ambiguities and uncertainties of the difference principle—it is *not* clear, unambiguous, and self-executing. Questions of who the least advantaged are and whether particular inequalities work to the advantage of all cry out for interpretation, as well as facts. Moreover, even if these concepts were unambiguous, all the difference principle accomplishes is to establish standards by which more particular laws are to be measured. And creating and developing those laws requires that we interpret the way that the difference principle applies in particular contexts.

If we need to interpret the principle, it stands to reason that one of the things we will look to in figuring out what it means and how it applies is the reason that we adopted it in the first place. Certainly that is one of the things lawyers and judges do in interpreting our Constitution and our statutes. And in the case of the difference principle, the reason for adoption is self-interest. Finally, the people who will be interpreting the principle—policy makers and judges—are people who have succeeded in society and are most likely to interpret this principle consistent with the self-interest that motivated it in the first place. The reason we would adopt the difference principle clearly is pretty important.

If we adopted the difference principle (or something like it) because we truly cared about each other, the limits would be quite different. Later in the book I will put this idea into a hypothetical framework that will allow us to explore this possibility. The important point for now is to realize that Rawls's understanding of motive anchors even his sharing principle in a strong assumption of autonomy.

Sharing and Autonomy

The difference principle is a sharing principle. Not only is it grounded in autonomous choice, but it is also, importantly (and like my own theory), designed to facilitate autonomy. The inequalities measured by the difference principle are inequalities in what Rawls terms "primary goods." Primary goods, "to give them in broad categories, are rights and liberties, opportunities and powers, income and wealth."[8] These are, according to Rawls, "necessary means" to achieving whatever else it is that you might want to achieve. Rational people, he says, prefer "more rather than less" of these goods. The participants in the original position want to assure themselves that they will have as much of them as possible.

Why are primary goods important? Why should they be fairly distributed? Rawls tells us that possessing a certain level of primary goods makes a person invulnerable to a variety of injustices.[9] They put you in a position to defend and take care of yourself. This makes a lot of sense. If you are well fed, adequately housed, and treated equally by the political system, you are more likely to be able to function in society than those who are not. The point seems so obvious as to be beyond debate.

Rawls's reason for establishing this threshold is based on his goal of ensuring equal autonomy. If people have adequate primary goods, they will be free of the need to spend their time acquiring additional resources and will thus be able to choose life plans that have real value. A life spent merely insuring one's survival is hardly the autonomous life that liberal theory aims toward. It is only when you are freed from making survival your life's focus that you are able to choose and live a life of real meaning. This is the realization of the liberal ideal of autonomy.

Perhaps, for example, you believe that you will live your life most valuably as a painter of abstract landscapes. If primary goods are distributed only through the processes of a competitive market, you might forgo this desire, for fear that you would starve, and instead become an investment banker. There's nothing wrong with investment banking. But it's not what you wanted to do. You are forced to live a life that is different from the one you want just so you can survive.*

For the first principle of justice—equal liberty—to work, Rawls must ensure that you are able to act autonomously. This requires that those who would otherwise be unable to exercise their autonomy be put in a position that enables them to so act. Fairness in the distribution of primary goods is thus an essential condition of liberal freedom.

Seen from this perspective, this principle looks much like the theory of fairness that I have alluded to and will develop further. But it is not. The reason is that Rawls and I begin from different presumptions. Rawls not only begins with the assumption of the philosophical importance of autonomy, he also assumes that the real-world baseline condition of most people is functional autonomy. This must be the case because his principle of equal liberty, which makes sense only if people are in fact autonomous, is more important than his difference principle and even trumps the difference principle when the two conflict. And by making the touchstone of the difference principle those who are worst off in society, he implies that disabling vulnerabilities will be excep-

---

* It may be, as one reader suggested, economically inefficient for us to encourage your artistic pursuits if you are not an especially good artist but an excellent investment banker. Perhaps so. But economic efficiency is only one value we pursue as a society, and it is not the principal ethic upon which our nation is built—liberal autonomy is. All the question does is to highlight some of the costs of pursuing autonomy as a principal goal by demonstrating that there may be efficiency losses that result from people's choices. The issue is further explored below in my discussion of Ronald Dworkin's theory.

tional. The story of the Lamberts (who almost certainly are not the worst off in our society and who almost certainly do have an adequate measure of primary goods) suggests otherwise.

The Rawlsian approach assumes that the need to raise people to the standard of functional autonomy is exceptional and is carved out of a world of radical freedom. I will have more to say about this later, but it should be clear that this posture creates a serious risk of replicating the problem of the vulnerable-as-other that I identified in Chapter Two and thus of ignoring or severely discounting the broader vulnerabilities that permeate our lives together.[10]

There is perhaps a more important but related problem as well. Rawls assumes that his fair distribution of primary goods, which in terms of material goods is not to make people equal but simply better off, will enable people to take advantage of the mechanisms of liberal society—the economic and political marketplaces in particular. Presumably these mechanisms are embodied in the processes and formalities that take a central place in the law: contracting and legal process. But substantial inequalities in material goods may well still exist, making it difficult for the lesser advantaged to utilize those processes fully, as we saw in the due process and equal protection contexts. More important, Rawls's rather materialist account of fairness fails to consider the emotional and other relational vulnerabilities that we saw arising in the cases applying family law and corporate law. Rawls's assumption that a fair distribution of rights and goods is sufficient to facilitate equal autonomy misses the vulnerabilities that often preclude even well-off people from exercising their autonomy. His coupling of autonomy and rationality thus leads him to miss the deeper implications of his fairness theory, implications I will explore in Chapter Seven.

Model II: Resource Equality as Equal Autonomy

The Basic Idea

Autonomy is also the starting point in Model II, fairness as equal resources, a model developed by Ronald Dworkin,[11] who teaches law at both New York University and Oxford. Through his regular essays in the *New York Review of Books*, in which he addresses some of our most pressing social issues from a lawyer's and a philosopher's perspective, and through his many books on these subjects, Dworkin has become one of our best-known and most influential legal and political thinkers. His basic project has been to develop theories he thinks present the most persuasive possible defense of liberal values.

Dworkin tells us that his goal in tackling the subject of equality is to provide us with what he believes to be the best philosophical account of equality (one that is consistent with our intuitions about fairness and justice). It seems pretty clear, though, that he thinks his model sets out a distributional account of fairness on its own terms, especially since he actually applies the model to argue in favor of a certain approach to health-care reform.[12]

We shouldn't be surprised that equality plays a role in a persuasive account of fairness. After all, when we say that elections are fair, we mean that each person has had the opportunity to participate equally. To divide a pie fairly at dinner generally means to give each person an equal slice. Equality as fairness, then, has strong intuitive appeal.[13]

Saying that we ought to be equal, though, tells us rather little. In order to evaluate an argument for equality, we have to know what we are measuring: In what respects are we to be equal? Should we have equal money, or happiness, or simply equal liberty? Dworkin begins his argument by showing us the ways in which kinds of equality other than equal resources are *inconsistent* with our intuitions.

He focuses, among other metrics of equality, on the concept of equal welfare. This is a familiar concept, especially to economists. It says that our collective obligation to one another is to ensure that each of us is equal in terms of his well-being. According to this theory, we are equal if we feel that we are equally well off, even though we may have different resources. You, for example, may be content with lots of money because it gives you a feeling of security or self-esteem. I might be equally content spending all of my time at the opera. And Sam might feel as well off as both of us simply knowing that the earth is round.

Different things provide each of us with different levels of welfare. So it makes no sense to give each of us the same amounts of the same things. Sam would be no happier with more money, and the strains of *Don Giovanni* do nothing for you. Welfare is obviously very much a matter of personal taste (and this is one of the main defects of the theory). But our welfare matters to all of us, so at some level it makes sense to say that fairness is achieved when we are equal in welfare.

We could, in theory, make everybody equal in welfare if we had the information to do so—that is, if we could identify the things and quantities of things that make each person happy and then come up with some way of comparing them, of comparing opera and money and the knowledge that the earth is round, so that we could equalize them. Even if we could do this, however, Dworkin tells us that it would be unfair to do so. The reason is that equalizing welfare permits me to impose the costs of my choices on you. Opera is expensive to produce; the knowledge that the earth is round costs nothing. (I suppose it's more accurate to say that the costs of acquiring that knowledge have, by now, been amortized.) Thus, I am entitled to a greater share of resources than Sam. If equalizing welfare means that we achieve fairness only when society provides me with my fill of opera, equal welfare permits me to exercise my autonomy, my freedom to choose, at Sam's expense. In a world of scarce resources, this necessarily limits Sam's ability to make and fulfill his own choices. Equality of welfare thus fails to match our intuitions of fairness.

Equal Resources as Equal Autonomy

A theory of equal resources does not share this failing of equal welfare. Dworkin says that our intuition tells us that fairness means that each of us gets to make our own choices, as long as we each bear the costs that those choices impose on everybody else. Simply put, I may park myself at the Met as much as I like—as long as I pay for it. In terms of our discussion thus far, fairness requires us to limit our autonomy, with the boundaries marked by our obligation to bear the burden of those choices. Permitting autonomous rational choice is what makes life fair. And so Model II, like Model I, is based on an ideal of fairness as equal autonomy.[14]

How, though, do we make sure that everybody has equal resources? Dworkin's answer is the quintessential mechanism of rational choice—the market. The market itself is, after all, nothing but an amalgam of people's choices. But Dworkin's theory is not simply a defense of free competition. Unlike libertarian theories of free competition, which tell us that we are entitled to what we get because we got it,[15] Model II demands that we all live lives that are equal in their share of resources. How do we do this?

Dworkin asks us to imagine that we have landed on a desert island and that each of us is given one hundred clamshells. We then conduct an auction in which we sell off all of the island's resources. In this auction, each of us has an equal opportunity to spend her shells as she likes. The end result, Dworkin says, will be a situation in which nobody envies anybody else, because each of us will have the bundle of resources she wants. This is equality of resources.

But Dworkin goes further. He recognizes that even if we start with equal resources, we will soon be made unequal by the processes of a dynamic market economy. This is because each of us has different talents and abilities. Andre Agassi is a gifted tennis player, and I am a modestly able pianist. Each of us is equally ambitious in making the most of his talents, and we work equally hard to do so. But the market is likely to reward Andre with a much bigger share of resources than it will give to me. People surely will pay more to see Andre play tennis than to see me butcher Beethoven. Andre will become rich; I will likely become poor. As a result, our initial equality will be destroyed by the market. The problem for Dworkin now is the extent to which these inequalities are acceptable if our goal is to equalize resources.

Luck and the Limits of Choice

The question is basically the same one we saw Rawls deal with: when does our ideal of fairness require us to redistribute resources from some people to others? Dworkin identifies two central issues in resolving this problem. The first issue has to do, as he describes it, with the role of luck in creating inequalities. The second, related to the first, involves the point or points at which we measure equality.

As we saw in the case of the Lamberts, luck plays a very important role in determining success or failure in a competitive society. What failings do the Lamberts seem to have besides their bad luck? They work as hard as they can. They try to improve their lot in life. But they don't seem to be able to do so.

Luck has a profound impact on success. Luck can mean that you were born with brains or with the athletic talent of Andre Agassi. It can mean that you were born on Park Avenue or in the South Bronx. It can mean that you are healthy or that you are physically disabled. It can mean that you meet the right people at the right time or that you always seem to miss the big chance.

Dworkin tells us that there are two types of luck: option luck and brute luck. Option luck is the result of choices, such as buying a lottery ticket or stock in Microsoft. It means you have made a calculated decision to risk your money, knowing that you may win or lose. *

Brute luck, by contrast, is not a matter of choice. Stuff happens. If your barn burns down because it is struck by lightning, that is bad brute luck. You did not choose to risk the destruction of your property by lightning, at least any more than anyone else did. An event like that is a risk you take simply by living in a world in which such a natural phenomenon is a (remote) possibility.

Model II treats you differently depending on the kind of luck you have. If your luck is the result of a choice you made—to plunk down your dollar on a lottery ticket or to take the time and pay the postage to respond to Ed McMahon—Dworkin suggests that it's fair to leave you with your winnings (and, by the way, not to compensate you for your losses). These kinds of inequalities in resources are entirely tolerable because they are the result of your choices. If you win or lose because of brute luck, however, because lightning struck your barn or a hurricane flattened your house, it seems fair for us to compensate you (and, conversely, to take away your winnings).[16]

It *seems* fair to compensate you for your bad brute luck, but, Dworkin tells us, generally it is not. This is because you could have bought insurance to compensate you for precisely those losses that are the consequences of bad brute luck. If there were an efficient insurance market (as there is in the case of your barn) and you had the chance to (but didn't) spend some of your clamshells on insurance against your barn burning, we have no obligation to help you out. The inequalities that result from such bad brute luck are perfectly consistent with the ideal of equal resources.[17]

This idea of insurance neatly converts the consequences of random natural events—of the lightning strike—into the consequences of free and autonomous choice.[18] If you lose under circumstances in which you could have but did not buy insurance, the losses are effectively your own fault—your own choice—and fairness requires that you live with them.

Equally important, this conclusion fits Dworkin's intuitive requirement that we each bear the costs that our choices impose on others; insurance rates will be set by a market in which each person has the

---

* I focus on money here as a proxy for resources. Of course, you might risk other things of importance to you in a manner that comes within the concept of option luck.

equal opportunity (and clamshells) to buy insurance, and fair rates will be determined by the risk pool and demand. If we had to compensate you even though you spent your clamshells on a BMW instead of insurance, you would be imposing the costs of your choice on us—after all, *we* spent some clamshells on insurance. This doesn't seem fair.

Of course, we don't have insurance markets that let you protect against every type of bad brute luck. Nobody is going to sell insurance against the possibility that you might not be as smart as you like or that I lack the genius of Horowitz. So Dworkin suggests an alternative—a scheme of redistributive taxation (sound familiar?). We tax the people who have more than you do because they have better brute luck and give it to you to compensate for your bad brute luck. It works somewhat like a golf handicap. We know the score that Tiger Woods is likely to shoot and we know what I am likely to shoot (and assume, with Dworkin, that I practice just as hard as Tiger does). It is just my bad brute luck that I lack his talent. So, to even things out a bit—to make it fair—I get a handicap.

How much of a handicap? Dworkin says that you get the amount that you would have been willing to pay for the premium and insure for had insurance markets been available against, say, being a lousy golfer. Of course, insurance against lousy golfing doesn't exist, but we can apply Dworkin's ideas to markets that do.

Luck, Resources, and Personhood

So far we have talked about the way your choices determine the kinds of claims you can make on the rest of us. But we haven't really talked about what it means to make a choice. The second part of Dworkin's theory determines the times when we measure resource distributions to see whether they are in fact equal (or legitimately unequal). He links the concept of choice to his conclusion that the proper time frame for this measurement is the course of a person's whole life. Choice and luck are critically related.

The idea that ties the two parts of Dworkin's theory together is his view of the "person." After all, liberal ideas of autonomy are based on your right to pursue your own self-fulfillment. We know that your ability to achieve this goal will depend partly on your talent and partly on your ambition. Are talents and ambitions part of the essential you, or are they external things (like that BMW) that you own?

Dworkin tells us that your tastes and ambitions are indeed part of you, while your physical and mental talents are simply a function of your circumstances. In other words, on one hand, you get credit for being energetic and hardworking and temperate in your wants and needs. On the other hand, your golfing ability or musical genius are just the way things are. Stuff happens. In other words, tastes and ambitions are like option luck, and talents are like brute luck. It should be clear that Dworkin thinks that our society is obligated to help you out only if inequalities result from the latter.

The distinction, while it may get fuzzy at the margins, is generally pretty clear. You may have mathematical abilities that could lead you to become a wealthy investment banker, but you decide instead to teach at a law school for (relatively) modest compensation. This is a function of your tastes and ambitions. It is a choice you make in your conception and pursuit of a life you think is worth living. This choice fulfills your ambitions, and you do not envy the wealthy investment banker because hers is a life you would never want to live—although you might like her money. Your choice is the quintessential exercise of your individual autonomy .

Perhaps instead you decide that, although your musical gifts are modest, a life lived in music—however unsuccessful by commercial standards—is the means to your self-fulfillment. You practice endlessly, and yet the limitations of your talents doom you to poverty. You look enviously at the career of Horowitz and desperately wish that you could achieve the same. This, too, is your choice. But fairness demands that you be treated differently. Your envy of Horowitz is simply a result of your bad brute luck—of not being born Horowitz.

How do we know whether inequality is the result of choice or circumstances? It is this sense of envy, present in the second case but not the first, that Dworkin tells us is the touchstone.[19]

Dworkin tells us that resources are equal between you and me if neither of us envies the other's life. Our ambitious but untalented pianist is willing to work as hard, or harder, than any prodigy, but his lack of talent means that he will be less successful than the prodigy and will therefore envy him.[20] The cause of this envy and these unequal resources is simply bad brute luck. Thus, an ethic of equal resources requires us to move wealth to the (equally ambitious) untalented from the more talented. How do we do this? The answer again is a scheme of redistributive taxation modeled on a hypothetical insurance market.[21] Our untalented pianist will be compensated to the extent that he would have been willing to buy insurance against being a poor pianist.

It should be absolutely clear that Dworkin's theory, like Rawls's, is based on the central value of free and autonomous choice. The question Dworkin struggles with, and that is at the heart of my project as well, is, when can we say that our choices are truly our own? Dworkin argues that there are often cases in which things that look like choices really are not, because unequal circumstances—vulnerabilities—restrict people from freely exercising choice. (I will later argue that the line he draws between talents and ambitions is entirely arbitrary; circumstances have a significant effect on the latter as well.)

But note Dworkin's solution: the way to compensate people for their inability to make autonomous choices is to provide mechanisms—insurance and taxation—that convert those vulnerabilities into the requirement that people make free choices. This seems to defeat his argument. And it does because, like Rawls, Dworkin assumes a baseline of autonomy.[22]

Model III: Wealth Maximization

Everyone remembers the famous line from the 1987 movie *Wall Street* in which the Michael Douglas/Ivan Boesky character tells a group of stockholders facing a corporate takeover, "Greed is good!" Perhaps this was a little crudely put (although it seems to have been the motto of an entire decade in America). But, crude or not, the line expresses in three short words a highly influential theory of fairness, the theory of wealth maximization—a theory that, not surprisingly, found its clearest articulation and strongest support in the 1980s. I was practicing corporate law on Wall Street at the time, and I can assure you that nobody was thinking of that feeding frenzy as fulfilling the dictates of liberal theory. But how nice to know that by grabbing all you can you are helping the world to become a better place for humankind!

What is striking about the theory of wealth maximization is not the way it elevates ruthless self-interest to the highest ethical principle (although for those of us raised on an ethic of social welfare it does seem rather jarring). It is, instead, that when you look at this theory together with the other theories we have discussed, their similarities may be more important than their differences—at least for an understanding of fairness. After all, what could fulfill the goal of autonomy more than to be told that you are to go out and serve yourself? To be fair to Rawls and Dworkin, there *are* important differences among the theories; I would rather live in Rawls's or Dworkin's world than one of wealth maximization, and for ethically important reasons. But the theory of wealth maximization does express the realization of equal autonomy in its rawest form. And, like the other theories, it starts with a presumption of autonomy-in-fact—with a vengeance!

Model III, the theory of wealth maximization, argues that the good society is one that aims to maximize overall wealth. This is accomplished when each person pursues that goal for herself. Implicit in this model is our familiar theory of fairness as equal autonomy—that everyone should more or less be left alone to pursue her self-interest.

Wealth maximization departs somewhat from classical liberal autonomy in that it privileges one view of the good—wealth maximization—above all others. But the reason it does so is to facilitate the realization of everybody's goals in a manner consistent with liberal theory. The theory of wealth maximization is also consistent with liberal theory in that, as we shall see, its leading proponent—Judge Richard Posner, formerly a law professor at the University of Chicago and currently a judge on the U.S. Court of Appeals for the Seventh Circuit—argues that everyone would consent to such a system, and in this way it resembles Rawls's social contract theory. I will use Posner's work as an exemplar of this approach because in his prolific, imaginative, and influential writings he stands as perhaps its most articulate proponent.

The Idea and Ideal of Wealth Maximization

Posner wears his ethical presuppositions on his sleeve. The good society is one that aims for wealth maximization. You are a good person if you produce surplus wealth for others. You will do this only if you maximize your own wealth.[23] Greed is good. Q.E.D.

The basic idea underlying Posner's theory is fairly simple. He starts by assuming that each of us wants to maximize his own wealth, which Posner measures in dollars. He further assumes that the only way you can maximize your own wealth is by engaging in business with others—you cannot go off and be a subsistence farmer in Vermont and expect to maximize your wealth. But I will trade with you only if I believe that the trade will be financially advantageous to me. And you will not offer me a deal unless you believe it will benefit you.

Here's an example. Imagine that I am an apple grower and you are a grocer. I want to sell my apples to you at the highest price I can get. But I cannot be a pig. I actually have to sell the apples to make a profit. If I charge too high a price, you will not be able to realize your goal of making a profit by selling the apples to consumers, and so you won't buy my apples. My offer to sell you apples must, then, promise you the opportunity to maximize your own wealth—it must be at the lowest price you can pay for apples, which will depend on the costs and incentives of apple growers like me. By the same token, your lowest price must be the highest price that I can get (consistent with the costs and incentives of grocers) or I will sell my apples to someone else who will pay a higher price. I, then, will sell all the apples I can grow at the highest price I can get, and you will buy them for the lowest price available (and in turn sell them for the highest price you can get). Thus, I can maximize my income only if it helps you maximize yours.

There's nothing very surprising about this. It is simply an explanation of the way that competitive market economies work. What is special about Posner's argument is the way he transforms it into moral theory.

Wealth Maximization and the Autonomy of the Wealthy

If we behave in the manner I described above, you and I are people of virtue. We are so by virtue of our commerce. And we, and people like us, are the only ethically good people in this society. Who can achieve this ethical status? Anyone who can act freely and who can rationally make choices in the market environment—autonomous people.

There is a catch. It is not enough that you try to maximize your wealth and fail. To be a good person, you must succeed. And if you are not a good person—if you try and fail or if you don't try at all—you should expect no public sympathy and no public support. For Posner tells us that the poor, "not those who merely lack ready cash, but those who have insufficient earning power to be able to cover the expenses of a minimum decent standard of living—count only if they are part of the utility function of someone who has wealth."[24] In other words, the only people who have an obligation to support you are those who care about you for some (nonrational) reason. But because you do nothing for society, society has no obligation to you.

To his credit, Posner stands up to the implications of his theory. But he believes himself to be in good company. All major ethical systems, he tells us, share the same basic implications. The reason appears to be that all of them accept a baseline norm of autonomy. Redistribution is unacceptable if you are truly committed to an ethic of autonomy, because "any policy of redistribution impairs the autonomy of those from whom the redistribution is made."[25]

Notice that the underlying idea behind this brutal realization is the same as Dworkin's—that you should not be permitted to impose the cost of your life on others. To be fair, Dworkin's application of the idea is more moderate than Posner's. Further, Dworkin argues that fairness demands that this ethic be located in a society of equal resources in an attempt to truly isolate choice from the uncontrollable forces of nature. But for our purposes—understanding that autonomy is at the root of the leading conception of fairness—their theories are essentially the same.

An ethic of autonomy is at the heart of Model III, then, just as it lies at the hearts of Models I and II. But its application seems to be different from those of the other models. For example, in Model I, we saw that Rawls limits autonomy in order to provide baseline benefits to the least well off. In Model II, we saw that Dworkin tempers autonomy by his requirement of equal distribution of resources. These seem to be dramatically different from a model that counts only the successful. But they aren't.

Wealth Maximization and the Social Contract

The reason they aren't lies in the fact that the system that embodies this ethic, like the others, is one that we would choose. In other words, the system that denies the value of autonomy to some is itself the product of the autonomous free choices of all. This, like Rawls's theory of justice as fairness, is justified by a theory of social contract. Both are derived from autonomous choice. Both are derived from the classical process of autonomous action—contract.[26]

To see why this is so, it is necessary to turn to Posner's version of Rawls's original position, the market. In doing so, we can see how Model III links up with both Model I and Model II in establishing a norm of fairness as equal autonomy.

Posner starts with the belief that some ethical theory derived from utilitarianism serves as the universe of choices.[27] Recall that utilitarianism, simply put, holds that the goal of political society is to maximize the utility of the society as a whole. Thus, utilitarianism permits each person's interests to count for one, and no more than one, in determining the course society will take. The corollary is that it permits each person's interest to be sacrificed equally for the good of the whole.

How does one measure social improvement in utilitarian terms? The answer is the concept of Pareto superiority, developed by the Italian economist Vilfredo Pareto. A political or economic decision that improves the utility of some, without decreasing the utility of others, is considered to be Pareto superior. But although this concept is simple enough, and even compelling in its logic, it is based on a fundamental flaw: we have no accepted way of measuring and comparing utility. Recall that this is what led Dworkin to reject the essentially similar concept of equal welfare: how can you measure the utility I derive from going to the opera, let alone compare it with the utility Sam derives from knowing that the earth is round? And if you have trouble measuring and comparing the utility of two people, imagine how difficult it would be to try to do this across an entire society.

Posner has a solution to the problem: he identifies the core ethical underpinning of Pareto superiority as the idea of—here it comes again—consent.[28] If everyone consents to the transfer of resources, the result must be an increase in resources or someone surely would have objected. Thus, if you and Sam and I and everybody else (or our surrogates in the U.S. Congress) are fully informed about all the relevant facts and agree that farm subsidies are a good idea, it *must* be the case that farm subsidies increase overall resources. If not, we would not have agreed to them. Thus, consent provides a substitute for the need to measure and compare utilities and so rescues utilitarianism from its fatal flaw.

Posner tells us that this idea of consent not only rescues utilitarianism but that it proves that it is a better theory than any other. For one, it is consistent with other liberal theories, such as Rawls's and Dworkin's, that attach ethical significance to autonomy.[29] For another, it facilitates economic development.[30] What could be better?

We have seen how Pareto superiority rescues utilitarianism through the idea of consent. But where does this consent come from? It is fine, as a theoretical matter, to say that all transfers of resources must increase wealth because we would have consented to them, but this begs the question, since we did not *in fact* consent. It will be a little complicated to get to the answer. If you stay with me, however, you will see at the end that it is all rather (frighteningly) simple.

Posner begins by answering that consent is implied in the market. In other words, we may not know that people have consented, but their actions prove that they must have. The very fact that resource-allocating transactions take place means that the parties must have consented, and we therefore assume that consent exists.

But the market poses a problem. Not all market transactions are free of third-party effects. Third-party effects (called "externalities" by economists) occur when a transaction between two parties has an effect on a person who has nothing to do with the deal. If my neighbor, Jill, sells her land to Sam, and Sam converts the land from a lovely suburban home in Bethesda to a pig farm, the unpleasant consequences to me of living next to a pig farm are third-party effects.

The problem that the existence of third-party effects poses for Model III is that the third parties—in this case, me—have not consented to the deal, and if Jill and Sam ask me how I feel about living next to a pig farm, I would tell them that I would rather not. In other words, Jill and Sam may achieve an increase in *their* wealth, but affected nonparties, like me, get nothing from the deal and have to live with pigs besides.

The deal between Jill and Sam is wealth maximizing, but it may not be utility maximizing. And there is no way to know, because there is no way to measure whether the overall increase in utility to Jill and Sam from the deal is greater or less than the decrease in my utility from it.

We can solve this problem too. The idea that a deal can be wealth maximizing (but not utility maximizing) and still be socially desirable is captured by the notion of Kaldor-Hicks efficiency. Remember that Pareto superiority is based on the idea that a transaction creates winners and no losers. Kaldor-Hicks efficiency is somewhat different—it begins with Pareto superiority as its base but goes on to argue that wealth is increased by deals in which there may be winners and losers but the winners gain enough to compensate the losers. So if Jill's profit from the sale of her land and Sam's profit from his pig farm are enough to compensate both of them *and* to allow them both to pay me the money I would demand to relieve my unhappiness (or at least to buy lots of room freshener), it is a good deal all around.

But there's a catch here too: Kaldor-Hicks efficiency doesn't require that Jill and Sam *actually* compensate me, only that they *could* have if they wanted to. And the odds are pretty good that they won't want to.

It should be clear that this notion of Kaldor-Hicks efficiency expresses Posner's social ideal as outlined above. Thus, he shifts the ethical defense from Pareto superiority, in which we presume consent because nobody is made worse off in terms of utility, to a system in which some people clearly are made worse off. In other words, Posner now turns to defend his disregard of the autonomy of the poor and unproductive, and he does so on the very basis of their autonomy: they are excluded because they have consented to be excluded.

This seems rather odd. Why would anyone consent to a social arrangement in which he is considered to be a nonperson? We saw that it was something like the fear of such an arrangement that led Rawls's people in the original position to develop principles that precluded this possibility. Can Rawls and Posner really believe that people are so different? Do we imagine that Posner himself would consent to a system in which he were potentially treated as valueless?

Posner's answer to these questions has a familiar ring. He says that people would consent to be losers in such a system because they have been compensated in advance. In other words, you have been paid to accept a losing position, and that pay was enough to get you to agree to be a loser.[31] You have chosen to be a loser (or at least to risk the possibility of being a loser), and so your losses are not really involuntary at all.

Posner uses lottery tickets as an example. He says that it is uncontroversial to say that the purchaser of a lottery ticket has consented to the loss.[32] The reason is that the purchaser has been compensated by the possibility of winning; in other words, he paid his money and he made his choice.

The reason the argument should have a familiar ring is its resemblance to Dworkin's theory of option luck. Recall that Dworkin argued that we have no social obligation to compensate people for inequalities of resources resulting from option luck—ambitions and tastes—because the people who suffered such losses in a sense chose them. Recall, too, that Dworkin demonstrated that losses from brute luck—talents and physical abilities—for which we appeared to have an obligation to compensate, could be converted to losses from option luck (which are noncompensable) through hypothetical insurance markets and redistributive taxation.

For Posner, compensation is consent (although Dworkin, perhaps for obvious reasons, strenuously objects to equating the two). The reason is that Posner's people are wealth maximizers. If, therefore, an arrangement maximizes wealth, they can be expected to consent because wealth maximization compensates them for their losses. If wealth is maximized, then everyone will be better off, even poor people, because overall wealth maximization implies that the poor will do better than under other systems. Even though Dworkin assigns his people a wider range of goals than simple wealth maximization, it should be clear that he and Posner ultimately come to the same place. And that place is autonomy.

Posner's theory also bears some resemblance to Rawls's difference principle. Recall that, to Rawls, inequalities are tolerable only if they benefit the worst off. Guess what? Posner is saying the same thing. The main difference between Posner and Rawls in this respect is that Posner thinks that the worst off would be better off *in general* if people were allowed to maximize their own wealth, and Rawls seems to leave the question of how to accomplish this to a case-by-case analysis. But the basic idea appears to be the same.

Conclusion: The Dominant Theory of Equal Autonomy

Despite their real and apparent differences, the three models of the dominant theory of fairness really present only one underlying ethic. That is the primacy of autonomy and free choice. Differences in the way the models describe and facilitate this ethic result from differences in the choices that the proponents of each model expect people to make—in other words, from differences in their concepts of rationality and personhood. It seems indisputable, however, that each theory assumes that, regardless of the nature of rationality and personhood, normal people are in fact rational and behave autonomously. They have the capacity to exercise free will and to make choices, and they do, in fact, do so.

At the same time, each of the theories imposes limits on the range of autonomous choices. In Model I, it is the index of primary goods and the difference principle. In Model II, it is the distinction between talent and ambition, between the circumstances and the person. In Model III, it is the constraint of the market that channels a rationality, commensurate with virtue, that works to the benefit of all. In each case, the constraint is designed to back up an ethic of autonomy and free choice with a means of protecting (or, in Posner's case, compensating *ex ante*) those who are unable to exercise the autonomy necessary to function in the system. Clearly each of these models treats autonomy as the normal human condition. But there is a safety net that exists to protect those whose inability to exercise autonomy makes them vulnerable, those whom the theory treats as abnormal.

None of the models satisfactorily explains why this safety net exists. The only model that attempts such an explanation is Rawls's, which is premised expressly on a Kantian conception of the person. But even Rawls falls short, for the Kantian conception of personhood is premised on rationality and the ability to exercise autonomous will. And without the help of Rawls's principles, the worst off in society are in fact unable to formulate and pursue their ends, are unable to exercise rational will. If the ethic of autonomy is desirable, if autonomy is the norm, why should we protect such people? Why, as Posner asks of Rawls, should such people have the right to participate in the system when they contribute nothing? [33] Why should we be concerned, with Dworkin, to assuage their envy? Why must Posner insist that losers are in some sense really winners?

The reason we care, I will argue in the next chapters, is that the dominant theory of fairness that is embedded in these models is wrong in its factual assumption of autonomy. That assumption is unrealistic and is not consistent with our motivations to develop these restraints on autonomy, these safety mechanisms. It is not consistent with our wish to be fair. This is why each of the leading models includes some argument to show that failure is protected (or *ex ante* compensated). And the fact that the line in each case is drawn in an arbitrary place suggests that the empirical assumption of autonomy is mistaken. The reality that instead leads to our caring, our motivation to limit our autonomy to the benefit of others, is the universal condition of human vulnerability.

6

Vulnerability

The Heart of the Matter

My family recently acquired a cat. We didn't want a cat—far from it. I am terribly allergic to cats, and my son is asthmatic. In fact, I don't even like cats. But several weeks ago, on a cold winter's day, a cat appeared on the deck behind our house. Although she was wearing a flea collar, and thus clearly was not feral, she was dirty and looked scared. Indeed, she was very timid and walked away whenever one of us would go out to look after her. She walked with sort of a limp, and her tail appeared to be damaged. She stayed all day, shivering outside our family room window, as we sat before the fire. I went out to buy cat food.

As I said, it was cold. So at the end of the day, after feeding her on the deck, we tried, with grave misgivings, to coax her into the house. She refused, much to my relief. But the next day she was back, and we repeated the routine. This time I put some old towels in a box and left it outside in case she needed warmth. But the next day she was gone.

Five days later she returned, and this time she stayed. Our consciences were somewhat eased by an unusual spell of January warmth, and so we were comfortable with her living beneath the deck. But winter returned, and the weather turned bitter. She seemed to want to come in but still was afraid. One night I returned home and opened the sliding-glass door that leads to the deck. After fifteen minutes, the room was cold, but she had only poked her nose in. Yet another fifteen minutes later, she came into the room. And there she stayed. We have engaged in the usual sign posting and newspaper notices proclaiming a lost cat (and *begging* its owner to call us). We have had the typical lack of response. My family and I have acquired a cat. Someday perhaps my eyes will stop watering.

Bert Bochove and his family lived in a small town in the Netherlands, not far from Amsterdam, where they owned a pharmacy. In May 1940, the Germans invaded Holland. He describes the beginning of the occupation as "pretty quiet. But in 1942 things started getting bad for the Jews." He goes on to describe the way he and his wife became Holocaust rescuers: "The way it started was, my wife's girl friend, her name is Henny, came to us. She was Jewish and she needed help. We didn't ever talk about it. It was something you had to do, and it was easy to do because it was your duty. And that was the beginning because when her husband came, that was all right too. And when the sister came, well, why not? And that was the way it went until there were thirty-seven people." [1] The Bochoves' attitude is not unusual among Holocaust rescuers. Interview after interview reveals that, when confronted with Jews in their desperate need—some known to them, some unknown—rescuers simply helped, typically at great personal risk and sometimes at significant expense as well.

To those of us who are not committed animal rights activists (and I am not), the differences between human life and that of a cat are significant. (If Beaver adversely affects Alex's asthma, for example, we will have to find her a new home.) Nor do I mean to compare our behavior to that of a Holocaust rescuer: they faced dramatic risks and were acting in cultures that were often not supportive; I risked sniffles and teary eyes, and, despite my (previous) dislike of cats, I don't favor killing them. By telling these two stories together, I in no way mean to trivialize the horror of the Holocaust (as an American Jew, far from it); nor do I mean to elevate my family's rescue of Beaver to the level of heroism. But there is at least one relevant parallel.

The parallel lies in what triggered our desire to help. A great deal of psychological research has gone into examining the motives of Holocaust rescuers, and I will not examine that work here. The issue I want to focus on is external to the rescuers' psyche and observable by anybody. Both the Jews rescued by the Bochoves and others, and Beaver, our new cat, came to us in conditions of extreme vulnerability. I don't think I need to explain the vulnerability of Jews in German-occupied Europe. And Beaver's vulnerability, given the weather, her evident fear, and her apparent physical condition, was obvious enough. If conditions were different, there would have been no need for Holocaust rescuers. If conditions were different, we probably wouldn't have taken in Beaver. In each case, though, a living being in desperate straits presented itself to us for help. And in each case, we had the power to help. Who could refuse? Listen to the words of Holocaust rescuer Stefan Raczynski, a Pole now living in Israel, explaining his impulse to rescue Jews: "It was a natural thing to do, like when you see a cat on the street, hungry, you give it food. When the Jews started coming from the forests and they were hungry, we gave them food and we didn't think anything of it."[2]

I have thus far simply asserted that others' vulnerability provides the emotional kick that leads us to be concerned with fairness and that the empirical assumptions of autonomy that underlie the dominant theory simply are wrong. But you don't have to trust me—I think your own intuitions will lead you to the same conclusion. In this chapter and the next, I will provide you with some opportunities to test your intuitions against both my argument and the dominant theory we have just examined. I will do so by way of presenting you with situations, both real and hypothetical, that will ask you to apply your intuitions and will, on behalf of Rawls, Dworkin, and Posner, draw out the implications of liberal theory in these contexts.

Intuitionism (and the emotions that help drive it) is not exactly the privileged methodology in Western thought. (Rawls himself relies explicitly on intuition in developing his argument but is very careful to establish a rational intellectual framework to give it parallel support.[3]) Reason has pride of place in our intellectual tradition, but even the hyper-rationalist Kant acknowledged nonrational aspects of human existence (and, unlike some theorists, did not attach negative judgments to them). But reason has its limits in telling us why we care. The philosopher Brian Barry has noted, "If it is true that moral motivation cannot be argued into existence from nothing, it is clearly of importance to know what are the conditions that predispose people to acquire moral motivation. I speculate that at any rate a part of the answer is going to be that the experience of dependence on others is an important predisposing factor."[4] I shall argue that such experience leads us to empathize with the dependencies of others—their vulnerabilities—and that this emotional response, and not our self-interest, provides our princi-pal motive to care.* Our emotions are a critically important aspect of our humanity, as many philosophers have come to realize and as psy-chologists have always known. To the lawyers, political theorists, and economists who make much of our public policy, however, this may come as news.

I am therefore at a disadvantage in presenting my ideas. In trying to affect the way we think about issues of fair political and economic dis-tributions, I confront a tradition that prizes carefully reasoned, logical explanation. Arguments made in that tradition are easier to make per-suasively, for they permit us to abandon confusing, sloppy, hard-to-describe, and often inconsistent emotions and lose ourselves in neatly ordered, carefully worded thought. Language and logic are inadequate tools to use in dealing with deeper, intuitive motivations. But I will try.

There is a scene in *Sister Carrie* in which Carrie is on the train from her small town to Chicago and meets Drouet, who attempts to establish a relationship with her. As he describes the scene, and the conversation of the two participants, Dreiser notes, "How true it is that words are but the vague shadows of the volumes we mean."[5] It is now time to open those volumes.

Testing Our Intuitions

I shall present much of the discussion in this chapter as an examination of a number of hypothetical cases before becoming a little more abstract near the end. Like any good law professor would, the early cases I give you will be fairly simple. The reason is that I want to test our intuitions in the obvious cases before moving on to situations that present com-peting values and that therefore require more nuanced thought and ar-guments. This will also give you an opportunity to test me—if your intuitions in these core cases differ significantly from mine, then you might not want to bother finishing this book. If they coincide, you can proceed on, trusting that we at least begin with a common ground.

Imagine that you are in the local shopping mall a few days before Christmas. I hardly need to describe the chaos you will encounter—if

---

* Self-interest is an almost infinitely malleable concept, and I am familiar with the raft of arguments that attribute any sort of altruistic impulse to a form of self-interest. I don't want to engage the details of that debate here. I think it is enough to note that one can stretch self-interest to a point where it becomes analytically meaningless.

you need illustration, run out to the local art museum and look at a painting by Hieronymus Bosch. As you attempt to negotiate your way through the crowd, you come upon a small child—say five years old—crying and obviously alone. You stop and ask the child what is wrong, and he tells you that he cannot find his parents. You have two options: you may shrug your shoulders and walk away, or you may help him try to find his parents, which for most of us will consist in taking him to the mall's security guards. What do you do?

I'm pretty confident that in the absence of extraordinary circumstances—say the onset of severe chest pains—you will do the latter. It's hard to imagine that you would pass up a child in such need of help, especially since the cost to you is negligible.

The more interesting question is *why* you would help—a pretty odd question I'd say, since I suspect that you probably would help without thinking much about it. One reason that might occur to you is that it would make you feel good to help—it would give you that warm, fuzzy glow that some people say comes to them from volunteering at a soup kitchen. But that's probably not it; you haven't actually looked for the opportunity to help—it simply confronted you. Most likely, you help without making a conscious choice—you just do it. And you do it because you can't imagine *not* doing it.

Why? Why is it so hard to imagine simply passing the child by? The reason, I think, is the same reason that we took in Beaver: the child is completely vulnerable. I suppose you could decide that if you don't help, somebody else will, or that a security guard or the child's parents eventually will find him. There certainly is psychological evidence that people in groups are less likely to help because, among other reasons, they anticipate that somebody else will—remember the Kitty Genovese story.[6] But the hypothetical I gave you says that *you* come upon the child, and, anyway, even if there were several people present I suspect that the only topic of discussion would be which of you would take him to the security desk. And not only do you come upon the child but, unlike the Kitty Genovese case, in which neighbors watched her murder from their windows, you are confronting the child face-to-face. You are looking at him, and he is looking (tearfully) at you.

You have no choice. The child cannot help himself. Without your assistance, he is likely to stay lost—and scared—for some time. The child is completely vulnerable and, importantly, now has become dependent on you. If you help, you might not get a warm, fuzzy glow. But

I bet if you walked away, you'd feel pretty bad. You'd have done the wrong thing.

Contrast this with a different case. You're in the same mall, at the same time. Instead of a tearful child, you come across a forty-year-old man who approaches you. To all appearances, he is perfectly capable—well dressed and with Bloomingdale's shopping bags in his hands. He even has a cellular phone on his belt. He tells you that he cannot find his wife, whom he last saw at Nordstrom's, and asks you to help him. What do you do?

My guess is that you will get away from him about as fast as you can. If you are particularly trusting, you might engage him in brief conversation to determine whether he is as competent as he appears. But if you are like most of us—certainly like me—you will find the situation rather creepy and suspect that the man had some nefarious reason for stopping you. Not only will you refuse to help—probably just by walking away—but you will ponder the situation for some time and may even feel a little violated. I suspect that you will not, however, feel that you somehow have done the wrong thing by walking away.

Why the different reaction? Why help the child with no hesitation yet scurry rapidly away from the man? Unlike the child, the man is not vulnerable. To all appearances, he is at least as capable of finding his wife as you are, and more so since he knows what she looks like. He certainly is able to find his own way to the security desk to ask someone there to make an announcement, or to go to the car and wait for her to show up. He appears to be perfectly capable of exercising his own autonomy, of making his own decisions and helping himself. And, I suspect, the fact that he appears to be so capable is an important part of what makes the situation so discomforting to you—why could this man possibly need your help?

Of course appearances may be deceiving. He could have Alzheimer's disease (not likely in a forty year old) or some other cognitive dysfunction that has no physical manifestation. If you had some way of knowing this (if perhaps he introduced his request by telling you), you would, I suspect, be very likely to help. And if you later heard that a disoriented and ill man meeting his description was found wandering the mall, you would probably feel somewhat bad that you failed to help him. But, given all appearances, your past experience, your reason, and your intuitions would probably lead you to walk away.

Now let's up the ante.

The Test Gets Tougher

Two important factors were missing from these first hypotheticals, certainly from the easy case of helping the lost child. The first factor is that our vulnerable victim made no choice that led to his predicament—it was completely involuntary (or at least involuntary in any meaningful sense). The second factor is that helping the child was virtually costless to you—at most it would take a few minutes of your time. When these factors are added back into the problem, our intuition to help is strained and we begin to identify reasons that may lead to different decisions. I will present two hypotheticals, each of which implicates one of these factors, and then put them together in a third problem.

Choice is a critically important issue in determining whether we will help. Classic liberal theory, as we have seen, asserts that choice is the manifestation of individual autonomy. What you choose reflects who you are, and permitting you to realize who you are—to live the life you choose—is a fundamental goal of liberal society. But your choices are not without consequences. An important corollary to the liberal ideal of freedom of choice is that, in general, we require you to live with the consequences of your own decisions.

Recall that one of the main reasons Dworkin settled on equality of resources as the fair measure of equality is that it permitted a system in which we each had to bear the costs of our choices ourselves. This implicates the issue of the cost to others of our choices, which I will explore in the next hypothetical, and is an important issue in a world of scarce resources.

But there is another reason liberal theory requires us to live with the consequences of our choices. If autonomy is not only the privileged state but the way in which we realize our value as human beings, then to interfere with a person's choices by mitigating the consequences of those choices is to interfere with another's personhood. Let's go back to my son, Alex, whom you met in the introduction to this book. When I tell him that his bedtime is 9:30, the principal reason that he protests is that he thinks his life would be improved if he could stay up later to read or watch TV. Of course I know (as does he) that he is wrong—if he does so, he will be tired and cranky in the morning, and the next day will be spoiled for him. If he were mature and rational, not only would he realize this consequence but most likely he would go to bed at a sensible hour without my compelling him to do so. He is ten years old, however, and not yet entirely rational. That is why I must make the decision for him, despite its interference with his autonomous choices. We call this kind of interference paternalism, and it comes from situations precisely like this one. I am his pater—it is my right and obligation to interfere.

If he disregards my command and, after my wife and I are asleep, turns on the light and reads until 2:00 or 3:00, he will be rather unhappy when we wake him for school at 7:00. It is likely—in fact, he has done so—that he will say that he is too tired to go to school, that he doesn't feel up to it. When we ask why he is so tired (we were, after all, asleep) and he tells us (he is a very honest child), should we take pity and let him stay home? No. He has an obligation to go to school. If he made the autonomous, rational decision to stay up and read as a means of asserting his personhood, then his choice is not complete until he bears its consequences. As a ten year old, he is not yet fully capable of rationally exercising his autonomy. But we still don't accede to his request, because if we want him to achieve meaningful autonomy one day, we must let him understand that his choices have consequences and that they are consequences that he alone must bear.[7]

So much for paternalism and the child. What about when the chooser is a (presumably) fully rational adult? To explore this issue, I will present a hypothetical (with apologies to Immanuel Kant and Victor Hugo). Let's say you have a friend named Valjean. Both of you are rather poor and have families to support. Valjean has been out of work for longer than you have, and he is at the end of his rope. His children are hungry, and he is too proud to beg. One day, the two of you are walking past a bakery, which emits the seductive odor of pastries into the street. Valjean turns to you and says, "I can't take it anymore. I'm going to steal a loaf of bread." You remind him that he knows that stealing is wrong and that the same pride that keeps him from begging should prevent him from stealing. On a more practical note, you also point out that Officer Javert, the local policeman, is standing across the street (although he is engaged in conversation and not looking in your direction). Despite your warnings, Valjean enters the store and emerges with a loaf of bread. Seconds later, the baker runs out into the street crying "thief." By the time Javert turns around, Valjean is gone. But Javert notices you. He approaches you and asks whether you know the escaping thief and where he lives. Of course you do, and you know that Valjean will be returning home to feed his children so that Javert will find him there if he hurries. But Javert has no way of knowing this. If you lie, it is likely that Valjean will escape. And there will be no consequence to you. What do you do?

My guess is that you probably would lie and help your friend escape. I would. After all, the crime is a modest one and Valjean is in desperate straits. If he is arrested, his children will surely go without food. He is, in short, highly vulnerable, both before and after the theft. And it costs you nothing (besides a pang of law-abiding conscience) to let him go.

But the answer is not so clear in liberal theory. In fact, Kant suggests an answer and it is, to put it bluntly, that you not only should but must rat on Valjean. One reason (which I will not explore here) is that lying is morally wrong. The more important reason for our purpose lies in your understanding of Valjean's autonomy, and this implicates the issue of paternalism that I mentioned earlier.

Valjean made his bed—he must lie in it. By choosing to steal the bread and run, he made an independent, rational decision, aware of the risks that he faced. For you to protect him deprives him of fully realizing his autonomy by preventing him from experiencing the consequences of his choices. And so giving Valjean his proper respect as an autonomous human being requires you to tell Javert where he lives.

This probably strikes you as bizarre—me too. But let's think about why it strikes us as bizarre, for this will tell us much about both the ideal of autonomy and our own moral motivations. It bothers me for several reasons. The first reason is that Valjean is my friend; the baker is a stranger. It is only natural to feel a greater obligation to those whom you know and like than to those whom you've never even met. An important reason for this is that I identify with my friend more closely than with those whom I don't know. If you will pardon the expression, I feel his pain. This is quite literally what David Hume meant when he said that our moral impulses come from our sympathetic identification with others and that the closer others are to us, the stronger are the impulses. Even Kant recognized this, although he rejected it as a basis for constructing moral rules. And Rawls even relies on it in explaining why people are motivated to care.

A second, related, reason this conclusion bothers me is that it seems unfair that society has placed Valjean in a position in which his choices are theft, mendicancy, or starvation. Assume that Valjean has done the best he can to make a living and that social circumstances and plain hard luck have consigned him to poverty (remember the Lamberts). His decision may be rational *under the circumstances*, but we at least ought to ask whether the circumstances themselves are fair. And if the circumstances are not fair, then it is hard to blame Valjean for making a bad choice—bad choices are all that he has. The problem is compounded by my knowledge that Valjean has children who are dependent on him. So I consider not only his vulnerability but theirs as well. This leads me to see that granting him his autonomy is harmful not only to himself but to others too.

My instincts are to help by lying. But liberal theory—in this extreme application—tells me that by doing so I am depriving Valjean of his essential personhood. I am behaving toward him in much the same way that I would have behaved toward Alex if I let him stay home from school. But while liberal theory permits me to rule Alex (and the mandatory school attendance laws back me up), because he has not yet attained full rationality, it prohibits me from helping Valjean. To do so would be impermissibly paternalistic.

Yes, Kant's rule is extreme. But this argument has played a very important role in constructing the society we have today. Versions of this argument arise especially in debates over issues like seat belt laws, speed limits, and motorcycle helmet laws, as well as drug laws and laws limiting drinking ages. These debates are complicated, of course, by the potential social costs that actions like irresponsible driving may impose on the public. But the argument from paternalism resonates powerfully in our liberal society.

It is important to see the assumption underlying this argument. It is that the choices that we make in these areas truly are free and rational. It is the same assumption that we saw underlying liberal philosophy—that people are generally autonomous in fact. If the assumption is right, then there may be something to liberal theory. If we make all our choices rationally, aware of all the potential consequences and the costs that we will bear if we choose wrong, and we still make bad choices, maybe we ought to live with them.

But if the assumption is wrong, the theory becomes a cruel joke. If you were Valjean, how would you react when I visited you in jail and told you that the reason I had ratted on you was to protect you in the choice that you rationally and autonomously had made. You probably would look at me as if I were crazy. What choice did you really have? And if you had no choice, then my ratting on you (and in fact Javert's arresting you) clearly is wrong.

But maybe not. There is one more arrow in the liberal quiver. Perhaps Valjean felt boxed in; perhaps *he* failed to see that he had a choice. But, the liberal argues, he did *in fact* have choices—after all, I am poor too but didn't steal. The choices he had were to steal the bread, beg, face starvation, or continue looking for work. And the choice he made—stealing the bread—impinged on the baker's autonomy. (We will have occasion soon to examine the issue from the baker's perspective in the tale of Heinz.) One purpose of law in liberal society is to help us make the right choices, which include respecting the autonomy of others. If we permit people to make the easiest choices without considering their effects on others, we will have anarchy, not society. In the future, after his release from prison, Valjean will see that he has such choices and, presumably, decline to break the law in the future. Autonomy for all is ensured only when we let people make choices *and* the chips fall where they may.

When we implicate the baker's autonomy, we implicate the issue of cost to others, a factor I left out of Valjean's story. Let's now look at the issue of cost alone, before we combine cost and choice in the story of Heinz.

Lightning strikes your neighbor's house and starts a fire. Before the fire department has arrived, the fire has spread and, by the time it is extinguished, destroyed a substantial portion of his house, making it uninhabitable. The family has lost most of its possessions and is disoriented and upset. Your own house is not very large, but you can squeeze your neighbor's family in. Assume too that all your other neighbors are out of town—it is August in Washington. Do you offer to let your neighbor and his family stay with you until they can make longer-term arrangements?

Your answer may largely turn on your feelings for your neighbor (although some of the Holocaust rescuers disliked the people they saved), so to make the problem easier assume that you get along perfectly well with him, although you are not close friends. My guess is that you probably would make this offer. Your neighbor and his family are in a state of vulnerability through no fault of their own. Although they may well have adequate means to find a hotel room (or insurance that will pay for it), they probably need a safe place to stay where they can regain their bearings and begin to make sensible decisions about their future. Putting them up entails some costs—the inconvenience of overcrowding your home and additional groceries (for which you may not ask for reimbursement). There is also the increased stress of having to get along with people with whom you are not accustomed to living. But the circumstances will probably lead you to disregard these costs and take in your neighbors.

Why? Because they're there, and so are you. They are vulnerable at a time when you are not, and you have the means to help them out. No questions of autonomy arise, because of course they did not choose to be in their helpless state. Of course they may refuse your help, and if they do so, you will respect that choice as rational (assuming that a falling beam didn't hit them over the head). But no questions of paternalism arise here, and the costs to you, while they clearly exist, are modest under the circumstances, although there could come a point when those costs could become excessive (more on that later). You might even feel that your neighbor would help you out if you were in the same position, which you surely could have been. There but for the grace of God go I, after all. But if you do help out, it will be because you recognize in yourself the same (contingent) vulnerability that your neighbor has experienced.

This is an easier case than Valjean's, both because it lacks the critical component of choice and because your resources are adequate enough to share them without causing you undue hardship—that is, the condition of scarcity is minimized. But the issue of autonomy is not entirely absent; if the costs to you became too great, your neighbors' presence would infringe upon your autonomy too severely and you would reach a point at which you might cut off help. In the next chapters, we will explore what that point might be.

As a last hypothetical, let's combine the problems of autonomous choice and cost to you. The story of Heinz powerfully tests our intuitions and leaves us with unsatisfactory answers. Heinz was first introduced to us by the psychologist Lawrence Kohlberg and was made more famous by his colleague Carol Gilligan in her groundbreaking analysis of women's psychological development, *In a Different Voice*.[8] It is the story of Heinz that Gilligan presented to boys and girls in order to analyze and contrast their responses. I have taken some liberties in modifying this story to serve my purpose, but the essential tale remains the same.

You are the local pharmacist. One day a man named Heinz appears at your counter. You know Heinz from the neighborhood, and he is your regular customer. Heinz and his wife (Mrs. Heinz) have always lived well. This fact has been the talk of the community—Heinz manages the local supermarket and Mrs. Heinz doesn't work, yet they always drive a new-model Cadillac, live in one of the nicer houses in town, and frequently dine out in your town's fancier restaurants. It might make the story more graphic (and Aesopian) if we agree that you are hardworking and frugal, living modestly and saving your pennies for a rainy day.

Heinz tells you a sad tale. Mrs. Heinz is gravely—indeed, fatally—ill and needs an expensive and rare drug. If she receives it, she has a good chance of recovering. If not, she will surely die. But Heinz cannot afford the drug. He tells you that he never bought health insurance (assume that his employer did not provide it) and that he and Mrs. Heinz not only have spent all of their money but have borrowed quite a lot. They have no children or other family—nowhere to turn. Heinz tells you that he knows that you can obtain the drug and asks if you will simply give it to him.

You can, like the ant in our Aesopian mode, tell grasshopper Heinz simply to go away. After all, two things are clear: Heinz and Mrs. Heinz have made the choices that have led them to this predicament, and giving them the drug will cost you a considerable amount of money. I think that there is little doubt that liberal theory will suffer no pangs of guilt in suggesting that we leave the Heinzes to their predicament.

And for good reason. What if we all behaved like Heinz? What if we all squandered our money and failed to protect ourselves? If people were obligated to help the Heinzes of the world, then soon everybody would behave like Heinz. To whom then would we turn for help?

Recall, too, Dworkin's argument—that an obligation to help Heinz would unfairly impinge on your autonomy because it would impose the costs of his lavish lifestyle on you. Besides, Heinz had the chance (and once had the money) to protect against this kind of bad brute luck by buying health insurance, and thus his bad luck really is bad option luck. He didn't, so tough (option) luck.

It might be easy to say this in the abstract, as you sit in your chair reading this book. But try to visualize how you would react if Heinz were standing in front of you, forlorn and helpless. (And leave aside as impractical a variety of other options, such as taking up a collection from the neighbors or seeking other forms of help.) *You* are the only person who can realistically help Heinz. Make it even more difficult: assume that Mrs. Heinz, although frail, is standing by his side as he pleads with you for help. Will you look Mrs. Heinz in the eye and tell her that she's just going to have to die?

I doubt it. I wouldn't. I might be resentful that my own brute luck has put me in the position to be faced with Heinz's request, and I might be angry that I have to spend some of my hard-earned money to help these people, but I wouldn't turn them away. And I doubt that you would either. After all, there but for the grace of God go you.

Or do you? You have, after all, made different and (as it turns out for the moment) better choices than Heinz. You have exercised your autonomy rationally and carefully, and Heinz has been profligate. You would probably not think that the Heinzes deserve your help, and they probably don't. But I think you would help anyway.

Why? For the same reason that my family took in Beaver, rescuers saved Jews during the Holocaust, and you would help the child in the mall. All of them were more deserving of help, sure. But their deservedness probably didn't enter into your calculation at the time you helped. You didn't assess whether the child seemed to be well behaved or willful and obnoxious; nor did the Holocaust rescuers evaluate the character of those they saved. They were there, they were vulnerable, and you had the capacity to help. You probably would have felt better about helping, and maybe even enjoyed it, if you knew that the people you were helping were good and decent people. But this would simply affect your attitude in helping, not the decision to help them in the first place.

So there it is. The Heinzes, wastrels that they are, have nobody to turn to but you in a matter of life and death. Mrs. Heinz is in a state of ultimate vulnerability. There are, to be sure, choices and costs involved. But she is staring you right in the face.

The philosopher Joel Feinberg explains the reasons for helping on a broader social level this way:

> We could let people gamble recklessly with their lives, and then adopt inflexibly unsympathetic attitudes toward the losers. 'They made their beds,' we might say in the manner of some proper Victorians, 'now let them sleep in them.' But this would be to render the whole national character cold and hard. It would encourage a general insensitivity and impose an unfair economic penalty on those who possess the socially useful virtue of benevolence. Realistically, we just can't let people wither and die right in front of our eyes.[9]

Feinberg is a liberal theorist, and he puts the argument in interestingly liberal terms. He gives two reasons for helping. The first reason, "we just have to help," is intuitive and I suspect derives from the same intuitions we have been developing so far in this chapter. But this argument is somewhat of a departure from liberalism—remember the coldness of Kant? That's what strict autonomy is about—we are not obligated to relieve you of the consequences of your choices and, in the extreme version, are obligated to ensure that you suffer (or enjoy) the consequences of those choices. Certainly Posner would deny that this intuition produces any obligation to help. Dworkin probably would too, assuming that Heinz and you had, over a lifetime, roughly equal resources. Rawls, too, I suspect, would agree that if the initial conditions of justice are met, the Heinzes must live with the consequences of their choices unless you simply choose to help because you want to.

Even Feinberg feels compelled to give a second reason, one that sounds like Dworkin. If we had no general obligation to help, so that the only helpers were those who chose to help, their helping would be more costly than if the obligation were spread out among all of us. In effect, this says that we must all sacrifice a little autonomy to prevent some from having to sacrifice a greater amount. This argument (unlike the intuitive one) is acceptable from the perspective of philosophical liberalism.

But the real reason we help, the one without explanation, lies at the end of Feinberg's statement: "Realistically, we just can't let people wither and die right in front of our eyes."

Why not? By now you know the answer. You just can't. And you can't because your ability to identify with vulnerable and suffering human beings, and their appearance right before your eyes, puts you in a position in which you simply can't say no.

I suspect too that Rawls, Dworkin, and Posner, finding themselves facing the Heinzes face-to-face across the pharmacy counter, would find it hard to refuse to help. Imagine the response: "Well, Heinzes, we're sorry, but you started out pretty much with the same advantages we did, but unlike us you made bad choices and squandered your resources, so we feel no obligation to help. Besides, helping you would cost us money, and that's unfair to us, so we're not going to do it."

Unlikely, I think. It's hard to imagine that they, any more than the rest of us, would ignore the concrete facts and their own emotions in favor of some abstract theory. And the fact that they wouldn't helps to identify the problem with the theories. As abstractions from reality, with a common supposed starting point, they ignore people. In describing how we ideally should be, they fail to see us as we are, as individuals with our limitations, our weaknesses, our vulnerabilities—and our emotions. It is the same problem we saw in characterizing the *Matthews* court's categorical approach to due process and the assumption of various courts that divorcing spouses typically act as economically rational agents.

But there is a critical difference between my hypotheticals and their theories—a difference that is captured in Feinberg's last sentence. The Heinzes are standing "right before our eyes." Hume was right, I think, in claiming that our proximity to others determines the strength and likelihood of our responses to them. We are more likely to help the helpless child who belongs to us and is standing before us than the one who doesn't. We are more likely to help our neighbor than someone far across the country whom we've never met.

The problem becomes more complicated when our help is compelled by anonymous government bureaucrats and dispensed by them as well. And, to be fair, this is the real problem that contemporary liberal theory attempts to solve: when can we use the coercive power of the state to help others, and when is it appropriate to help them?

Liberal theory starts with autonomy. In doing so, I suggest, it has buried the very intuitions that I have thus far tried to recapture. We could (and in the rest of this book I shall) take those intuitions and use them to create a theory of fair social obligation that fits those intuitions.

There is one last point to deal with before undertaking that task. I noted that the face-to-face aspect of our encounters with the people we were inclined to help was important in leading us to help. I also let our liberal theorists at least partly off the hook by noting that they were attempting to build theories for society in general and for a society—ours—that is remarkably heterogeneous. As a result, they needed to be abstract and to deal with problems at a general level.

But there is another effect of distance and abstraction, and it is one that I think you'll see is quite familiar. Just as proximity in distance, time, and relationship lead us to help, their absence has the opposite effect: not only do they tend to negate our intuitions to help but they may exacerbate negative feelings about helping—remember our resentment toward the Heinzes?

Distance Makes the Heart Grow Cold

Let me start by summarizing the moral theory that lies at the base of my argument (and our intuitions). David Hume and his protégé, Adam Smith, claimed that moral development relies on the similarities among people and their physical and situational proximity in the world. They described the feeling this produces as "moral sympathy." It may be easier to understand the concept if you think of it as empathy, which comes closer in contemporary usage to what they meant. The term *empathy* is also free of the implications of pity that we often associate with sympathy in modern usage. I will continue to use the word *sympathy*, because it is what they used. Where I use that word, you may substitute *empathy* if you like.

The ideas are straightforward and intuitive. It is precisely what Bill Clinton means when he uses the phrase for which he is roundly mocked, "I feel your pain." Think about how you react when you see another person in pain. Typically, we identify with that pain and, in a sense, feel it ourselves. Do you flinch when you see a particularly violent scene in a movie, or turn in horror when the evening news presents yet another person's tragedy? If so, you feel their pain in the sense that Clinton (and Hume and Smith) mean. If you do, you understand moral sympathy.

But we don't just feel pain. We have a similar reaction when we witness another's happiness. We take pleasure in the success of friends and loved ones and those we admire. We've all experienced the effect of feeling grumpy and walking into a room full of happy people—it's hard to remain grumpy.

We experience these reactions because the pain and happiness that others are experiencing are within our own experience as human beings. They are experiences that are common to us and part of what makes us human. Think of a particularly moving rendition of a sad song, Frank Sinatra singing "Send in the Clowns," for example. (Those of you who are not Sinatra fans can think of your own examples.) The performance evokes feelings of sadness in us (or at least in me). It does because the words, the music, and Sinatra's interpretation aim directly for our own suppressed experiences of failed love and regret and lead us to identify with the singer's feelings.

It works for happiness too. I remember a day not long ago when I returned home from work in a particularly foul mood. My son was bouncing around the house, giggling and singing, because he had done especially well in school that day and had been praised by his teacher. It wasn't long before my bad mood disappeared.

Although we react similarly to pain and happiness, our sympathetic reactions differ somewhat in each case. Adam Smith described this effect: although our sympathy with others' sorrow is both stronger and "more universal" than our sympathy with their joy, "our propensity to sympathize with joy is much stronger than our propensity to sympathize with sorrow." The simple reason is the discomfort and pain that the latter causes us. As Smith put it, "Nature, it seems, when she loaded us with our own sorrows, thought that they were enough, and therefore did not command us to take any further share in those of others, than what was necessary to prompt us to relieve them." [10]

Hume and Smith also recognized that these sympathetic reactions are strongest to people closest to us—emotionally and physically. The further the emotional and physical distance, the weaker they become. [11] So, for example, while I am pleased when my neighbor's child wins her swimming race, I am happier when my son wins his violin competition. While the world was horrified by the tragic bombing in Oklahoma City, the reactions of those of us at a distance were undoubtedly less strong than those of the residents of that city. [12] Trauma counselors were brought to Oklahoma City, not to Manhattan.

Something similar happens with respect to the recognition of vulnerability. We are most sensitive to our own vulnerabilities and those of the people closest to us. We are often more vulnerable to those who are close to us (and they to us) in ways that we are not to others. [13] We are emotionally vulnerable to our spouses, friends, and children, and our children (and sometimes our parents) depend on us to meet their needs and give them support. And we are aware of some vulnerabilities that we acknowledge within ourselves—a lack of aptitude or ability in certain activities we pursue, for example.

Distance and separation make it hard to extend this appreciation of others' vulnerabilities. And, for the reasons given by Smith, as well as others I will discuss later, we are less inclined to expend our sympathy on others' problems. [14]

As difficult as it is to sympathize with those who are distant from us, it becomes all the more difficult to appreciate vulnerabilities when our legal and social institutions are structured on the basis of autonomy. Because we assume autonomy, we see autonomy, particularly in millions of faceless others with whom we have no contact or experience. And because we value autonomy, we tend to treat vulnerability negatively. The language of our law and institutions is that of autonomy and preaches the virtues of autonomy. That language has a powerful effect in helping us mask the reality of vulnerability.

Legal scholar Mary Ann Glendon notes something like the same phenomenon in what she calls "rights talk," the contemporary language of strong individualism. We see it all the time, particularly when activist organizations protest or bring litigation. It is what the militias argue when they claim their independence of the federal government, and what women's rights groups argue when they oppose limits on abortion. It is, in short, the American way of making claims for ourselves—standing on our rights. As to this rights talk, Glendon claims: "In its relentless individualism, it fosters a climate that is inhospitable to society's losers. . . . In its neglect of civil society, it undermines the principal seedbeds of civic and personal virtue." And again: "By making a radical version of individual autonomy normative, we inevitably imply that dependency is something to be avoided in oneself and disdained in others." [15] Relentless individualism is a corollary (even if not a necessary corollary) of a strong ethic of autonomy. It has the potential to lead us to disregard our commonality with others and thus to fail to identify with their vulnerabilities.

As a result of our denial of vulnerabilities, and our use of institutional devices to mask their existence (remember the laws I talked about in Chapter Two), we tend to recognize and acknowledge as vulnerabilities only extreme cases of emotional, physical, or economic dependence. That is, we acknowledge only those vulnerabilities that we can't help but recognize. By viewing these vulnerabilities as qualitatively different from our own, we see people with these vulnerabilities as somehow different.

One commentator sees this tendency both to deny and to distinguish vulnerabilities, at the same time that we fear them, as leading to prejudice against the extremely vulnerable: "Negative views of handicapped persons also result from fears and anxieties of non-handicapped individuals about their own vulnerability to disability." [16] And admit it, most of us look away uncomfortably when we see a seriously handicapped person, no matter how hard we try to avoid this reaction. The consequence is that we fail to see that our motivation and sense of commitment to deal with the vulnerabilities of the handicapped stem from precisely the same source as our motivations and desire to relieve our own. One result of this tendency to deny the normalcy of vulnerability, which we saw in case after case in examining our legal doctrines, is that we tend to assume that all but the most extreme vulnerabilities can in fact be relieved by processes that ensure autonomy.

This tendency to transform differences and vulnerabilities into negative feelings that ultimately mask vulnerabilities is supported by recent examples of dehumanizing speech. You may recall the furor caused by President Clinton's remarks, after the Oklahoma City bombing was revealed to be the work of right-wing extremists, that hateful talk about the government and liberals, particularly by conservative talk-show hosts, may have been a catalyst toward violence.[17] The particular province of the talk-show hosts President Clinton seems to have had in mind is not so much hate as mockery, a genre in which Rush Limbaugh is the reigning grand master. The danger of this use of mockery is less that it produces or exacerbates hatred than that it creates disdain and disrespect for its subjects. This disrespect, in turn, dehumanizes its subjects and helps create an atmosphere in which they can be either demonized or discarded. It is, as the Nazi propagandists well knew, a form of speech far more powerful than simple hate. For the basic rights and courtesies we accord to all who are human, including the right to let live, we do not grant to those who are not.

One of the most effective propaganda devices the Nazis employed when they began their campaign against the Jews was to use every opportunity to depict Jews as subhuman. Such a sustained attack on our basic personhood helped create an atmosphere in which the suppression of Jews' rights did not produce outrage, because the rights allegedly suppressed were the rights of humans, not Jews. While I am not claiming that the right-wing talk-show hosts have a Nazi-like intent or agenda, it is the similar dehumanizing effect of their rhetoric of which the president spoke. So when Limbaugh produces a mouse trap–like "homeless trap" and advocates its use on the streets, he is encouraging his listeners to think of the homeless as rodents. And of course we can trap and dispose of rodents—they have no rights. He further dehumanizes those he dislikes, less explicitly perhaps, when he picks on the physical characteristics of government officials (or their families) and when he dismissively identifies particular ethnic or racial groups simply as groups instead of people ("some Indians," "the blacks," "immigrants").[18] This way of speaking reifies the members of these groups—it turns them into objects instead of persons. It thus leads listeners to stop thinking of them as persons. And when we stop thinking of others as persons, we certainly disregard their vulnerabilities and their needs to have them redressed.

My suggestion that our denial of vulnerability leads us not only to fail to recognize the vulnerabilities of others but to acknowledge only extreme vulnerabilities and give them an extraordinary status is supported by David Hume's explanation for the basis of morality in the passions. It is worth quoting at length:

> Now 'tis obvious, that nature has preserv'd a great resemblance among all human creatures, and that we never remark any passion or principle in others, of which, in some degree or other, we may not find a parallel in ourselves. The case is the same with the fabric of the mind, as with that of the body. However the parts may differ in shape or size, their structure and composition are in general the same. There is a very remarkable resemblance, which preserves itself amidst all their variety; and this resemblance must very much contribute to make us enter into the sentiments of others, and embrace them with facility and pleasure.[19]

When we deny this resemblance, or fail to see it because of our repression of unpleasant similarities, or dehumanize others because of their differences, our ability to sympathize with others is bound to suffer.

If Hume and Smith are right about the role of the sympathies in morality, and if I have been right about your intuitions, it stands to reason that our sense of moral obligation to those with whom we are less sympathetic, to those with whom we fail to identify, to those whom we dehumanize, will diminish. We fail to see their vulnerabilities, because we fail to see that they are just like us and that our experiences are just like theirs. Liberal philosophy provides a justification for this blindness by comforting us, by telling us that the world truly is as we would like it to be, not as it is. By doing so, it tells us that we can disregards others' pain and ignore their vulnerabilities.

I think that we have sufficiently worked through our intuitive responses to a variety of situations to see whether we are on the same wavelength and to see why. It doesn't matter if you think you would be less willing to help than I in some of these circumstances. All that really matters is that you understand that it is the vulnerability of others that led you to help in any of these situations and that when that vulnerability was absent—or self-inflicted—your impulses to help diminished. If you have been with me thus far, and see the way in which sympathetic reaction combines with vulnerability to motivate us to care for and help others, then we can go on to the project of using these insights to begin to see how we can construct a fair society.

1

Vulnerability and American Liberalism

Our intuitions are at odds with the underlying assumption of liberalism. And liberalism, with its grounding in autonomy, is, as we have seen, deeply embedded in our institutions, our language, and our consciousness. The result is that our intuitions, at least at some level, conflict with our institutions.

This conflict, I suspect, is part of what lies at the heart of the talk about rootlessness and lack of values in our society. It is what has led us to favor selfishness and fostered much of the mean-spiritedness in recent political debate—imagine taking free lunches from needy children so that we can lower our tax bills. It has contributed to the growth of a generation of young Americans who, at least as the popular press and novelists portray them, have little sense of self, nation, or society. Although I don't want to overstate the case, the Canadian philosopher Charles Taylor has blamed the radical individualism that comes with modern liberalism for creating in us a sense of aloneness in, and detachment from, the world.

In an atmosphere like this, it is little wonder that we seem to have lost our ability to sympathize with each other and our sense of responsibility to each other. The 1996 welfare "reform" bill is just the latest in a series of events that proclaim that—regardless of circumstances, regardless of fault, regardless of social structure, and regardless of vulnerability— we expect each adult (and in some cases each child) to stand on his own two feet like the rugged individual that American mythology tells us he is. Take care of yourself—look out for number one. In our attitudes, and increasingly in our policies, we are getting perilously close to the world according to Posner.

Is this a reason to throw liberalism out? Does liberalism have to lead to pathological individualism? I don't think so. There are good reasons to retain liberalism's core values. The idea of individual autonomy, of individual self-determination, resonates quite strongly within us. Some theorists, notably the philosopher Alasdaire MacIntyre, think that the reason liberalism holds us—but also leaves us empty—is because of the regrettable decline of traditional values. But I think that, at least in America, there are positive reasons we find liberalism attractive.

The Attraction of Liberalism: Cooperation and Independence

Consider the following. You are shipwrecked and find yourself on an island with several other members of the crew. Each of you has a different ethnic, religious, or racial background. There is a Hindu from Calcutta, a Roman Catholic from Italy, a Jew from England, a Moslem from Iran, a Taoist from Japan, an African American Baptist, a Confucian from China . . . you may extend the list as far as you like.

Some of you are men, some of you are women. Assume too that you know the island is off the main shipping routes; suspend your faith in modern technology, and assume that you will not be rescued. Fortunately, the island is rich in resources, and you have managed to save enough tools and supplies from the trip to enable you to begin to build lives for yourselves.

To get along, though, you need to set up some social and legal rules. But whose rules will they be? Those of the Vatican? The Koran? The Torah? Whose social norms will govern? Those of the United States? Of India? Let's assume that you agree to settle the matter democratically and vote. Each of you has only one vote, and each of you has a different preference. And assume that each of you believes strongly in your own traditions and will vote in favor of them. You will come to no resolution.

So you have two choices. You can divide up the resources in some fairly equal way (assume that you can agree on at least this and you undertake a Dworkinian clamshell auction) and each go your separate ways as multiple societies of one.[1] Or you can agree on a minimal set of rules that are sufficiently strong and clear to ensure cooperation and also to ensure that each of you will let the others alone in pursuing their own private religious and cultural beliefs.

If you do the latter, which seems to me to be the only route to long-term survival, what will those rules look like? They will probably look like the rules of liberal American society. They will, perhaps, be based on something like Rawls's first principle of justice, providing for as much liberty as is consistent with liberty for all. You are not likely to persuade anybody that your beliefs are the ones that should govern. The next best alternative is to make sure that you are each secure in following your own ideals.

We can now begin to see the attraction of liberalism in America. Our society is much like the island society I have described, a society of people with many different backgrounds and many different—and often inconsistent—fundamental beliefs. To survive as a nation, we have had to develop ways of accommodating those inconsistent beliefs within an overall structure of social cooperation. The crowning glory of liberalism is its ability to achieve this goal. It is why we have not abandoned liberal ideals, and it is why we are not likely to abandon liberal ideals.

We have managed to provide for our (relatively) peaceful coexistence—for our *modus vivendi* to use Rawls's phrase—by creating institutions and structures that help us to cooperate at the same time that they allow us to pursue our independent goals. They facilitate cooperation by asking each of us to make the minimum contribution necessary to sustain our common life. And they give us our freedom by protecting our liberties of speech, religion, association, and the like.

We are required to do very little in our society to make our necessary contributions to cooperative life. We have laws of taxation, military conscription when necessary, and the obligation to obey the laws that keep the peace. If you doubt that these obligations are minimal, think for a moment of what they entail. We (almost) all agree that taxation is a necessary burden, although we disagree about how much taxation is appropriate. And paying our taxes is an affirmative obligation of citizens; it is something we actively have to do. Military conscription, which we impose only in times of national necessity, is also something burdensome that we affirmatively have to do.

But what else do we have to do? Most of our legal obligations are not affirmative—they are negative. It's not that we have to do certain things, but rather that we are prohibited from doing certain things. We must not kill, steal, cheat, or force others to do our bidding. Once we get past these rather basic prohibitions (with which most of us, I suspect, find it rather easy to comply), even our legal prohibitions are pretty slim. Sure, there are rules governing contracts, say, but these are designed to facilitate the institutions of exchange, association, and the market, not to burden them (although we might argue about whether more or fewer rules are optimal to accomplish this goal). And nobody forces you to enter into any contract or association unless you want to. You can't use your property in ways that harm others, but this is simply another instance of the general principle that we can't use our own liberties to interfere with those of others.

If you're still skeptical about the minimal nature of liberal obligation, think about other societies that reject liberalism. Communist societies are perfectly happy to intrude on the most private aspects of people's lives to serve the common good. Hierarchical societies—traditional Indian society, eighteenth-century English society, theocracies like modern Iran, and even the celebrated (but limited) democracy of ancient Athens—all compel their members to live lives they might not freely have chosen and to fill social roles with clearly defined obligations in order to serve the society as a whole. Even liberal America imposed restrictions on members of our society—from African slaves to women— that were far more limiting than the restrictions we now face.

So we demand just as much cooperation as we need to keep the organs of our political and social infrastructures going—and no more. This is also the way we ensure our liberties. We say that as long as you have fulfilled your minimal obligations of cooperation, your responsibilities to the group are over—we will not interfere with the way you choose to live your life. You may say what you think, practice any religion you choose, observe the cultural traditions you find attractive, and generally enjoy privacy in all of your endeavors. You may do as you like, as long as you don't interfere with other people's rights to do the same. And so, as on our desert island, we don't have to agree on the religious ideals, cultural traditions, and other values that enrich each of us to get along—all we need to do is leave each other alone.

The autonomy ideal that we have seen as the heart of liberalism is thus attractive, valuable, and important to the survival of American society. It is the ideal that each of us is free to seek out the good, to reach our own conclusions about the best way to live our lives. At the same time that it is attractive, though, this ideal is sometimes hard to sustain. Our modern lives are filled with strife fostered by our disagreements over what the good life is and the extent to which the government may rule that certain visions of the good are unacceptable. We see this in disputes over issues such as the right to abortion and the right to die, largely fueled by the fundamental religious or ethical beliefs—the fundamental understandings of the good—of one group against another. Every December brings new stories about creches in the town square, and graduation season invokes concern over school prayer. Maintaining the liberal ideal is a struggle. We are constantly at odds over its proper boundaries.

We are extremely cautious about imposing obligations on one another precisely because it is difficult to maintain liberal society. This, I think, explains part of the problem with liberalism, a problem that is at the heart of this book. It is hard to use law to keep such a diverse group of people cooperating with each other without dominating each other. And so we limit our mutual responsibilities. This limitation may be part of what makes liberal society work. But it also tends to isolate the individual at the same time as it leads us to treat other individuals as abstractions. Thus, there are two related approaches that enable us all to be equal: take care of yourself, and don't worry about anybody else. *

The problem is that the mechanisms of liberal society don't work as well for some as for others. If we are left to our own devices, only the strong will prosper.† In Chapters Three and Four we saw the law struggling—and generally failing—to incorporate this reality into

* Of course we are free to worry about others, but only to the extent that such worry is part of our own vision of the good. As philosopher Will Kymlicka points out, the autonomy that is at the heart of liberalism doesn't mandate selfishness—one could find the good in civic or communal life. See Will Kymlicka, *Liberalism, Community, and Culture* (Oxford: Clarendon Press, 1989). My point in the text, though, is that our liberal social and political structures leave such concern as a matter of individual determination—we are not compelled to adopt a vision of the good that demands that we take account of the concerns of others. And as I have begun to argue and will continue to do so in this and the following chapters, the absence of a socially articulated (and perhaps somewhat compelled) understanding of community, combined with a culture that mythologizes self-fulfillment, leaves us with a society in which self-determination and selfishness often are congruent.

† Although, as we will see in the next chapter, strength is at least as much a function of social starting position as it is of natural ability.

legal doctrines. And in Chapter Five we saw liberal philosophers also trying—and failing—to reconcile liberal autonomy with observable vulnerability.

Why the failure? Because, I suspect, of the fear of lost autonomy that comes with obligation. We are terrified of imposing our values on others; if we do, they will feel that they can impose *their* values on *us*. We tend to see every attempt to impose greater obligations on us as an imposition of someone else's values on us. We resist obligation to protect autonomy. And as we do so, we lose our sense of obligation and interdependence—our sense of being stranded together on a desert island.

Liberalism's Mistake

Does liberalism have to result in pathological individualism? I don't think so. The seeds of the pathology rest on a critical mistake. If we fix that mistake, we can begin to correct for the failings of liberalism.

The mistake is this. We fail to recognize the difference between having someone else's essential values imposed on us and structuring a society that takes account of the reality of human interconnection. This failure is caused by our elevation of the right to do whatever we please to the level of essential value. It is our failure to recognize this difference that focuses us on autonomy, and obsesses us with ourselves, at the same time that it buries our intuitive understanding of our common humanity.

Think about our desert island again. You and the other castaways come up with rules to facilitate cooperation at the same time that you avoid imposing anyone's beliefs on anyone else. But let's imagine what life in this society will be like. Will your cooperation be limited to a business arrangement, in which each of you participates as necessary and at the end of the day returns alone to your grass hut? Not likely. Think about yourself for a minute. You move to a new town, you start a new job, you arrive at your dorm to begin college. Do you simply hang out by yourself, having only the minimally necessary contacts with your neighbors, your colleagues, or your classmates? I doubt it. Most of us are pretty social people, and even those who are more withdrawn than others find it hard to deal with people day to day without developing some relationships that go beyond the minimum with at least some people. That's what being a person is.

So even if your initial contact with your fellow castaways is minimal, it is likely that over time you will develop friendships (and perhaps enmities as well) that will deepen your relations. You may, despite your different beliefs, even come to share a group purpose in establishing and sustaining your new community. Look at the way that neighbors come to identify with their communities, employees with their businesses, and college students with their college (and later alma mater). There is a richness to relationship that goes beyond simple cooperation and that doesn't rely on full agreement on matters of fundamental value but that simply derives from common humanity in similar circumstances.

Of course all of these relationships are voluntary. And so the liberal would find them perfectly consistent with the basic minimalism of liberal principles. But the fact that we need these relationships—indeed seek them out—suggests that the liberal focus on autonomy fails to capture an essential aspect of human being.

There is another argument that supports my conclusion. Imagine how the other citizens of your island republic would think of you if you behaved in an isolated and withdrawn manner. Imagine how you would react to someone like that in your midst. You would probably, at the least, be somewhat suspicious of that person. The reason is that he would not be acting the way you expect a normal person to behave under the circumstances. You may discover reasons for the behavior—the person is seriously shy, for example—but you would probably try to bring the person into your island society. Normal human beings don't live in isolation from other normal human beings.

The isolating properties of liberalism probably wouldn't cause us much of a problem if we were a relatively small-scale society with fairly close extended families and adequate social support organizations—a society that perhaps we never really were.[2] But we are not now that society nor, despite the hopes of some libertarians, are we likely to become so.

The essential problem, then, as I see it, is that we have retained a strong concept of liberalism at a time when the institutions and practices that could make liberalism tolerable, that could prevent its collapse into pathological individualism, no longer seem to serve that purpose. Religious organizations, civic associations, social clubs, service organizations, and the like have lost some of their pull and don't provide the unifying force that perhaps they might. We have also—irreversibly, I think—committed to our governments many of the support functions that in a simpler society were provided privately.[3] To the extent that we collectively help one another, it tends to be through faceless government bureaucracy—we no longer even realize that we help one another. By failing to realize that we are in fact helping one another, and that others need our help, we become blinded to their vulnerabilities. The interposition of bureaucratic institutions between ourselves and helping blocks our view of the vulnerable. And when we do realize that we are helping—when welfare becomes an issue, for example—we tend to resent helping because we no longer see it as the norm. This resentment about helping has contributed to making radical individualism the norm; it has led us to suppress or justify away our intuitive motives to help.

Here's one consequence of these problems. American law generally provides that no person has any obligation to help another in distress, a principle that comes under the inaccurate description of the duty to rescue. Go back to the lost child we encountered in Chapter Six. I noted there that your (probably strong) impulse would be to help. The reason was that the child is vulnerable—helpless—and you have the power to help at minimal cost. But our law does not demand that you help. Moreover, that legal precept is quite strong.

Make it more complicated. Instead of coming upon the child in a mall, assume that you are driving down a deserted rural highway at nightfall and pass a small child standing by the road. There are no other cars around—no signs whatever that there is an adult within range of the child. Let's even say that the child raises her hands, clearly imploring you to help. As far as the law is concerned, you may simply drive by. You may even drive by if there is an adult present and it is clear that he is abusing—even murdering—the child. You may continue on your way as if nothing at all were happening, without even bothering to pick up your car phone to call the police. You have, in short, no duty to rescue.

The cases are frightening. One of the most famous involved a woman who was repeatedly raped in a bar in New Bedford, Massachusetts. Despite her pitiful cries for help, the patrons of the bar, which was full at the time, did nothing. Well, not quite nothing—they watched, laughed, and cheered.[4] Or remember Kitty Genovese, murdered outside her apartment while several dozen neighbors watched from their windows, not one of them moving to pick up the phone to call the police. None of these people had any legal liability—they had no legal obligation.

We are so reluctant to impose positive legal obligations on others that even the state has very limited obligations to help persons in distress. Joshua DeShaney was put in the custody of his father following his parents' divorce. The Winnebago County (Wisconsin) Department of Social Services learned that Joshua might be a victim of his father's abuse. Joshua had been hospitalized on several occasions with various injuries consistent with beating. The department investigated and, at one point, took Joshua into custody for several days, returning him to his father after determining that there was not enough evidence of abuse to keep Joshua in custody. The department was notified of further hospitalizations, and a caseworker made monthly visits to Joshua's home, where she observed a number of injuries. Two years after the department was first notified of potential abuse, Joshua was hospitalized in a coma after sustaining injuries from his father that left him profoundly retarded and requiring lifelong institutionalization.

The Supreme Court ruled that the Department of Social Services was not liable to Joshua or his mother for failing to protect him.[5] It noted that nothing in the Constitution required the state to protect one citizen from another, although in very limited cases (in which the state had a person in its custody), it might be required to do so. Therefore, without a state law obligating the state to protect him—and there was none[6]—the department had no obligation to Joshua. A strong dissent pointed out that since the state had taken over the obligation to perform protective functions, it effectively signaled to private citizens that they had no need to help, and this deprived Joshua of the private help he might otherwise have received—but to no avail. Our laws of nonobligation are so strong that even the state can benefit from them. *

This absence of obligation—private or state—is symptomatic of the broader consequences of an obsession with autonomy. If we don't have to help a little child in danger, even when the costs to us are minimal, why should we have to help those who are less immediately (although perhaps not less severely) vulnerable? The absence of a rescue obligation also reveals, in each of these contexts, that we are not in fact entirely independent; we have countless relationships with others—good and bad—and frequently rely on others or are at their mercy. Why does the law then create this obviously fictional world of independent beings? The reasons I have given thus far begin to provide an answer.

---

* The *DeShaney* case of course raises somewhat different issues than the absence of a private duty to rescue. But it does illustrate the dissent's point (and mine above) that when the government assumes certain duties, it diminishes our perceptions of our need to help.

Our laws work to discourage us from helping in another important way that also originates in our concern for autonomy. Helping another may be viewed as intrusive, or may merely be misconstrued, in ways that could result in legal problems for the helper. There are many ways to make this point, but I'd like to rely on a (modified) story related to me by a law professor during a colloquium on this book. He was in a public men's room and saw a small boy trying to reach the sink—and obviously upset that he could not do so. There were other people in the stalls, including, as it later turned out, the boy's father. This law professor's first instinct was to help the boy by lifting him up, but he resisted. He resisted because he was afraid that someone would see him and misconstrue his actions.

His caution may have been excessive, but it is a reaction with which I suspect most of us can identify. In a variety of situations, helping can be misconstrued as assault—even by the person you are trying to help. Sometimes your help, as in a rescue situation, can produce harm to the victim. And even if the victim suffers considerably less harm than he would have suffered in the absence of your help, the law sometimes provides him with a cause of action against you for the harm you caused. Obviously these laws are designed to protect us in our personal and physical integrity—in our autonomy—from one another. But it is important to see how they work to counteract our helping instincts and preserve the value of autonomy in the same way as does the duty to rescue doctrine.

We would come up with far more rational social policies if we allowed ourselves both to see that we have an obligation to help (even the rescue cases are full of moral condemnation of those who refused to do so) and to recognize, as I argued in Chapter One, the extent to which we already are helped—at the same time that we continue to retain the autonomy we find so valuable. We have to find a way to incorporate the intuitions we exposed in Chapter Six into a social structure that preserves the freedoms that we want to determine the course of our lives. We have to reconstruct liberal theory in a way that preserves the value of autonomy at the same time that it recognizes and takes account of the reality of vulnerability. How do we do this? How do we construct a society based on obligation that avoids domination?

I'm not going to be able to give a complete answer—I don't have it yet. And I know that this will disappoint those of you who like answers to questions. Answering this question, though, will require work far beyond the confines of this book. After all, liberal theory has been around for a few hundred years.

But neither will I leave you hanging entirely. I am going to suggest some beginnings of answers. The most important thing I will do is suggest an entirely new way of thinking about the problem. If we start to think along the lines I suggest, it may become far easier to develop the answers.

Old Questions, Old Answers; New Questions, New Answers

The Old Question

What kind of society would you chose to live in if you didn't know what place you would hold in it, if you didn't know what your talents and abilities would be, if you didn't know what your fundamental beliefs would be? This is the question that Rawls asks the participants in the original position. It is really the question that underlies all of liberal theory. One of the major reasons that liberal theory clings to this question is that it reflects the social contract model on which liberal theory was founded. And the social contract model is so appealing because it permits us to see the structure of our government and society as the product of our autonomous choices. Autonomy is the desired value, and we get there autonomously. Sort of circular, no?

This circularity provides a philosophical trap. A system that starts with autonomy—that assumes that autonomy is the normal state of being—works only to serve autonomy. This system provides convincing explanations only if you buy into its assumptions to begin with—kind of like pre-Galilean astronomy. Since we find liberalism attractive, and since these theories are pretty much what are available, we have had little choice but to buy into their assumptions. Further, we want to buy into their assumptions since we evidently find self-reliance to be an attractive quality. Once we find ourselves in this philosophical system, its assumptions seem quite natural to us. We are persuaded by the conclusions, and so the fact that we even made assumptions in the first place disappears from our sight.

This is a perfectly natural phenomenon that we have all experienced in other contexts at one time or another. Magic provides one example.

Magic is a perfect example of a practice that plays on assumptions that we don't even realize we are making. When a magician shows us an empty box, closes it, and then pulls out a rabbit, we are impressed and left wondering how he did it. Of course we assume that the bottom of the box that he showed us is in fact its only bottom—we assume that boxes have only one bottom, and his is constructed in a way to make it appear that his does too. But our assumption is wrong. There is a cleverly masked false bottom that conceals the rabbit hiding underneath. Once we drop our assumption—presto, chango—we can figure out how the magician did the trick and the magic becomes a mere illusion.

We also often experience hidden assumptions as the basis of humor. Sam walks into a restaurant, sits down at a table, and orders a bowl of soup that the waiter then brings. The waiter walks away, but after a few moments Sam motions him to return. "How can I help you?" asks the waiter. "Taste the soup," Sam responds. "What's wrong with the soup?" "Taste the soup." "Is it too cold, is there something in it?" "Taste the soup." "Okay. Give me your spoon." "Aha!" Sam exclaims. The waiter, conditioned to respond to complaints, assumes, as do we, that there is a problem with the soup. In fact, Sam merely wants a spoon. It is our (and the waiter's) assumption, and Sam's exploding of it, that makes the joke work.

Assumptions can be useful. They make magic magic. They make jokes funny. And they also establish the basic underpinnings necessary to allow any theory to proceed without having to reexamine the entire world. Assumptions create problems only when they either are clearly implausible (the moon is made of green cheese) or are proven wrong or inadequate (Newtonian physics). When we forget that we have made the assumption in the first place, we forget the contingent nature of all of our theories. We unquestioningly accept the assumptions as reality, which allows the theories to take on a possibly unwarranted realism as well.

We have seen that autonomy is the assumption underlying liberal theory and that liberal theory has led to a (relatively) minimal set of social and political obligations. But we have also seen that vulnerability provides a powerful motivation for us to help others and in fact lies at the heart of an important set of obligations we perceive we have. I have argued that liberal theory, combined with the phenomena of difference, distance, and time, have led us to suppress those motivations in constructing a social vision of fairness. But, as I hope Chapter Six made clear, those motivations remain an important part of reality, and the assumption of autonomy is wrong.

So, if we can construct a social theory that preserves the *values* we find in autonomy with the motivations and intuitions that lead us to care about others, to identify with them, and to perceive ourselves as part of a common humanity—that is, if we can construct a theory that combines what we know is real with the ideal that we would like to achieve—we will have done a better job than liberal theory in aiming toward the same goal.

But we have a problem. Although I tried to explain the basis for our intuitions and motivations to help, they remain for all that mired in our inarticulate emotions and hard not only to describe but to generalize. As I also noted, we have problems perceiving the vulnerabilities of others who are distant and different from us—we have trouble feeling their pain—and this makes it hard to extend to them the sense of obligation that we experienced in my hypotheticals in Chapter Six. I would therefore like to get at the problem indirectly and to do so by adopting the methodology of social contract theory that Rawls used to such powerful effect.

The New Question: Toward a New Answer

Remember that social contract theory asks the following question: what kind of society would *you* choose to live in? Take a moment and look at the hidden assumption in this question. It is of course the assumption of autonomy. The question assumes that *you* are what is important and that you are the only person competent (and morally permitted) to choose the structure of your society. The basis of this assumption should now be familiar. It is the Enlightenment belief that we all are born equal and free and that our equality and freedom may be abrogated only with our own consent. This is the political counterpart of the liberal ideal that only you can choose a life that is of value to you and that for anyone else to do so is impermissibly paternalistic and interferes with your right to choose the life you care to lead.

It also assumes, as Rawls makes explicit, that you are rational. Recall that classic liberal theory defines rationality, at least in part, as the ability to look out for your own interests. Your interests may be broad; they may involve other people—even Posner recognizes that. But although your interests may go beyond yourself, they are always defined with reference to *you*. Liberal theory isolates you as an individual being from the concerns and interests of anyone else. The classic liberal is, by definition, self-centered, if not selfish.

Let's try a different question: what kind of society would you choose for your child to live in? What principles would you agree to that would dictate the structure of your institutions and the content of the laws you would pass? Let's assume that, like Rawls's participants in the original position, you have to make this decision together with a group of people who are asked to decide on the very same basis. This is a very different kind of question than the one asked by liberal theory.

This question contains within it all of the aspects of human being that I have argued that liberal theory leaves out, at the same time that it seeks to preserve much of what is valuable in liberal theory. In contrast to liberal theory, I have asked you to make these decisions on the basis of another's interest, not your own. I suppose you could argue that because your happiness may depend to some extent on the happiness of those close to you, my question implicates a type of self-interest. But it really is quite different from the other question. I have not asked you to choose principles that will maximize *your* share of primary goods, or ensure *you* the opportunity to pursue your own life plan with equal resources, or maximize *your* wealth. The principles you choose may account for these issues if they are important to you, because you will then consider them important to others, although you will at least think about whether they are important to others.

You might even come up with principles similar to those of Rawls or Dworkin or Posner. Recall that Rawls thinks that he is doing what I am—forcing you to account for others' interests because he puts you in a position in which you have no idea who you will be.[7] This has the presumed effect of forcing you to share their vulnerabilities, because their possible vulnerabilities could also be your vulnerabilities. But recall too that I criticized Rawls's approach as faltering on the altar of self-interest, in that principles developed on the basis of self-interest will always limit the extent to which you will take care of others.

My question changes your perspective because it directly demands that you take care of others. You may find some of Rawls's (or Dworkin's or Posner's) principles attractive. But you will likely formulate them very differently and impose different limits.

You will probably want to ensure your child's essential liberty. But your concern for her will lead you to ensure that the principles also take account of both foreseeable and unforeseen contingencies, so that she will be adequately protected. You will insist that these principles be fair. And your understanding of fairness will be premised on an appreciation of the vulnerabilities of those who are dependent on you.

You cannot create a society dominated by your child (even in the unlikely event that you thought this was a good idea). The fact that there are other participants in this project who must agree to the principles will prevent that. And since each participant at least knows that his child will be a different person than yours, the participants have real conflicting interests to work out.

The very posture in which my question puts you ensures that a concern with others' vulnerability will be foremost in your mind, and this will lead you to make provisions for those who are needy on a more coherent and defensible basis than do the liberal models I presented. The question incorporates the motivating effect of vulnerability in three important ways. First, it puts you in the posture of deciding for another person, and that necessarily makes the person for whom you are deciding vulnerable to you. Remember our discussion of fiduciary duty—it was the fact that you are in a power position over another who is completely dependent on you that causes the law to impose a duty to act in her interests. My question puts you in this fiduciary position in an inescapable way.

My question presents vulnerability in a second way. I have asked you to construct a society for your child. Children are of course a model case of vulnerability—they are not entirely autonomous and rational, not generally able to fend for themselves. Thus, the perspective of vulnerability deepens. You may argue that this is unreasonable, that the society you are structuring is not for children but for rational adults and so my question forces you to be unreasonably paternalistic. I will answer this objection more fully in the next chapter. For now let me say that the choices we are dealing with are the intrinsic selfishness of liberalism and the intrinsic care of paternalism. While unbridled paternalism may be unattractive, I will later explain why I think the argument from paternalism is highly overstated and in fact protects the self-centeredness of liberalism; I am arguing for a middle ground.

Third, and finally, my question asks you to employ one of your faculties that typically is absent from the liberal calculus—your emotions.[8] We saw in Chapter Six that confronting vulnerability face-to-face raises an emotional response within us that leads us to help the vulnerable. My question accomplishes the same goal but deepens it by making the subject of your power your child.

Why *your* child? First, most of us love our children and want only the best for them. (If you don't have children, or do but don't especially love them, then choose someone else who is important to you.) We care that they will live good and happy lives more strongly than we care about almost anybody else. And this implicates the second reason for introducing your child—it overcomes the problems of distance and difference that Hume tells us weaken our moral response. The fact that our children are, in every way, closer to us than anybody else (except perhaps our spouses) suggests that if we consider the welfare of our children we are more likely to have a strong helping response than if we consider the welfare of anyone else.

Notice how this solves the Humean problem in political deliberation. If I am right—that we care about our own children more than we care about anybody else—and if each of us has to deliberate with our own children in mind, then we are forced in effect to care about everybody's children. The very act of structuring a society for our children extrapolates that love and concern to all the members of the society we are creating. And so the problems of distance and difference that make it so hard for us to care for others—to feel their pain—disappear.

Let me ask you, then, to deliberate. But let's, in Rawlsian terms, make the deliberation fair. Deliberate on the following basis. You know you have a child, and each other participant in the deliberations has a child as well. None of you knows whether your child will be smart or dull, healthy or sickly, emotionally secure or deeply troubled, talented or ordinary. Nor do you know your place in society—your own wealth, profession, circumstances, and opportunities.

What principles would you construct for a society in which your child will live? How will you reconcile your concerns for your child with the concerns of the other participants for their children? Will you come up with a society like Posner's, in which your children will be cared for only if they succeed financially (or are loved by someone who does)? Will you come up with a society like Dworkin's, in which their ultimate well-being depends on their making the right choices? Will you come up with a society like Rawls's, which provides a safety net but limits their upside potential? Or will you come up with a society like ours, which leaves them on their own unless they are seriously and obviously impaired?

I will have more to say in the next chapter about the principles you are likely to adopt. But one thing is certain. Whatever the specific principles you construct, you will ensure that the society will not exploit your child's vulnerabilities and that it will be designed to permit your child to live as full and happy a life as is possible given her circumstances. You will reject Posner out of hand, and probably Dworkin too. (You will understand that your child's abilities, choices, and circumstances interact in more nuanced ways than Dworkin allows for and that makes questions of choice—as I will later discuss—murkier than they appear.) You will be reluctant to develop rules that treat your child as a member of a class or category based on particular characteristics and that leave her to the processes of politics and the markets. You will probably be concerned that even Rawls's more caring society—developed as it is with reference to self-interest—will at the margins neglect your child's needs. And you will probably find the rescue doctrine, which leaves your child at the roadside or otherwise subject to abuse, pretty unattractive.

Perhaps you doubt me. Let me then bring some realism into this game and invite you to test your responses against only one aspect of the current state of American society—income distribution. Surely you will want to ensure that your child has some measure of economic well-being. So let's look at the figures. In 1993, 40.4 percent of American families earned less than $25,000 per year, 71.4 percent earned less than $50,000, and only 12.5 percent of American families earned more than $75,000 per year.[9] My guess is that most of the readers of this book will see $50,000 a year as a rather modest income indeed, yet you get that only if you are earning at the top of the cohort—that is, better than 70 percent of all Americans.

The odds are pretty clear, then, that a person entering such a society, whether by birth or immigration, is likely to have, at best, modest means. You might choose to gamble that your child will be in the top 13 percent, but I doubt it. We know that where you start out has a strong effect on where you wind up. In our deliberations I said that you know nothing about your own position and so you don't know where your child is going to start. You might decide one way if you are in the top 13 percent of earners or better. You might decide differently if you were in the Lamberts' situation—or worse. We saw earlier that in American society, as in liberal philosophy, where you start has a pretty big impact on where you come out. Whatever else is clear, I am sure that you would at least think carefully before creating a society in which your children could face the overwhelming odds of the poor and the working poor who constitute such a large part of American life.[10]

You also probably wouldn't be too happy with institutions based on an ideal of fairness that was formal and process-oriented. Such a system would, as we saw with the approach to fairness prevalent in our laws, tend to classify your child and treat her as fungible with all members of the same class. It would overlook what was distinctive about her, her strengths and weaknesses, to fit her into an abstract model of autonomy.

If we ask my question, instead of the liberal question, we put ourselves in a position to extend our natural sympathies over all of our society. We are in a position where we can overcome the problem I posed earlier, that distance in space and circumstance leads us to deny universal vulnerability and to fail to extend our sympathies to others. Asking my question puts us in a position to construct our ideas of fairness using the full range of our humanity.

Notice how this shift in orientation maintains the values of liberalism at the same time as it confronts its weaknesses. As I noted, you will surely want some measure of autonomy for your child. You will want her to be able to do the things that make her happy, to live a life she finds fulfilling. But you will also see the price of a strong model of autonomy and attempt to construct a society in which it is most likely that she will be able to realize her goals. Since you know nothing of her abilities, your social and legal rules will be designed to try to address her individual needs. You recognize, of course, that such a society will be more willing than not to lavish attention and resources on those who are needy, weaker, less talented, more vulnerable. This will mean that if your child is highly successful, she will have to share some of this success with those who are weaker. But if she is among the more vulnerable, she will be the beneficiary of that.

You will also notice something else. A society that cares for your child will be a society in which your child cares for others. The ethic of the society is one of mutual concern with its participants' well-being. If the ethic is strongly present, it may be that we won't need much in the way of laws to coerce, and ideally stimulate, caring. It may be that the ethic itself will lead people to exercise their autonomy in favor of caring, instead of self-interest. A social environment of even modest obligation—say one that requires a duty to rescue in circumstances of low risk or cost—is more likely to breed a genuine (yet self-chosen) concern for others than a society whose laws permit you passively to watch a rape or murder.

It is important to remember that our society of strong autonomy is not a product of nature but of choice. And, as we explored in Chapter Six, that choice may well be contrary to our nature. But even if human nature is indeterminate, or itself a meaningless concept, it is clear that we can and do make choices regarding not only our personal values but those of our society. Once we have created that society, its governing ethics become predominant and largely self-fulfilling. Asking the question I posed to you—and seriously contemplating your answer—should raise doubts about whether we have made the right choice.

8

The Selfishness Surplus
A Matter of Choice

He Who Has the Gold . . .

akers in late-nineteenth-century America faced dangerous and unhealthful working conditions. Evidence suggests that the work was strenuous and subjected the workers to occupational hazards and diseases that tended to shorten their life spans significantly. The New York legislature passed a law that prohibited employers from employing bakers to work more than ten hours a day or sixty hours a week.

In the famous case of *Lochner v. New York*, the Supreme Court held that the law was unconstitutional.[1] Why? Because it unreasonably interfered not only with the employers' liberty but with the liberty of the bakers to sell their labor on whatever terms they saw fit. Liberal theories of autonomy, strictly enforced, argued that it was impermissibly paternalistic for New York to limit the bakers' self-determination, even with the laudable goal of protecting them. If bakers wanted to work longer hours for additional compensation and accept the risks that came with it, that was their choice to make, and theirs alone.

Of course the bakers didn't necessarily *want* to work longer hours—they didn't have much choice.[2] I admit that there was choice in the Kantian sense of extreme autonomy—in the sense that Valjean had, as we saw in Chapter Six, a choice of whether to break the law or permit his children to starve.

But unless you view starvation as both a realistic and a legitimate option, the bakers had no choice at all. There was a dramatic disparity in the bargaining power between the bakers and the employers—the relationship was one of free contracting only in form. Clearly the employers dictated the terms and the bakers had to accede or go without work. Yet the court looked only to the form and not the reality of the situation—at the bakers' apparent autonomy, not their true vulnerability.

Lochner and other cases of its era have been discredited. But it would be a mistake to think that the formal approach to jurisprudence has disappeared. Think only of the courts' attitudes toward Cristina De-Lorean, James Gallagher, and James Ingraham. The formalism that presumes autonomy still largely dominates, as we see in law, philosophy, and the social attitudes we examined in Chapters One and Two.

This formalism—embedded in the structure of our society—has real economic consequences. Look at the effect of the *Lochner* decision on the welfare of bakers and their employers. The employers saved money by hiring fewer employees and working them harder. The consequence to the bakers was a more miserable existence. The relative circumstances—the differences in their bargaining power—combined with a laissez-faire theory of strong autonomy, created a surplus for the employers. The invalidated New York law would have eliminated this surplus, created at the expense of the bakers, by caring for them in circumstances in which they could not care for themselves. By invalidating the law, the court excused the employers from caring and restored their surplus. The employers' surplus was thus enshrined by the court as a matter of constitutional law, based on a very strong theory of autonomy. Although we have abandoned the legal approach of *Lochner*, structurally sustained surpluses like that in *Lochner* persist, in more subtle forms, in American society today.

This is another way of looking at the practical consequences of the problem we have been discussing. It is that the structure of American society—politics, law, and markets—has embedded within it this surplus, which I shall call "the selfishness surplus." It appears in a variety of forms, some of which you have seen and some of which I will discuss. But they all stem from the proposition that we are entitled to do pretty much what we like and we get to live with the results of our successes and failures. A consequence of this proposition is that we also have minimal obligations to others, so we can pretty much disregard their needs in pursuing our goals. In such a system—it should be obvious—the strong usually win.

We are permitted to keep what we acquire because the myth permits us to believe that our achievements truly are our own, that our successes are the result of our talents, our ambitions, our energies. Some of this is true. But we can now begin to see that there is another cause of our success: our political and economic systems are set up in ways that ensure that those of us who start out ahead—in practical terms, those of us who are able effectively to exercise our autonomy—tend to stay ahead. And this has a corollary: those who start out behind tend to stay behind. This is not logically necessary; it is not an essential truth about the world. But it is a practical consequence of the system we've adopted.

The system pretends that we are all free, rational, and equal and is structured in a way that works for free, rational, and equal people. It does this by reducing the vulnerabilities to which we are all pretty much subject—to spoiled food, for example, or bank fraud—and pretending that other vulnerabilities don't impair one's ability to succeed. It also creates hidden advantages for those who already are advantaged—like the tax deduction for home mortgage interest and federally subsidized securities markets that can be used only by those who are reasonably well off.[3]

What about other vulnerabilities? As the Lamberts showed us, it may be disabling enough to be born lower middle class (as we now define it). With that economic status comes parents who are constantly struggling to make ends meet and are exhausted by the effort; barely adequate, or inadequate, schools, including, if you're lucky, community college or a third-tier state college; limited opportunities to expand your talents; and limited job opportunities. It's not that it's impossible for someone in these circumstances to succeed—many have. It's just that it's considerably harder for such a person to succeed.

On the other hand, it is considerably easier for a person born to relatively wealthy parents to become a success. Because of our limited obligations, that person's parents are free to devote their resources to their own children, who will attend good schools, have good health care, be exposed to extras like music lessons, sports, and summer camps and vacations, and have a degree of social and economic security. It's not that it's impossible for a person growing up in such circumstances to fail—many have. It's just that it's considerably harder for such a person to fail.[4]

You might at this point ask, "So what? The well-off child's parents earned their well-being—why shouldn't they devote it only to their own child?" But this question assumes the reality of the myth again, for not only does it fail to see the fallacy of strong self-reliance, it also fails to see the extent to which the system probably gave that child's parents the same head start that he has. And the system exacerbates that head start partly because it doesn't require them to care about anybody but themselves and their own children.

In short, the selfishness surplus is the difference between a successful person's welfare in the system we now have and what that welfare would be if it ensured that every person had a fair obligation to care for the welfare of every other person; if every child—my child, the Lamberts' children, and children from the ghetto—had the same real prospects for a decent life; if, that is, we created a society based on my reconception of the original position. * And although I will not pretend that you can quantify the selfishness surplus precisely, I will, for those of you who like math, express it mathematically:

$$SS = AS - CS$$

where SS = Selfishness Surplus, AS = Autonomy Society, and CS = Caring Society based on the principles we would develop by playing through the original position as I formulated it in Chapter Seven. Let me explain it further.

Rich Man, Poor Man; Poor Man, Rich Man

Please meet three (fictional) ten-year-old children whom we will encounter throughout this chapter.

Johnny is a lucky boy. His parents both are college educated—in fact, his father is a lawyer in their small East Coast suburban town and his mother works at the public library. They live together in a comfortable

---

* I will use welfare to mean a general state of well-being including reasonable economic security, freedom, leisure, and happiness. It is well beyond my mission in this book to attempt to specify and quantify welfare or the selfishness surplus; my goal is simply to introduce the concept and demonstrate that it is a consequence of American liberalism as it is practiced today.

house, and Johnny goes to an excellent public school together with other children like him. The schools are provided with computers (all on-line), and the PTA supplements the school's programs with courses in literature and music. Johnny plays on the sports teams sponsored by his town government and has violin lessons (although he hates to practice). Each summer he spends a month at a camp in the mountains, together with other children like him, and his family takes a vacation together.

His mother's hours are flexible, and at least one of his parents is always available to attend school events, sports games, and music recitals. The weekly housecleaning help allows his parents to conserve their energies for him. They take him to museums and concerts and ensure that he has good books to read. His friends all enjoy similar circumstances. There is no doubt that he will go to college, and, despite its cost, his parents have easily been putting aside sufficient money to finance his education. In fact, 95 percent of the children in Johnny's high school district attend college after high school. Johnny's parents assume that he will become a professional just like them—they don't say it but it is a clear subtext of daily life. At worst, he will become an artist or pursue some other intellectual or aesthetic endeavor. Money is almost never discussed. It never appears to be an issue (although Johnny is unaware of the fact that his parents sometimes have to delay major purchases, like a new car, to enable them to do other things).

Susie lives in a medium-sized industrial city in the Midwest. Her dad, who was born in rural Appalachia and began working at sixteen to help support the family, works the night shift at the local factory. He'd rather work days, but nights pay better. Her mother is a waitress in a diner. On weekends, Susie's dad works at an auto repair shop to help make ends meet. Susie's parents are both too busy to spend much time with her or to follow her school progress closely and must communicate with her teachers over the phone (although they are somewhat intimidated by the teachers and don't do this often). Susie's school is the best that her industrial town can afford, but there isn't enough money around to raise the taxes needed to pay better teachers and buy better books. The school library has one computer and it is often broken. The school district recently suspended the school athletic program because of lack of funds. Besides, Susie and her classmates—all kids like her—have little time for play. As soon as they are old enough, they will all hold after-school jobs to make some pocket money and, when necessary, help out their parents. Susie is often home by herself and has to shoulder a number of chores, including cleaning the house, doing yard work, and helping to prepare dinner. During the summers, Susie spends almost all her time doing nothing but hanging out with her friends. Her parents cannot afford to take her on vacation, except for an occasional trip to visit family in the next state, and there are few cultural amenities within driving distance. In the evenings, Susie does her homework and watches TV, often while listening to her parents at the kitchen table arguing over the bills to skip that month.

Susie and her parents don't assume that she will attend college. If she does, she will have to find a way to pay for it herself. Few of the students in her high school go on to college, and most of those who do wind up enrolling in the vocational programs at the community college, typically working during the day and studying at night. Susie and her parents expect that she will work at the factory or one of the other businesses in town. They don't discuss her future much, but Susie is aware that their expectations are not high—they've seen too many disappointed people.

Jerry lives in an inner-city neighborhood in a West Coast metropolis. He shares a two-room apartment with his mother. Jerry's father left home when Jerry was two. Jerry's mother works hard, cooking and cleaning houses in a wealthy neighborhood, and her long commute on public transportation means that she must often leave before dawn and return home well after dark. She'd like to find work closer to home but hasn't been able to find anything that pays as much, and she has rather limited time to look for new work. Jerry is thus responsible for getting himself to school, preparing his own meals, and—often—getting himself to bed at night. Although he is fairly responsible, he, like any boy his age, is inclined to skip school when he doesn't feel like going and to eat meals of questionable nutritional value (although his mother always leaves him decent food). When he skips school, he hangs out at the playground, which during the day is populated by unemployed men, drug addicts, and the occasional dealer.

School is a dubious affair for Jerry. There are thirty-five children in his fifth-grade class, all from Jerry's neighborhood. Many of them, like Jerry, often have to fend for themselves because of their parents' (usually mothers') work schedules and tend to be undisciplined and undernourished. Lunch (provided by the school) is the only balanced meal that most of these children receive. A number of the children come from families on welfare. (Jerry's own mother spent six months on welfare last year because she was sick and unable to work.) The teacher spends most of her time trying to control the class, and when she is able to engage in academic instruction is hampered by a lack of books. The books she does have are out of date. Several drug dealers take up positions outside the school at the end of the day, and Jerry knows a few children who already have tried a variety of drugs. He also knows several people who have been killed in random or gang violence, including his older brother, whom he very much loved and admired.

Jerry's mother put him in the Head Start program when he was younger, and that has enabled him at least to stay on grade level at school, which makes him unusual among his friends. Clearly leisure-time activities are few. Summers are spent hanging out, sometimes at the local community center. Jerry's mom has tried to get him sent to camp by the Fresh Air Fund, but the waiting list is long and he hasn't yet been chosen.

If Jerry keeps his grades up, he may well be able to go to college thanks to financial aid and perhaps affirmative action programs.* Jerry knows of several teenagers from his neighborhood who have gone to college. But, for now, Jerry and his mother simply would like to survive.

If you know nothing more about Johnny, Susie, and Jerry, who would you vote as most likely to succeed? I understand that success is a very personal concept but assume that it includes reasonable financial security, a satisfying job, and some amount of leisure time. I think you would agree that Johnny is the obvious winner.

Why? Is he smarter? Does he have better character? A more highly developed work ethic? He might have some or all of these qualities. But I didn't say so. No, the reason he is obviously more likely to succeed is that he is a fairly typical child of his class, and he begins with all the advantages of that class. Jerry—if he survives—will at least have a good shot at a college education, but only thanks to the helping hands of financial aid and perhaps affirmative action. No matter how bright he

* Affirmative action would, of course, be available only if Jerry were African American or a member of another minority group recognized by affirmative action programs. (See Richard D. Kahlenberg, *The Remedy: Class, Race, and Affirmative Action* [New York: Basic Books, a New Republic Book, 1996] for an insightful argument in favor of class-based affirmative action.) I have deliberately not specified the race of any of the three children. While it may be relevant to the likelihood of their being in any of the particular positions described, it is far less relevant to the advantages or disadvantages held in each position.

is, his precollege educational opportunities are unlikely to make him competitive at a good school. Susie has a chance to make it out of the lower middle class, but it will take more effort for her to succeed than it will for Johnny. Johnny wins most likely to succeed for no better reason than that he is lucky.

Of course Johnny's luck may not help him. It may be that deficiencies of intellect or character will lead Johnny to be a failure. But the odds against his succeeding are much lower than those of the other two children. Besides, if Johnny fails, his fall is likely to be cushioned by his parents' affluence and position.

Albert Szymanksi surveyed and evaluated data dealing with American class mobility in the twentieth century.[5] He found what common sense tells us he would find. The greatest determinant of your ultimate success in the United States is the wealth and position of your parents. The second most important determinant of your ultimate success is your educational attainment.[6] And the most significant determinant of your educational attainment is—surprise!—the wealth and position of your parents. The strong stay strong; the weak stay weak. This evidence is powerfully supported by extensive data provided by sociologist Claude Fischer and his colleagues at the University of California at Berkeley in their 1996 study, *Inequality by Design*.*

Let's make the obvious more graphic. Assume that Johnny lives in Scarsdale, New York; Susie lives in Toledo, Ohio; and Jerry lives in Compton, California. According to one estimate, the 1995 average household income in Scarsdale was $241,495 and the median was $150,001. This would result in a per capita income of $76,642. In Toledo, the average was $35,736 and the median was $28,731, for a per capita figure of $14,011. For Compton, the numbers are $37,654, $28,943, and $9,022, respectively.[7] The per capita figure for Compton is less than 12 percent of that for Scarsdale and only two-thirds that of the hardly wealthy resident of Toledo. Regardless of how one feels about radical economic inequality, it defies common sense to suggest that Johnny has anything but a dramatic head start and that Susie is likely to do better than Jerry.

But there is another point. Johnny's parents, the best off by far of the three, get to keep almost all of their advantages—they have no obliga-

---

* It is also worth looking at the summary of statistics provided by Kahlenberg in *The Remedy*, pp. 88–90, which supports the point in the text.

tion to help Susie or Jerry at all. Sure, they pay the taxes that helped fund Head Start and that gave Jerry's mom welfare when she needed it, but their accountant has worked hard to keep their taxes to a minimum. As far as tax dollars to help the poor go, Fischer and his colleagues found that in 1992 the federal government spent about $5,900 per low-income person, of which almost half was spent on medical care, and only $2,100 per person in the form of cash and food stamps.[8] And this takes no account of the millions of working Americans who, like the Lamberts, effectively are poor. Johnny's parents believe that the fact that they pay taxes (which they complain are too high) is enough to discharge their social obligation. They don't feel it's their responsibility to take care of other people—it's enough that they take care of Johnny and themselves. Besides, they think they have earned their success and the right to enjoy it.

But they've achieved their success at least in part because our society is set up to make sure that they succeed. Johnny's parents are educated professionals and clearly have advantages over other people. They undoubtedly had to work hard to achieve their success. And it may be—we don't know—that Johnny's parents grew up like Susie (or even Jerry) and managed to succeed despite their starting disadvantages. We do know one thing, however: they were able to achieve their success without regard for anybody else. Like the bakers' employers, they were advantaged by a system that is structured to deny the obligation to care.

But we don't need to pick on Johnny. Let's change the story a bit. Jerry's mother continues to struggle, and Jerry is one of the fortunate few of his friends to stay out of trouble and do reasonably well in school. He is recruited by several fine colleges and winds up attending an Ivy League school. There he receives some additional assistance provided for disadvantaged students, as well as a full scholarship. He again does reasonably well and is admitted to a top law school, where again he receives special help and full financial aid. After law school he is recruited by a number of prestigious law firms, works for one, and is made a partner.

We can and should admire Jerry's diligence. It takes a special kind of person to overcome his adverse circumstances and succeed in our society, even with the help he received. But now he is a wealthy partner at a major law firm. What are his obligations to the other Jerrys of the world? How is he obligated to repay the help he has received? Not at all, except to pay his taxes (which he can work with his accountant to reduce).

Let's vary the story a little more. Johnny succeeds as we expected he would. He graduates from high school with an A average but goes to his second-choice college. (His first choice has reduced the number of students it takes from Johnny's school district to make room for students from disadvantaged backgrounds.) But don't cry for Johnny—his second choice school is still in the Ivy League. He does very well there too, and after a year at a major New York investment bank he goes to a prestigious business school. Johnny then goes to work in the finance department of a major corporation. When he is forty-five, the company is taken over in a hostile tender offer, and Johnny finds himself out of work. He has enough money to get by for a couple of years, but his children are approaching college age and his net worth (combined with the value of his home) ensures that they will not get much financial aid. Johnny looks very hard for new work, but jobs at his former level are scarce and generally are given to younger people. Besides, Johnny spent twenty years with the same company, and his expertise is highly specialized. Johnny sells his house and raids his retirement savings to pay his children's college tuition. Eventually he finds a job, working for a small company at a third of his former salary. But the benefits are poor and the health insurance inadequate. Johnny's wife becomes seriously ill (remember Heinz?). His kids are still in college. Who must help him get her treatment?

Class advantages make a huge difference. But vulnerability and autonomy are contingent and transitory. Despite their advantages, the strong may become weak, and, although it is relatively less likely, the weak may become strong. Luck, talent, ambition—circumstances and nature—have profound effects on our lives. But our society is structured in a way that assumes that you are either independently strong or debilitatingly weak. There is little in between. When you're up, you're not obliged to help; when you're down, there will be little help. *

A wonderful example comes from the Republican revolution of 1992. Newt Gingrich and his minions took over the House of Representatives in a sweeping electoral victory, proclaiming a platform of individual responsibility, self-reliance, and a drastic cut in government welfare

---

* The Welfare Reform Act of 1996 makes such help even more unlikely.

programs. When they took office, Gingrich, as Speaker of the House, chose to appoint a new House historian, an old friend of his named Christina Jeffrey. Jeffrey and her family moved to the Washington area.

Shortly after her appointment, Jeffrey was enveloped in controversy as a result of allegedly favorable comments she had made about Nazi Germany. She was forced from her post and had to return home. But she and her family had incurred major expenses in moving to Washington, expenses she could not now recoup. In desperate straits, she looked to the government for reimbursement. When that failed, she sued Gingrich personally. Gingrich was himself facing a $300,000 fine for campaign finance violations and spent almost four months deciding whether to pay the fine out of his own pocket or his campaign funds—other people's money—before finally settling on a loan for $150,000 with favorable terms from retired Senate Majority Leader Robert Dole.[9]

Ironic, no? American.

Let's change Johnny's story once again. Let's say that those music lessons have paid off and Johnny becomes a fine violinist. Instead of going to business school, he opts for Juilliard. As good as Johnny is, he never quite makes it as a soloist. Instead, he joins the faculty of a small college, giving extra violin lessons on the side and performing occasionally with community orchestras and a quartet of his friends. He doesn't earn enough money to approach his parents' standard of living—in fact, he does only a little better than Susie's family—but he's happy with his choice and makes enough to get by. Unlike him, his children will have to borrow money to go to college, although their grandparents will help out. But the town has good schools, and the college where Johnny teaches provides opportunities for Johnny's children to study music and enroll in other enrichment programs. Johnny sometimes travels with the quartet and often brings his family. Johnny's social life extends to other professors, local professionals, and the like. In short, Johnny's economic status doesn't severely burden his social status.

Should we treat Johnny like Susie? Johnny still benefits from his starting advantages: he has chosen (in a meaningful sense of the term) a life that he wants to live, making sacrifices of one kind (financial) for benefits of another (career satisfaction). The conditions under which Johnny made this choice pretty much were ideal—he could have done anything he wanted to do. And so we may believe that Johnny's trade of money for music was a true expression of his autonomy.

It is hard to imagine that Jerry and Susie have quite the same freedom of choice. Certainly the limiting conditions under which they are forced to make their choices have to give them the feeling that they have less freedom than Johnny. And in fact they have less freedom. Susie has to pay for her own college education, if she goes at all, so it is unlikely that she will feel free to choose a career that promises relatively low income, especially when she will have debt to pay. And her background and experience suggest that she is unlikely to perceive the range of choices that Johnny has. Unlike Johnny, she cannot assume that she will have occasional financial help from her parents. Besides, her parents—unlike Johnny's—have little wealth available for their own retirement. She has to bear in mind that she might be called upon to help them out someday.

Jerry has seemingly even fewer choices. Although college might be free, should he ever get there, he must in the meantime overcome a series of impediments and disadvantages that most of us would find hard to imagine. His choices are bounded by the need to survive in a crime- and poverty-ridden inner-city ghetto. His circumstances may give him a strong incentive to work to get out. It's entirely possible, however, that he will be beaten down by them and consigned to a life like his mother's, for no better reason than that he happened to be born into the circumstances that he was.

What about Johnny's children? Johnny didn't ask them to approve of his choices. Still, their disadvantages are relatively minimal. They have to borrow money for college and may qualify to receive some financial aid. But they, like Johnny, come from a background of educated parents, high expectations, and social sophistication. Johnny's profession gives him a relatively large amount of independence and leisure, which allows him to spend time with them and to help them grow. There is no reason to expect that they will not succeed and make their own life choices, although they are still not in the ideal position from which Johnny started.

So here is the problem. Our system ideally is designed to reward effort and initiative, as we saw in Jerry's case. But a consequence of this structure is that it more dramatically rewards advantage, as we saw in Johnny's case.[10] While I assume that it is legitimate and, for reasons I will discuss, necessary to reward effort, it is illegitimate to reward advantage—that is, pure brute luck. The reason, as we have seen and as Dworkin and Rawls make clear, is that luck is in a very real sense undeserved; it has nothing to do with the qualities that make you who you are. Luck is even more undeserved when the system is arranged in a way that makes that luck hereditary, as we saw in the case of Johnny.

We can now refine the notion of the selfishness surplus further: the selfish surplus is that portion of the advantaged's greater welfare that comes from advantage, not effort. Mathematically again, we can say: SS = (AS − E) − CS, where the new variable, E, stands for effort and initiative.

I admit that expressing the issue this way oversimplifies the problem and ignores some legitimate objections. The most significant objection, I think, focuses on the apparently paternalistic nature of the caring society and the seemingly devalued role of choice, which, after all, is at the heart of autonomy. The major oversimplification is that expressing the issue this way ignores the costs of creating a caring society and the difficulty in determining the numbers one might plug into the equation. I will take up these issues in the balance of this chapter. I will first discuss choice, and then costs, by way of answering what I call the argument from incentives. While I do not propose to quantify the variables, I will suggest some ways of thinking about them that can at least begin to establish their parameters. At the very least, it will enable each of us to begin to assess the extent to which our advantages are earned (and thus deserved) and the extent to which we have obligations to address the vulnerabilities of others.

The Role of Choice

Choice is an important defense of the autonomy society. We could say that it defines the autonomy society. As we saw in the Kantian answer to Valjean, choice is the expression of autonomy, and so we ought not to interfere with it.

It will be easier to see the relationship among choice, vulnerability, and luck by considering some hypothetical cases on the background of my argument in Chapter Six, that our instinct is to do something to help the vulnerable person, and my reconception of the original position in Chapter Seven. What happens when we see a person's vulnerabilities as the product of his own choices? And how do we understand the meaning of the concept of choice in the first place? Let's assume that Valjean was present at Dworkin's clamshell auction and that he used his clamshells to make choices. Assume that Valjean invested his clamshells in a business that, despite his best efforts, failed, leaving him in his current destitute state, which left him the choice to starve or steal. What do we mean by this choice?

A Matter of Luck

There is something hiding in this question—a matter of luck. A proper understanding of the role of luck brings us closer to appreciating the universal nature of vulnerability that leads to the motivation to fairness. It leads us to question our confidence in the conclusiveness of choice. Luck involves at least two issues: the circumstances in which we make choices and our abilities to evaluate those choices and their consequences.

Luck and Circumstances

We saw that Valjean had a limited universe of choices. He could let his family continue to starve while he looked for work, beg and hope for charity, or steal the bread. None of these choices is particularly good. But these choices are the outcome of other choices. And those choices are the outcome of yet other choices, and so on. How good were those choices? Do they make Valjean's present predicament his own fault? *

I modified my story earlier to say that Valjean's poverty was the result of bad business investments. This lets us stop what could be an infinite regression of choices at an early level that most of us would agree was a respectable choice. Valjean has some money—perhaps from inheritance, perhaps from earlier jobs. He could spend that money on consumption—his own necessities and enjoyment—he could give it away, he could put the money under a mattress or in a bank, or he could invest it. He chose to do the latter by starting a business. And it was a sensible and conservative business, say selling umbrellas from kiosks on the streets of Seattle. Hard to imagine that he could lose.† But, unluckily for Valjean, shortly after he opened his business, Seattle experienced its first, historic, year-long drought. Valjean had to liquidate his inventory at bargain prices by selling it to jobbers in San Francisco just to support his family. The money ran out, and work was scarce.

---

* Fault itself as a basis for justifying outcomes is a concept worthy of debate that I do not intend to engage in. It is enough to note that fault—in the sense of bad results stemming from choice—is sometimes assumed as a basis for liberal arguments over distributional justice.

† Let us also assume that insurance against business failure caused by adverse market conditions was unavailable.

Did Valjean deserve his failure? Hardly. The decision he made was rational and respectable; the bad luck that plagued him was unforeseeable. He did everything that American society said he should. So we cannot say that his current set of bad choices is the result of other bad choices; we cannot say that it is his own fault, just bad luck. And there it is—all of the choices that face Valjean are bad.

When we get to the point where the only set of choices that face a person are bad, can we rightfully blame him when he picks one? One way of answering this question is to ask whether we would have made the same choice ourselves if we were in his position. But this seems like a bad way of resolving the question. In the first place, we can never really know how we would act in a given set of circumstances. In the second place, surely we are entitled to set a reasonably high standard of behavior, as long as most of us can attain it.

Aristotle, echoed by Aquinas, favored legal standards that were higher than the ordinary level of conduct on the theory that people would first comply with those standards because they are the law but eventually would internalize those standards and adopt them as their own. The legal scholar Alexander Bickel saw this same effect as a major benefit of certain Supreme Court decisions, such as the desegregation decision in *Brown v. Board of Education*.[11] Bickel observed that the change in law, from segregation to desegregation, expressed a new social norm that many people were not ready to embrace fully as their ethic. They had to comply with the law, however. Over time, their habitual compliance with the law led them to begin to internalize its norms and to make them their own. So it may be with our prohibition against theft, even when you are starving.

So maybe we don't want to lower our standards, even if we think that we would have acted as Valjean did (and especially if we don't). But if we are to expect good behavior by good people who find themselves in desperate straits, maybe we have to be sure that the choices they face include good ones as well as bad ones. Our legal standards may be attainable by most of us. But we must realize that others, because of vulnerable circumstances and not simply because of character flaws, may be unable to attain them.

The recent development in criminal law of the battered woman defense is a good example. Some women accused of murdering their husbands have been acquitted on the ground that the horrible and frightening circumstances of their marital existence left them, in their minds, no realistic choice but to defend against violence with violence.[12] We never want to say that murder is permissible. That would lower our high legal and moral standard and diminish our appreciation of the value and dignity of human life. But accepting a battered woman defense is a way of reflecting our understanding that we sometimes find ourselves in circumstances in which we can reasonably perceive that our normal range of choices—the range in which our laws and moral standards operate—have drastically changed. We cannot expect that people who encounter these conditions can make good choices.* We cannot expect, perhaps, that Belinda Williams faced a real choice as to whether to sign the antenuptial agreement. We can wonder whether Valjean faced a real choice as to whether to steal.

There are ways in which we can improve the conditions of choice. Maybe, for example, we are obliged to ensure that adequate public assistance is available for Valjean and his family while he looks for work. And maybe we have to ensure that adequate jobs are available so that Valjean can find work. Certainly we need to guarantee that Valjean has enough education and training to qualify for available jobs and to make a decent living. Otherwise, we are being not only unfair but cruel. If we do not assume the responsibility of providing Valjean with decent choices and the tools to make them, we are essentially treating him like the convict who is given a choice of execution methods—we are making a mockery of the meaning of choice.†

We don't have to look to the economically disadvantaged to understand the unrealistic way our society treats choice. Remember Belinda Williams? What does choice mean when you are religiously observant

---

* I want to be clear here that I am neither endorsing nor attacking the battered woman defense. I only provide it as an example of our ability to understand the ways in which vulnerability can constrain choice and lead to otherwise irrational results.

† Some of you may think that the choice of one's method of execution is indeed a meaningful choice. In response, I present the words of Robert Frost:

> Some say the world will end in fire,
> Some say in ice.
> From what I've tasted of desire
> I hold with those who favor fire.
> But if I had to perish twice,
> I think I know enough of hate
> To say that for destruction ice
> Is also great
> And would suffice.
>
> "Fire and Ice"

in a small Bible Belt town, pregnant, single, and faced with the alternatives of marriage with a one-sided antenuptial agreement or single motherhood? Our system is pervaded by an emphasis on choice without regard to the conditions in which choices are made. Here's an example drawn from finance law.

Oak Industries was a corporation in financial trouble.[13] Facing a bad business environment and burdened with debt, it was on the verge of bankruptcy. Allied Signal agreed, among other things, to make a large cash equity investment in the company, on the condition that at least 85 percent of the company's public bondholders agreed to exchange their bonds for new bonds, with substantially less protection than the bonds they held. To be sure that enough bondholders agreed to this exchange, the company required each bondholder who took new bonds to consent to changes in the old bonds that stripped them of their protection and substantially reduced their value.

This condition was pretty clever—the old bondholders were widely dispersed and had no practical way of contacting each other. They couldn't coordinate their actions, and they didn't know how each other would act. If one bondholder refused to participate in the exchange but most of the other bondholders did, he would be stuck holding almost worthless bonds. So each bondholder had no meaningful choice than to tender.

The bondholders realized this and sued, arguing that they were coerced into exchanging their debt against their wishes—that they had no choice. The court disagreed. It held that for the word "coercion" to have meaning in this context—in the sense of overcoming real choice— the court had to determine whether the coercion was wrongful. After all, it noted, some types of coercion (parents coercing children to study by withholding allowance) were legally permissible. In this case, the bond contracts did not prohibit the deal the bondholders found objectionable. It was not, therefore, wrongfully coercive. In other words, the bondholders did have a choice, at the time they bought the bonds, to insist on a provision precluding coercion of this type. They didn't make that choice, and so any resulting apparent unfairness was their own fault. *

---

* Note the parallel with Posner's argument. The clear implication is that the bondholders were compensated *ex ante*, with a higher interest rate, to bear the risk that such coercion would occur.

Maybe there's something to that. But of course it begs the question. We again have to look to the conditions under which the initial choices were made. If the bondholders had ample opportunity to negotiate, and if coercive deals like this were reasonably foreseeable, and if the bondholders had alternatives to buying the bonds, then the court is probably correct. But if any of these conditions were absent, the court is seriously stretching the concept of choice.

The conditions of choice are powerful determinants in how we feel about the fairness of outcomes (and our resulting obligation to help or not). We can see this more clearly if we look back at Johnny's story, this time at his choice to become a violinist. His financial position is probably acceptable, although not great. But even if he were doing poorly, we would wonder whether we ought to help him. The reason, I suspect, is that the conditions under which he made his choice—reasonably wealthy and supportive parents, excellent education, an understanding that financial difficulties were probable, and a knowing trade-off of financial success for a life in music—were good conditions of choice (at least as good as our society can provide). They suggest that Johnny's choice to become a violinist, unlike Valjean's decision to steal or Belinda's decision to sign the contract, was a true expression of his autonomy, a true reflection of his conception of a valuable life.

Having said that, though, we need to reconsider Johnny's children. I suggested earlier that we didn't have much of an obligation to help them. After all, even though they didn't choose their financially disadvantaged state, they lived adequately well and in an educated and supportive atmosphere that provided them with a good environment in which to make choices. Unlike Johnny, however, they faced more costs in making choices that would breed even better choices, especially the decision to go to college. Johnny's parents paid for his education; the choice to attend was, for him, largely costless and didn't burden his future choice of a career. His children would have to finance their own education, and this comes with significant costs.

If we look at the situation this way, we can extend Dworkin's thinking a bit. Johnny's choice to become a musician imposed costs on his children—the cost of financing their education—that they did not choose to assume. For much the same reason, then, that Dworkin argued in favor of a system of equal resources—it requires each person to internalize the costs of her own choices—it seems reasonable to conclude that we have some obligation to help Johnny's children receive an education. To fail to do so would be to burden his children's autonomy for his benefit. Obviously this conclusion implicates issues of costs and incentives. I will take these up later.

So much for the circumstances of choice. Dworkin, you will recall, tried to distinguish choice from ability. In doing so, he hoped to identify what is characteristic about each of us—what reflects our considered exercise of our autonomy—and to separate it from what is contingent about each of us—our luck. His understanding of choice is incomplete, however, as I hope is clear by now. Choice is at least in part determined by luck for two reasons. The first, more obvious reason is that the set of real choices we are presented with is a matter of luck. Johnny clearly has a better set of choices than either Susie or Jerry. Valjean's choices are— unluckily for him—all bad. And it is at least questionable whether the Oak Industries bondholders had a meaningful choice. Dworkin tries to compensate for this by equalizing resources, but he cannot actually equalize circumstances.

The second reason is that the types of choices people make are also conditioned at least in part by circumstances. Dworkin tells us that talent is a matter of luck while tastes and ambitions are things we determine. But this is an obvious oversimplification. At some level, the distinction between talent and ambition is a matter of degree. Why is it that the mythology of the self-made person means so much to us? One reason that I mentioned in Chapter Two is that it gives us hope that we too can overcome our circumstances to succeed. But another reason is our simple admiration of those who have transcended their circumstances, who have, unlike their peers, glimpsed the possibilities beyond their station and prevailed.

In other words, the range of choices you actually have may be broader than you see but the circumstances in which you are living may make it unlikely that you will see them. Jerry's circumstances are such that the choice of working hard, attending a top college, and becoming a lawyer may well appear as likely to him as conducting the Boston Symphony Orchestra appears to me. In Dworkin's analysis, Jimmy's failure to attend college would be seen as a matter of choice, whereas my decision to write this book instead of boning up on Beethoven is a matter of talent.[14] That much clearly is true. But it is clearly wrong to attach moral consequences to this distinction.

Economists recognize this problem; they call it bounded rationality. This means nothing more than that the scope of your rational behavior is limited by the choices you see are open to you. The consequence of bounded rationality is that the choices you do make may well be second best or worse, because your information is limited. But that your choices are bounded is a consequence of your circumstances—you simply don't have the information or the tools fully to process them.

Put this in terms of our three children. Johnny clearly has the widest range of choices. His decision-making ability is about as unfettered as it can get. Susie and Jerry are, to increasing degrees, limited in their decision-making abilities by their circumstances. We cannot expect them to make as good choices as Johnny, even if they are as talented. And what about Valjean? He does not see that he has any good choices (as perhaps he doesn't). The circumstance of hungry mouths to feed may blind him to other possibilities than stealing or starving.

The reality of bounded rationality should limit the consequences we impose on choice. Bounded rationality explains why the decision in *Lochner* was so wrong. The Court said that the bakers had to be free to contract to work on terms that were acceptable to them. But the circumstances in which they lived made a fiction of the concept of choice—they had to accept the terms that were offered to them.

We saw the way the Court's decision provided the employers with a surplus born of circumstance. We can now see the selfishness surplus from which Johnny (innocently) benefits. Johnny's choices are broader and freer at least in part because we have chosen to let Jerry's choices remain constrained by his circumstances. One of the reasons Johnny is as well off as he is is that our social structure permitted his parents to get and keep what they could, without paying attention to whether Jerry and his mother had enough. Johnny benefits from the fact that he and his parents don't have to help.

Why is this wrong? Let's get at it this way. There is a television game show called *Supermarket Sweeps*. To simplify a bit, the competitors line up with shopping carts and, at the starting gun, are free to gather as many groceries as they can within a limited period of time. The person with the highest value grocery basket at the end is the winner.

The show is pretty amusing, at the same time as it is vaguely disquieting. Does it provide a good model for society? I bet you think it doesn't. But if you think about it, *Supermarket Sweeps* is a metaphor for American society, although, like all metaphors, an oversimplification. And this is why I think the show is both appealing and disturbing at the same time.

Who wins *Supermarket Sweeps*? The swiftest, strongest, most aggressive, and, within the boundaries of the rules, most ruthless participants. The game is set up so that these people win. It is also set up in a way that brings out the most aggressive and acquisitive tendencies in the contestants. And this is part of its entertainment value. We laugh as we see housewives abandon all restraint on the way to the meat aisle and frantically toss steaks into their baskets. Their overwhelming focus of concern is their own success, and the devil take the hindmost. All that restrains the contestants from violence are the rules of the game, and perhaps some deep moral virtues. The ethic of the game—the goal they are taught to aim for—is to acquire all they can.

American society is not a game, at least in the ideals we set for it. But, like *Supermarket Sweeps*, it is set up so that the fastest, the swiftest, and the most aggressive will have overflowing grocery baskets and the weaker will lose. The winners keep what they can grab, and the losers are left to take what they can get.

Johnny's parents are *Supermarket Sweeps* winners. So Johnny can choose among steak, chicken, fish, or vegetables. Jerry's mother is a loser—despite her best efforts, Jerry is stuck with dry cereal. While I don't want to belabor the metaphor any further, it is obvious that Johnny is presented with more options than he possibly can chose. Jerry has few options indeed. But Johnny's extra options don't go to Jerry—they just get wasted.

Johnny's excess—the selfishness surplus—ensures that he has a range of good choices and that if he chooses to eat dry cereal it will be a meaningful expression of his autonomy. We can never know whether Jerry's choices express his autonomy, because his range of choice is so severely limited. We need to rethink the emphasis we place on choice.

Luck and Judgment

There is another way in which choice is limited by circumstances. I earlier introduced the concept of bounded rationality. In discussing the range of choices people have and the circumstances under which they are made, I have been focusing on the "bounded" portion of that phrase. It is also worth spending a few moments on the "rationality" part of that phrase. We will then see that our legal and political understanding of choosing is flawed as well.

Let's say that you are an avid bicyclist. You enjoy the thrill of the open road, and you are a skilled rider. But you hate to wear a helmet;

you find it constraining, and it detracts from your experience. Besides, you are careful and have never had an accident.

One day while you are riding down a shady lane (within the speed limit), a child darts out in front of you from behind a tree. You veer away to avoid hitting her and hit a tree. Falling off the bike, you strike your head and sustain a severe injury. What have you chosen to do?

It seems pretty clear that you have decidedly *not* chosen to bash your brains in. But arguments about choice tell us that, in a meaningful sense, you have. You have, after all, chosen to ride a bicycle without a helmet, aware of the possibility that you could be in an accident and sustain a head injury. Such an injury was a foreseeable consequence to you of riding without a helmet. Because it was foreseeable, it was a matter of your choice. Put in Posner's terms, you have been compensated for your injury in advance by the pleasure you derived from riding a bicycle bareheaded.

The idea that you have chosen to smash your skull is ridiculous on its face. But it is not ridiculous to say that you should be held to the foreseeable consequences of your choices. This is the "rationality" component of bounded rationality. Part of our understanding of the concept of rationality includes our ability to assess the likelihood of a range of outcomes of our choices. If we make the choice aware of the risks (and under circumstances in which we have meaningful choices), then we are legitimately stuck with the consequences.

The work here needs to be done both by the broader concepts of rationality and foreseeability. We talked about rationality earlier, in Chapter Three, when we wondered about the formal application of that concept in antenuptial agreements and saw how the emotions of love and hate predictably alter the range of rational thought. But foreseeability is a related issue. How do we deal with it?

We have a legal concept that deals with foreseeability in accident law. Our legal standard tells us that a result is foreseeable if a reasonable person would have foreseen it. How do we know what a reasonable person would have foreseen? Typically we ask a jury. While the jurors have some freedom to interpret the concept, the legal standard is phrased in a way that they are asked to imagine—as objectively as possible—what a rational person would have foreseen. What it fails to ask is what *this* person actually foresaw. Thus, the concept is collapsed into the artificial understanding of autonomy that we have continued to see.

Legal scholars have begun to expose the problems with this concept.

Feminists have explored the ways in which this standard expresses a particularly male-centric view and the modifications one might predict if a
"reasonable woman standard" were applied.[15] But we don't need to generalize over gender groups; it is enough to see that the standard fore-
closes inquiry into individual circumstances—individual luck.

If we extrapolate this issue to the broader problem of choice, we begin to see the way in which our attitudes toward the conclusiveness of
choice ignore the luck of circumstances. Some people—our bicyclist,
for example—are temperamentally attracted to risk. To his mind, he is
not behaving recklessly; he is behaving normally. We view his actions
as reckless only because most of us—averse to risk—view risk taking as
somewhat pathological.

Or perhaps he is behaving perfectly rationally because he does not
foresee the risk. As I told the story, he is a skilled and experienced
driver, and accidents are beyond his experience. Perhaps he truly believes that he will not have an accident. Can we (should we) say that his
belief is irrational?

We should have an easier time dealing with the first account—risko-
philia—than with the second. It may well be that our biker has a taste
for risk. But his risk taking imposes costs on the rest of us: we have to
send an ambulance, clean up the mess, and take care of him if he is
uninsured. Even if he is insured but winds up in long-term care, those
costs are eventually borne by more careful insurance buyers. We might
feel we have a right to say: if you ride without a helmet, you will get a
ticket. We might even extend this to say that if his head gets bashed in
we will do nothing to help him—although, for the reasons I gave in
Chapter Six, I doubt it.

Dealing with the second case is harder; the biker honestly didn't see
the risk. How much responsibility should we give him for having his
head bashed in? How much of the consequences will we say that he has
to bear on his own? Is it right for us to say that because *we* would have
foreseen the risks from our decidedly different set of circumstances that
he must also be held to have seen them?

I don't know the answers to these questions, and I don't propose to
resolve them here. But I do want to illustrate a point. Our circumstances, including our personalities (over which scientists increasingly
tell us we have little control), help to determine the choices we make.
When someone like Dworkin, then, makes a distinction between talent
and ambition, between circumstances and choice, he cannot really be

making a descriptive claim—that talent and choice are qualitatively different. Instead, he is making a normative claim—that talent and choice *should* be treated differently. The reason—again—is the liberal value of autonomy, backed up by the probability that we have more control over our choices than our talents. But that control is limited. And when we assume that each of us has equal control—equal autonomy—we do so at the cost of ignoring the vulnerable circumstances that also affect those choices.

The False Problem of Incentives

Assume that you agree with the core of my argument. Our society is one of radical inequality. That inequality is perpetuated by a system that rewards and reinforces the advantages with which some people start out and does little to ameliorate the disadvantages of others. Those advantages are largely contingent and are, for the most part, undeserved. Some sort of redistribution would make our society more equitable and more fair, placing everybody in a position in which they could meaningfully exercise the autonomy that we believe is so important.

There remains a significant problem. Where is the money going to come from? The standard argument goes like this: Even if we want to take money from Johnny to give to Jerry—even if a redistribution from the children of Scarsdale to the children of Compton betters the lives of Compton children without significantly damaging the lives of Scarsdale children—redistribution will damage the incentives that Scarsdale parents have to work hard and earn lots of money. If Scarsdale parents don't work as hard, tax revenues will go down and there will be even less money than there is now to help the Jerrys of America. The argument, of course, is the inverse of the trickle-down theory that led the Reagan administration to implement the policies that have helped to accelerate American inequality over the last two decades[16] and is the practical implementation of the Posnerian vision—an ethic of wealth maximization lifts all boats. Human nature is acquisitive, and people thus respond to incentives that increase or decrease their share of the pie. Redistribution would destroy our economy.

The argument is not entirely wrong. While I have no intention of exploring the thorny question of the characteristics of human nature, there certainly are enough historical examples to demonstrate that people respond favorably to incentives that enrich them. At the same time, however, we have seen in this book that there are other aspects to human nature as well. In particular, our caring impulse—our motivation to fairness—is strong. It is the reason Posner, for example, must tell us that even the poor would benefit under his system, because such an explanation is needed to make Posner's theory even remotely ethically acceptable. But, like the acquisitive impulse, we have seen that the caring impulse also responds to incentives, and those incentives have increasingly become negative ones—they have led us to bury the caring impulse.

You may disagree with me and believe that there is an identifiable core to human nature and that is selfish acquisition. If so, my answer to you, which we will get to in the last chapter, is that it is unquestionably in your self-interest to create a more caring and equal society. But by this point you probably agree (if you didn't already) that people are more complex than that.[17] The evidence suggests that this is true.

For starters, the United States has by far the largest ratio between chief executive and average worker compensation in the world. The significantly more modest pay of chief executives in other industrial countries has hardly prevented their corporations from becoming substantial and powerful economic forces. Remember the cries of American executives for government subsidies to enable them to compete that we saw in Chapter One? Moreover, substantial economic evidence suggests that more equal societies grow faster than societies with greater inequalities; even the U.S. economy grew faster in times of greater equality than it has recently, and during the last two decades the more egalitarian European economies grew at faster rates than ours did. So it is not at all clear that inequality is necessary to spur growth—to get people to work harder.[18]

But there is a more important point, an ethical point, that lurks beneath the standard argument. If you think that there is nothing unfair about radical inequality, there is no reason to read further (and you've wasted your time reading this book). But if you agree that the current structure of American society is unfair, then you must question an argument as breezy as the incentives argument. You must question whether the argument provides too easy a justification for doing less than we otherwise might. You must question whether the incentives argument, like the American myth in general, gives us an excuse to perpetuate the selfishness surplus.

We might start to think about the issue this way. In the days before the school desegregation cases and federal civil rights legislation, a substantial portion of the American population believed that racial separation was both necessary and right. This belief was reinforced by a variety of laws that helped to perpetuate that separation in society at the same time as it incorporated the racist ethic. There was also a time when our society believed that it was natural and right for women, in effect, to be the property of their husbands and that their God-given role was to stay home, bear children, and keep out of business and politics. And the law helped to reinforce "nature."

While American society is hardly perfect, I think it's pretty safe to say that those ethics have changed. Some of the change is due to cultural development and maturation. But a significant part of the change has been aided and accelerated, if not caused, by legal and structural changes. When white Americans were compelled to mingle with black Americans in their neighborhoods, schools, shops, and workplaces, they began to develop a greater appreciation of the humanity of those they had shunned. The Humean moment was able to occur. And as blacks and women assumed new roles in society—and demonstrated their abilities to discharge them as well as whites and men—our earlier beliefs in the limitations of "nature" began to dissipate.

Is the incentives explanation of human nature different? We don't know for sure; for one thing, we haven't really tried to alter it in America—and that in the face of evidence that "nature" may, in this respect, be different in other industrialized countries.* The burden of proof ought to be on those who argue that human nature determines the incentives argument in ways that are different from the human nature arguments for racism and sexism.

There is another point, a moral point. We choose our social structures and the ways in which we behave within them—they are not given by God or nature. We have chosen the system that rewards advantage and perpetuates inequalities. We have chosen a system that channels our incentives toward acquisitiveness and selfishness. We can choose to

---

* I am of course aware of the difficulties that some of the European socialist democracies have been having in sustaining their social programs. By itself, however, this hardly controverts my argument. One explanation for the problem in those societies is perhaps that they are helping beyond their means, not that people refuse to work hard because of redistributive policies. And these countries all experienced dramatic economic growth at the height of their implementation of social welfare programs. The issues are sufficiently complex as to be beyond a single explanation.

change that system. The choice is simply a matter of individual and collective will.

If there is anything to our belief in human autonomy, it must be that we can make choices about the way we are to live. If we accept that selfish acquisitiveness is determined by nature, then we have made our ethic of autonomy incoherent—we have confessed that we really have no choice as to how to live.[19] All autonomy means in such a world is that we are free to determine the methods by which we accomplish our (common) predetermined end.[20] If that is so, we should recognize our mythology for what it is and abandon it. But if we believe that we are free to make choices as to the good in life, which is a necessary belief for the justification of our ethic of autonomy, then we must examine the choices that we make. If we believe that the structure of American society is unfair—if we reject the ethical legitimacy of the selfishness surplus—then we must choose to change it. Arguments about natural incentives provide no excuse. The failure to change it is an acceptance of this structure as ethically right. We must face the morality of our own decisions.

9

Fairness and Games

There is another way of talking about fairness that I have only alluded to but not yet discussed. That is the way in which we draw our ideas of social, economic, and political fairness from the model presented by games. In Chapter Eight I said that, unlike *Supermarket Sweeps*, American society was not a game. But I didn't explain why.

The distinction between American society and games is important. Fairness in games has provided many thinkers with their models of fairness. Rawls himself describes a principle of fair play that he draws from the idea of games. It is from the world of games that we draw our metaphor of a level playing field, which many policy makers assert as the goal of American political and economic justice.

Metaphors are useful. They help us simplify and think clearly about complex problems. But they are dangerous as well. For the conclusions that we reach about the problems we are examining are only as good as the metaphors that help us to reason our way to those conclusions. If the metaphors are bad, the conclusions will be bad. And the game metaphor is a bad one to use in looking at fairness.

Fairness in games shares many of the presuppositions, and therefore many of the flaws, of the leading models of fairness. In particular, fairness in games is premised on the same idea of equal autonomy that we have seen is embedded in our laws, institutions, and philosophy. If autonomy is the wrong basis for structuring fair institutions, as I have argued it is, then drawing our reasoning from games is probably a bad idea.

Imagine that you arrive at work one day and your boss, with whom you do not especially get along, tells you that the company is going to have to lay off some employees. Only one person will have to be let go from your department, which consists of five people (in addition to your boss). To determine whom he will fire, he has decided that you all must compete in a tennis tournament and the loser will be fired. If you do not compete, you will be fired. It just so happens that, as the boss knows, each of the other four employees was a member of his respective college's varsity tennis team. And none of them is over thirty-five. You, however, are nearing fifty and, while an avid chess player, were never much of an athlete. You play in the round-robin tournament he has set up and—guess what?—you lose! I suspect that you wouldn't think this was a fair way of making employment decisions. You would view the choice of the contest as irrelevant to your professional abilities. And even if your supervisor innocently chose the game, you would curse your bad luck that it was tennis and not chess.

This little story illustrates three distinct characteristics of games that make them a particularly inappropriate form for modeling fairness. First, one important purpose of fairness in games is to induce people to play. Second, we typically get to choose not only whether to play but with whom we play. Third, games are designed to provide winners and losers in a way that our social and political institutions are not.[1] In short, games present a highly stylized and constrained model of rational choice that is abstracted from reality in ways that are inconsistent with a deeper understanding of fairness. They assume a high level of autonomy and present the players with an artificial universe of choices. These are the same presuppositions that I have argued are present in our leading models of fairness.

The first observation is that games do not provide an appropriate model for fairness analysis because, ultimately, nobody is forced to play games.[2] In fact, fairness in games is designed, at least in part, to induce people to play when they do have a choice and thus resembles fairness as it is understood in the social contract model. Rawls partly characterizes fairness as something that is appropriately applied in situations in which people have a choice and distinguishes it from justice, which he says applies where no choice exists.[3] In making this claim, Rawls reveals his transformation of fairness into justice as he develops a theory of justice (no choice) based on fairness (choice).

Assuming for purposes of discussion that this distinction between justice and fairness is correct, this importation of fairness into justice mixes concepts that apply in different contexts. Justice *as* fairness is incoherent. For, although social contract theory posits a cooperative enterprise freely entered into, people have no choice but to exist in society. Thus, fairness modeled on choice does not apply. For there is no choice.[4] Such a choice exists only in the world of philosophers, not the world in which we live. To understand fully how this observation disqualifies games from providing a model of social fairness (and similarly discredits Rawls's model as well as the dominant theory), we need to consider how games come to be and why we care about their fairness.

How do we know that chess is chess? How do we distinguish it from tennis? The answer lies in the rules of the game that define it. Chess is chess precisely because that is what we call the series of rules that dictate the creation of a board with a particular pattern and pieces of different sizes and shapes, rules assigning different characteristics to those pieces, and rules that dictate how the game is begun, played, and won. Before these rules are created, there is no such game as chess and so the concept has no meaning.

Assume now that chess does not exist. To create a game that ultimately will be the game we call chess, I sit down and imagine a board game that can be played quietly and that requires a great deal of concentration and some intellectual skill to be played well. The opportunity to create the rules gives me a chance to tailor them toward my strengths. If, for example, I know that I am particularly good at planning complex strategies in my mind, I will structure the game so that people, like me, who have this particular ability will have an advantage. But I cannot go too far. After all, if I invent a game that capitalizes so thoroughly on my idiosyncrasies that I always win, I will eventually wind up playing by myself.

So my game must be reasonably balanced. In some sense this need to induce others to play is a self-interested motivation to be fair, preventing me from advantaging my abilities too heavily and thus giving others a chance to win. But this understanding of fairness holds only for as long as I am playing the game. Assume that I invent my game, call it chess, and market it heavily and successfully. The percentage of chess games that I will play as a percentage of all chess games played will be quite small. And it is only in those few games that I play that fairness in the guise we have been discussing will be of any concern. It is true that players who are like me in talents will probably have some advantage because of the way I designed the game. But the likelihood is that chess will really only appeal to people with my talents and tastes—that is, people who are attracted to a quiet board game requiring intense concentration and some intellectual ability, including the ability to develop and maintain complex strategies in their heads. Thus, the fact that I created chess to suit my tastes and talents is an advantage that quite rapidly dissipates. This leaves chess as a series of rules that are impartial among the players that approach the game.

When the players approach this chess game, there is no initial inequality. That is, assuming that each player is fully familiar with the rules and demands of chess, each approaches the set of rules that define it as equals. One player might be more talented than the other, but this is beside the point, for between two people who are approaching a not-yet-played chess game, the rules are entirely neutral. They favor neither player, although a player can use the rules once the game has begun (through her skill and perhaps her luck) to capture an advantage. But this is what the game is about. It is designed to produce a winner and a loser, and as long as the rules are balanced in a way such that neither player is inherently favored, we say that the game is fair. It is fair because the players have freely chosen to play, and, within the neutral constraints of the rules of the game, they play as autonomous equals.

We can see the distinction between fairness in games and institutional fairness most clearly in the comparison of this game model to criminal trials conducted in accordance with due process. After all, due process is one of the paradigmatic cases that manifest our concern with fairness, and the similarities between the game hypothetical and a due process trial are striking. Philosopher John Chapman has drawn precisely this parallel, arguing that fairness is a concept we use to refer to procedural balance and impartiality and that we save the term "justice" to refer to some of the kinds of things I have been suggesting we mean by fairness—in particular, the outcome of the process (winners, losers, distributions, and the like).[5]

The parallel is formally interesting. It is, however, not a parallel at all. One does not choose to participate in such a trial. Moreover, once one is compelled to participate, it is not as an equally autonomous player.

In the chess hypothetical, I suggested that if I wanted to induce others to play chess with me I would have to develop rules that would be accepted as fair, that would neutralize my advantage as the game's creator. I also noted that the rules had to be impartial to induce others to play generally and to make the game widely successful. But criminal trials are coercive. You are invited to play by an indictment backed by all the force of the state. If I am invited to play the game of a criminal trial, I cannot resist, without at least dramatic disadvantage to myself. I might be able to strike a plea bargain, but since this too subjects me to the coercive power of the state, it hardly seems analogous simply to refusing to play a game, which thereby entirely avoids a loss.

The same problem may not appear to exist when I sue the government in a civil context. I do, of course, have the option of refraining from suing the government. Assuming, however, that I am suing because I have been deprived of a government benefit, or have been subjected to government interference I believe myself to be entitled to live without, it is again the coercive power of the state that has created the situation. The ensuing lawsuit merely is a reflection of the preexisting inequality. A similar state dominance exists in disputes between seemingly private actors, as such disputes occur against the background of the law of the state and sometimes in a state's court. Such laws are created by the less vulnerable through the political process.

It is precisely this situation of the state, with its coercive power, under law it has created, arrayed against the individual, that gives rise to due process concerns in the first place. To put it in the context of our game model, it is precisely because the game's creator, the state, is *always* a player that we worry about fairness in trials and proceedings in which the state is involved. But the rules, including the rules that are meant to ensure fairness, are designed by the game's creator, the state. If my rules of chess are truly unfair, nobody will play with me. No such choice is presented to the litigant. The parallel between games and trials is, therefore, falsely drawn.

There is a way in which the game analogy appears to provide a useful model of fairness. Two players may be unequal in ability. This type of inequality goes to the issue of vulnerability, which I argue is at the heart of fairness. Why doesn't this inequality of ability raise precisely the kinds of problems that vulnerabilities do—the same problems that underlie our concern with fairness?

This is the second basis for distinguishing games, and it comes in two parts: one practical and the other theoretical. The practical distinction is simple: we get to choose not only whether to participate in games but also with whom we play.[6] The average person knows that Andre Agassi will always beat her at tennis, and therefore if she hopes to have any chance of winning (or even playing a competitive game), she will not play against him. Likewise, Bobby Fischer in chess. In contrast, a defendant in a legal proceeding against the state does not have the opportunity to choose her opponent in the trial. It is always the state.

More broadly, one generally does not get to choose the persons one deals with economically and socially, even if social contract theory posits a hypothetical choice. Jerry's mother, for instance, will have a limited choice of places to purchase food and necessary goods. She will have a limited choice of employment opportunities and places to live. Her relative lack of choice, particularly in contrast with the (presumably) greater options of the grocery chains, or the owners of the clothing store, or potential employers, or landlords, by definition puts her in a position of vulnerability that one simply lacks when one decides to play a game. When this distinction between choice and coercion is therefore highlighted, the inequality of ability that may exist in games appears almost trivial, and hardly analogous to our legal and societal concerns with fairness.

These reasons suggest why the game analogy does not provide an appropriate general model of social and political fairness and starkly illustrates the problems of attempting to develop such a model abstractly. Your life in society is a given fact. Most people have little choice but to live in the society into which they are born, under the political system into which they are born. Each person has some opportunity to participate in and influence this system, although for most people that opportunity is quite limited. Even those who participate the most have limited abilities to influence the structures and principles on which our institutions are organized. It is like being compelled to play chess against the creator of the game, with no opportunity to shape the rules. Human society is not a game.

There is another important theoretical distinction between games and society that lies in the nature of games themselves. With rare exception,[7] games are designed to have winners and losers. That, in fact, is the point of games. While our motivation for playing a game may be to relax, or have fun, or to develop or challenge our abilities, our motivation while playing a game is to win.

The same is not true of society. Take the example of criminal trials. Although the trial produces winners and losers, the ideal of the system, however flawed, is to accomplish justice or, at a minimum, to resolve the dispute in a fair manner.[8] So too with our administrative laws and our laws governing private disputes. This goal also applies in the broader contexts of our political, economic, and social life.

No matter how much we may wish to achieve or accumulate as much as we can,[9] which in a society of scarce resources often comes at the expense of others, we generally do not declare those who fail to succeed to be "out."[10] Losers of a game get nothing; there is no consolation prize. But given the nature and purpose of games, there need not be. It is fundamental to our instincts and to our common humanity, in contrast, that we do not throw the "losers" in society out of the game. Rather (and this is a key to fairness), we attempt to provide them with enough so that they can remain in the "game." We do not, ideally at least, leave the losers to starve. So the very purpose of games suggests that they do not provide a satisfactory context for a general theory of fairness.

This leads me to the third basis for distinguishing games, one that directly addresses game theory. There are two principal types of games identified by game theory: competitive games and cooperative games. Game theory does not address my first point, that individuals in our society have no choice but to play the game and so fair games present a distinctly irrelevant model of fairness. Game theory does, however, address the idea that games, at least competitive ones, have winners and losers and so present an inappropriate model for social fairness. This leads to cooperative games as a possible answer to my argument for the poor match between games and fairness analysis.

Cooperative games do not necessarily have winners and losers. Cooperative games can lead to results in which the spoils are shared. One measure of fairness in cooperative games is provided by the concepts of Vilfredo Pareto, which I discussed in Chapter Five. Game theorists often use the concept of Pareto optimality to evaluate the fairness of games. Pareto optimality says that the outcome of a game is fair if nobody could be made better off without making others worse off.[11] But you have to start somewhere—you have to set up the rules of the game. Social justice theorists who look to cooperative games as a model for fairness thus focus on the starting position of the players—the baseline in game theoretic terms. If the baseline is unfair in some way, then the game will also be unfair even though its result might well be Pareto optimal.[12]

How do we know whether the baseline is fair? Game theory doesn't tell us. So we need some independent conception of fairness to evaluate the baseline. A number of suggestions of how to determine the fairness of the baseline have been made by theorists. R. B. Braithwaite—in his inaugural lecture as Knightbridge Professor of Moral Philosophy at the University of Cambridge—even suggested a baseline that incorporated whatever starting advantages you have to begin with.[13] He told a story of Luke and Matthew, who live in adjoining apartments and who can hear pretty much everything going on in each other's apartment. Luke is a classical pianist, and Matthew is a jazz trumpeter. Their schedules permit them to practice only at the same time. But Luke cannot practice while Matthew is playing, and Matthew would prefer not to practice while Luke is playing. Their preferences among mutual silence, mutual playing, and individual playing differ slightly, and the game is not entirely cooperative but not entirely competitive either. How do they allocate their practice time fairly?

I will spare you Braithwaite's mathematics. It is enough to report that Matthew gets to play more than Luke, because Matthew is not as bothered as Luke is by both of them playing together. The cooperative surplus, the gains that each can achieve by coordinating his practice schedule with the other, goes disproportionately to Matthew, because Matthew has the greater "threat advantage"—he can make Luke more miserable than Luke can make him. The allocation of surplus, then, is directly related to the starting advantage of each player. This is the same basic result we saw in looking at the structure of American society—it is just like the selfishness surplus. And it occurs for the same reason: each player pursues his self-interest from a given starting point.

Obviously the baseline could be different. The evident wrongness of Braithwaite's approach to cooperation for a social structure doesn't doom game theory to irrelevance. But it does highlight the importance of the baseline—where you start, in game theory, largely determines where you come out. And the fact that the players operate from the basis of self-interest merely replicates the problems we've seen with liberal theory.

We have to do more than simply establish a fair baseline, though. We also have to know how to measure the fairness of the results. Like the measurement of the fairness of the baseline, this also comes from outside the game. Thus, if Pareto optimality is a fair result in games, it is because we already have decided that Pareto optimality is the appropriate measure of fairness. But this cannot be determined from within the game itself. So even cooperative games fail to provide us with a way of understanding fairness, at least without appeal to external standards.

The nature of games is so different from that of our broader social coexistence that to draw a definitional or conclusive analogy between games and society is at best misguided, and at worst dangerous. Games provide a carefully constrained universe, voluntarily entered, within which the parties are free to operate as they choose. Fairness is of minimal concern, for the parties have freely chosen to play, with knowledge of the rules. They can, therefore, protect themselves through the exercise of their autonomous free choice. But most people are stuck with the society into which they are born. Their autonomy is constrained from birth. Moreover, it is not troubling that vulnerabilities may arise during games as a result of unequal abilities or better choices, because the aim of games is to win.

As I have demonstrated, the leading models share the flaws of game theory. While they may be suitable for establishing the justice of a cooperative enterprise, they are far too abstracted from reality to provide a satisfactory theory of fairness. Like games, justice needs an underlying metric of fairness against which it can be judged. When justice swallows fairness, the latter disappears, much as the means of evaluating the fairness of a game disappears into its rules. The transition from fairness to justice in law and politics thus incorporates the same problems that make games an inappropriate tool for modeling fairness. Understanding the basis of fairness in vulnerability provides a needed corrective.

10

Fairness, Trust, and Responsibility

et us return to Alex and his bedtime. The point, you will recall, was that formal structures of fairness can conceal deep unfairness by replicating the intrinsic advantages one group has over another. We saw, and have seen throughout this book, that the systemic advantages given to and retained by some people can turn even the fairest processes and structures into situations of fundamental unfairness. We all can sympathize with Alex's distress at losing a vote that was procedurally fair but was in fact rigged.

Our contemporary ways of talking about fairness ensure that arguments like his will never win the day. As long as we assert that individual autonomy and self-reliance are our ethic, and as long as we assume that people generally are autonomous and self-reliant, we will build structures of formal fairness—like our family vote—that guarantee that the strong will always win. This is precisely the insight that lies behind Lani Guinier's arguments for proportional voting— the arguments that helped to keep her from appointment to a high position in the Clinton administration.[1]

The problem, as we have seen, goes beyond politics. It is built into our economic structure as well, where our market economy, characterized by formally fair rules and a reasonably formally level playing field, works to perpetuate the advantages of those who start out ahead. We each, as a formal matter, have access to the same opportunities and advantages and, in a society of individual choice and self-reliance, are free to use them as we wish. But as the stories of Johnny, Susie, and Jerry illustrated, this freedom is a practical illusion.

Our assertions that we help the disadvantaged are also illusions, as we have seen in examples ranging from marital contracts to the duty to rescue to dramatic income disparity and minimal—and decreasing—social welfare spending. The illusion is compounded by our failures to see vulnerability as a far more widespread and subtle phenomenon than we have chosen to see it. We see vulnerability, and thus the need to help, only in people who are dramatically different from us. We don't see vulnerability as the normal human condition. We don't see it in ourselves. As a result, we don't see helping as the normal human obligation.

I have thus far made the argument for helping as a moral argument. We ought to recognize the roots of fairness in vulnerability and, in so doing, be motivated to help a broader range of people and to help them more broadly because, deep down, we know it's the right thing to do.

But there are important social and political realizations that come from this argument. As examples from history prove over and over again, an unfair society is an unstable society. Profiting from Marie Antoinette's example, we no longer simply tell the downtrodden to eat cake, but the structures we have built into our society have the same effect.

My argument in this chapter—and the concluding argument of this book—is that unfairness breeds mistrust, and mistrust creates substantial social instability. It didn't take long for Alex to see through the formal fairness of our family vote and cry foul. And I suspect that if we limited his participation in important decisions to similar formal procedures, he would find it increasingly difficult to accept and respect the results. We would then be able to assure his compliance only through coercive means.

Nor will it take long for the disadvantaged in America (whom we can now see are a much larger group of people than our mythology identifies) to cry foul either. We have made it this far because our rhetoric of individualism has been tempered, at least for much of this century, with reasonable attempts to rectify social imbalances, from New Deal legislation to civil rights laws. We said that we cared, and our actions sometimes showed it. Even when our efforts fell short, it was clear that we were heading in the right direction—our aspirations were noble.

Today, and at least since the election of Ronald Reagan as president, both our direction and our rhetoric have changed. When President Clinton signed the Welfare Reform Bill of 1996, it was just the latest in a series of measures—some enacted, some simply proposed—that signaled an end to our caring efforts. As important as this action was, the language in which the president's action was wrapped—the language of rugged individualism—is perhaps even more significant. That language reflects the culmination of years of telling ourselves that the best way to help others is to take care of ourselves—and let others fend for themselves.

There may be some value in that. It is the value of liberal autonomy. But what I have shown thus far is that we have serious misconceptions about who can take care of themselves—and what it means to take care of yourself. The Lamberts take care of themselves, but to what end? They may be forgiven for asking whether it is worth the effort. Jerry's mother is trying to take care of herself, but the odds are long that it will get her anywhere. Why, as we wondered in Chapter Two, should anyone work hard to reap meager benefits?

The answer was that we told people that if they worked really hard, they could achieve a level of meaningful prosperity that would enable them to live lives of their choosing—to live the American Dream. But that doesn't seem to be true. They work as hard as they can and still get nowhere. Instead of living rich lives of liberal autonomy, they spend their days and nights just trying to survive. It seems unimaginable that they will ever attain the level of prosperity, comfort, and autonomy that I have. They haven't had my luck.

So if it comes down to luck, why should people like the Lamberts trust us? Why should they trust the American way? They'd be almost as well off on welfare, or buying lottery tickets. It is only rational for the Lamberts to trust our society if we provide them with some assurance that if they make the right choices—the choices we say are socially useful—they will reap appropriate rewards. It is only rational for them to trust us if we can assure them that their ultimate success or failure is more than a matter of luck. Otherwise, like Valjean, with his perceived universe of bad choices, we cannot expect them to trust us. And if they fail to trust us, they will, like Valjean, be led to choices that disrupt and destabilize our system.

Trust is a two-way street. If we are going to restructure our society to help the vulnerable—to help Valjean, and the Lamberts, and Jerry and his mom—if we are going to give up some of our advantages to be sure that they too have good choices, we will have to believe that they are reasonably likely to make those choices and not simply take advantage of our good will.[2] The flip side of our obligation—our responsibility—to help the vulnerable is the obligation of the vulnerable to respond responsibly. Once we have discharged our obligation to ameliorate their vulnerabilities by providing them with good choices and the realistic ability to take advantage of them, they must respond by making good choices to help themselves and ultimately to put themselves in positions to ameliorate the vulnerabilities of others. Only then can we sustain the trust between the powerful and the vulnerable that is necessary to maintain social stability.

How do you build trust from mistrust? There's a (stupid) game we used to play as boys. One would approach the other and say, "Let's see who can hit the hardest. I go first." Of course the idea is that the boy who hits first will hit very hard indeed, and the other boy may be too incapacitated to respond (at least immediately). Or perhaps a fight will ensue. The rational response is to refuse to play the game, because you have no reason to trust the motives of the other. Another rational response is to insist that you go first.

The rational response is easy here, because the motives of the boy who initiates the game are obvious. One could refuse to play the game. But, as we saw in Chapter Nine, American society is not a game—you have no meaningful choice as to whether to play. And so we are left with the second alternative: each boy insisting that he gets to go first.

I think that this pretty well describes the situation of American society today. Certainly the rhetoric of welfare reform is couched in language of abuse. We don't want to provide additional help even to those who we see are vulnerable because we do not trust them to take our help responsibly—that is, to use it to help them better their situation—instead of living lives of handouts. But we can also see that refusing to help yourself is a rational response, because the opportunities for self-improvement are so limited. If we look at the Lamberts, we see that responsible behavior doesn't get you very far if you start out far enough behind and your luck is bad.

We do help a bit. And we do find abuses. One way of dealing with the problem of abuse is to cut off help. That seems to be the response we have chosen. If we cut off help—stop welfare payments and other entitlements—people will have no choice but to help themselves or starve. They will have no choice but to go out and find work and improve their living situations.

But this assumes that the choices they are left with are meaningful choices. It assumes that they are equipped to find work, that work is available, and that it provides reasonable rewards. And, as the story of the Lamberts tells us, the incentives to work hard when your prospects are dim are limited indeed. If we leave the vulnerable with only bad choices—starve or eke out a subsistence living—we cannot expect them to trust the system we have established. We can expect them to behave like Valjean. And, perhaps, if we give them no reason to trust us, we may well wind up like Marie Antoinette.

There is some evidence that we are afraid of this result. In a 1994 report in *Mother Jones* magazine, Dale Maharidge noted that four million people live in gated communities across the United States—housing developments that are walled off from the rest of town and that can be entered only through a gate attended by security guards. (A 1997 *Wall Street Journal* article gave the number as more than eight million.)[3] Maharidge visited Dana Point in Orange County, California, where nearly one-third of the city consisted of these gated communities. The principal reason for this, he found, is the fear that wealthy residents have of increased proportions of poor immigrants and the crime that arises from their situation. In a balanced assessment based on a set of interviews with people on both sides of the walls, Maharidge concluded: "Walls are a result, not a cause, of society's problems—at least for now. But I've been to Third World countries and have seen how the rich have lived behind walls for generations. Removed from reality, they can't see why wars start against them."[4] Neither could Marie Antoinette.

If we don't trust the vulnerable, we can hide. If they don't trust us, they can revolt, either on the individual scale of crime or perhaps eventually on a larger scale. Trust based on fairness is a better solution. How do we develop trust in an atmosphere of such mistrust?

So we're back to our hitting game. Who goes first? Game theorists have modeled the problem in the game they call prisoner's dilemma. * In the classic prisoner's dilemma game, two conspirators have been ar-

* In the last chapter I argued that games were not especially useful for modeling social fairness. They do have some use in helping us understand the development of trust and cooperation. My use of games here does not contradict my earlier point.

rested and are being held in separate rooms, unable to communicate with one another. The police have inadequate evidence to convict them and so need one of them to testify against the other. Each is told that if he testifies and the other does not, he will go free. If neither testifies, they will both be released. If one testifies, the other will go to prison for four years. If both testify, they will go to prison for two years each. The best response of course is for neither to testify—they will then both go free. But they have no way of communicating with each other and— honor among thieves aside—do not trust each other. The rational response, then, is not the optimum response. The rational response is for both to testify. Neither trusts the other, and without the ability to communicate their responses, each does as well as he can by testifying and reducing his jail term. The result, while an improvement for each of them, is hardly ideal.

Like the prisoner's dilemma, the problem we are facing is one of trust. We are waiting for the vulnerable to show signs of responsibility just as they are waiting to be shown that the system is fair—that it's worth their effort to play the game. Although we have some evidence that shows us that welfare hasn't worked well, we have other evidence that suggests the reason is the failure to provide meaningful opportunities for self-advancement. The result is a stalemate.

Well, not quite a stalemate. In the prisoner's dilemma situation, the power of each prisoner to determine the fate of the other was equal. But as we have seen, American society today is one of radical inequality. Thus, even the second-best solution to the prisoner's dilemma doesn't work for us because the game is unfair. Like our bedtime vote, one side holds all the power. And that side is starting to exercise that power by taking away any help for the other.

The economist Robert Axelrod developed a computer-run contest of repeated games of prisoner's dilemma, inviting others to participate by submitting a program. The winner was a program called "tit-for-tat," in which one player did exactly what the other did. Thus, if the starting player were nice (cooperative), so was the responding player; if the starting player defected, so did the other. Axelrod found that the consistent winner was the "nice" strategy—start out cooperatively and respond in kind.[5]

The starting player in our society is us—the group to whom I have been referring as the advantaged. We hold all the chips. If we expect the vulnerable to trust us, we must make the first move. And the first move requires real helping, followed by real opportunity. Otherwise, there is no reason to expect the vulnerable to respond responsibly.

We might need to be more patient than Axelrod's computer programs. The players in that game had no prior experience with one another—no relationship outside the game. We, however, have been living together for a long time. Our national atmosphere of mistrust that arises from unfairness has taken time to develop and has been with us for a while. We can't exactly play tit-for-tat. It will take patience and tolerance, as well as real sustained fairness, for the disadvantaged to trust American society.

Who needs trust? Why is it important? There are other ways of ensuring some degree of social stability. Surely we can use the forces of the state to keep the unruly in line. Lenin and Stalin found that this approach worked—for a while. But even if it works, it seems like an unacceptable approach to the world in 1998 and does not even deserve discussion. What are the other alternatives?

One is to rely on simple self-interest. As in Posner's world, we can set up a system (much as we have) in which the greatest rewards come from looking after yourself and in which self-interest is pretty much the only way to get what's coming to you. That system doesn't require much trust, only a few rules against cheating and stealing. Beyond that the state can largely wither away. If Posner is right, we will all do better that way. So why not simply perfect the system we have?

One reason, as should be clear from the preceding chapters, is that such a society goes very much against our moral grain—against our deepest intuitions. Another reason is that such a society is not much of a society at all. It is likely to be devoid of any meaningful sense of common purpose and community. Adam Smith acknowledged that a society based on rules that simply prohibited people from hurting one other and permitted them otherwise to pursue their self-interest would probably work. But he also lamented that it would be a fairly dreary society in terms of the human connections that make life worth living.

Like fairness, trust has a moral dimension. It is necessary for community. But even more fundamentally, it is necessary for communication. And communication, as the philosopher Lon Fuller pointed out, is essential for human life and happiness. If preserving human existence is moral (as our laws against murder surely imply), then ensuring coexistence also is moral. And coexistence in any meaningful way—a coexistence of even rough equality—requires trust.

Brave New World

Let's imagine, then, a world ruled by self-interest, to see the level of trust one might expect to arise and be sustained, and the consequences of that level of trust for the society as a whole. I will model a fairly extreme case to illustrate my point—of course issues like this are always a matter of degree. But the case I present is not so far off from the situation envisioned by a number of prominent legal scholars and philosophers, not to mention politicians, not so far off from public policies we increasingly attempt to pursue. And so it is worth taking the extreme case seriously.

Such a world would have fairly simple laws. They would prohibit all the cruder sorts of crimes and injuries that people can inflict on one another. We do, after all, have some moral values like the sanctity of human life. But we don't need to resort to morality to prohibit theft and violent crime. A society that lacked these prohibitions would be one in which people had to devote a large portion of their time and energy to protecting themselves, and this would leave little available for the pursuit of self-interest. So a society that looked something like Hobbes's famous state of nature would be inconsistent with a governing ideal of the pursuit of self-interest, if that concept is taken to mean anything more than mere survival. This society would, in a paradoxical way, be practically inconsistent with the society of self-interest envisioned by the more extreme forms of liberal (and libertarian) thought. A society built on the liberal ideal of self-interest would need some form of state to enforce these laws. This is why, according to Hobbes, we have a government in the first place.

The principal (nonviolent) way in which people pursue self-interest is through voluntary exchange. And so we would need laws of contracting to facilitate exchange through a set of standardized rules. This probably isn't essential; people could make them up as they went along. But even if they did, customary practices would probably soon develop, both to save time and to ensure some certainty in transacting. If we establish these rules through law, the standardization is clearer and easier to achieve than through custom alone.[6] Of course if we think about it, we can see that rules of contract serve, at least to some extent, as a surrogate for trust. If you don't know the person with whom you are dealing, and have no reason to think that he cares at all about your interests (which you don't in the society I've postulated), then you need some other measure of security that he will perform as he promises. The law of contract, backed by courts willing to enforce contracts, serves this purpose rather neatly. It sets out standardized procedures for making contracts, requirements for enforceable contracts, and remedies in the case of breach. Of course you probably believe that your contracting partner intends in good faith to fulfill his end of the bargain, or you wouldn't go into the deal to begin with. But it sure helps to know that the law provides an enforceable remedy in case things go wrong. It probably is worth noting that you most likely also trust the legal system itself. If you didn't, then the fact that it exists would give you little help.

So contracts provide a backstop. But contracts also have their limitations. To begin with, you need to make the contract. And this requires some level of trust.

Consider the example of a negotiation between you and me for the purchase of my used car.[7] I know that the car is basically in good repair but that it will soon need a new water pump, at a cost of $250. Knowing this, I might ask $250 less for the car than I otherwise would. You would undoubtedly also like me to tell you about the water pump, because you would sooner replace it at your convenience than have the car break down on the highway. Yet I am afraid to reveal this information to you because if I do you might try to take advantage of me by insisting on a lower price. And you might reasonably do so, if you do not trust me when I tell you that I already have adjusted the price to take the water pump into account. The consequence is that I will neither adjust the price for what I know to be the cost nor tell you about the water pump, and you, suspecting that I am withholding information, may attempt to negotiate a price lower than one that reflects the cost of the water pump. (In other words, you will discount the price to compensate for your uncertainty as to its condition.[8]) Our lack of trust might lead us to forgo a deal that both of us want. If we do complete the deal, neither of us will be especially happy because I will have received a lower price than I would like and you may break down on the highway. If we trusted each other, we would make a better deal and each of us would be happier.

It would be hard even to reach agreement in an atmosphere of extreme distrust. But contracts have other limitations as well. Whether written or oral, contracts are expressed in words. And the fact that, despite our best efforts, words are necessarily somewhat vague means there may come a time when the contract needs interpreting.

Not only will the contract need interpreting but, if it is to be performed over some period of time, situations may arise that you didn't think of. Notice how this element of foreseeability is related to the problem of foreseeability I discussed in Chapter Eight when talking about choice. There I said that the problem was whether we ought to hold people to the consequences of choices they did not foresee. Here the problem is one of dealing with a new issue in the context of a bargain that has already been struck.

In either case, you or your contracting partner may be in a position to take advantage of the other. If we limit the contract to the words on the page, and attempt to interpret them literally, it may be that one side obtains an unfair advantage.

But to protect ourselves from each other would pretty much be the reason the state would exist. We might need a limited set of other kinds of laws. For example, antidiscrimination laws are simply another kind of law that ensures that everyone has an equal opportunity to exercise autonomy by ruling certain kinds of behavior out of bounds. In this respect, such laws are somewhat like the rules of games we talked about in Chapter Nine that attempt to create a reasonably level playing field. Antifraud laws, like those that are contained in our securities regulations, work to the same effect.

But one could argue (as some economists and lawyers have) that in the self-interested society even these laws are not necessary. Discriminating on the basis of characteristics such as gender and race would be against most people's self-interest—it would limit the universe of people with whom you could strike advantageous bargains. Let's say that you are a racist white man and want to sell your house. The best offer comes from a black woman. Your self-interest, rationally perceived, will lead you to sell the house to her, even if you hate her on sight. You might choose to act irrationally and refuse to sell her the house. If you do, you will be precluding an economically advantageous transaction. So we might want antidiscrimination laws to protect you from your own irrationality and ensure that economically efficient deals occur. But most people would eventually figure out on their own that discrimination is not to their economic advantage and behave accordingly.

The same may be true of antifraud laws and of a variety of other regulations, from food and drug inspection to implied warranties. Surely some people will behave badly, and some of those who deal with them may get hurt. But eventually we will be able to identify the bad actors and refuse to deal with them. If nobody deals with them, they will do poorly. So even those who are inclined toward bad behavior have extra-legal incentives to act decently.

A society of self-interest, properly understood, would have little need for domestic government beyond some rather minimal functions.[9] This society is, in fact, a classic liberal's dream. Each of us would be free to pursue the life course we desired, dealing with others of our own choosing on terms of our own choosing. This is the goal of autonomy of liberal theory, and it is the ideal that is embodied in the social and philosophical thought I have presented in this book.

Let's look at our lives in that society. Say, for example, that you had some extra money and wanted to invest it in the stock market. How would you go about choosing a company in which to invest? We'll make it easier by assuming that you have decided that the computer software industry promises the best long-term growth and so you limit your investment alternatives to software companies. Now you must choose a specific company. You certainly will want to know something about the company's financial position, its products, and its prospects. With no government regulation to force companies to disclose this information, how will you get it?

If the management behaves in accordance with its rational self-interest, it will disclose this information voluntarily. After all, it knows that people will not invest without some information, or if they do they will not pay nearly as much for the stock (to discount for the increased risk that goes with a lack of information). It also knows, even in the absence of antifraud laws, that the information should be honest and accurate or people will not buy the company's stock in the future. For these same reasons, you might be able to rely on the integrity of management—dishonest managements go out of business.

Some people will be dishonest and some merely incompetent. Eventually, this will be revealed in the market by their dishonest or incompetent actions. But if you bought stock before you were aware of these facts, you will lose money. So you will not invest in a company that is not well established. And neither will anybody else. Even if the company is fairly well established, you will have to do some research to figure out what's going on. You might rely on analysts and brokers to some extent, but of course these people present the same problems that the company does—you need to determine their trustworthiness and reliability. And doing so will take you some time and money.

But even if you determine that management is honest, you will still hesitate. The society, after all, is one in which self-interest is the governing norm. So you know that management will behave well only to the point where it is no longer in its self-interest to do so. The managers' only responsibility is to look out for themselves, so that they may fudge things at the margins, or take more money from the corporation than they are entitled to, if they think they can get away with it. And you will worry that this is true of all managers, because all are responsible only to themselves (which means that they are responsible to you only to the extent that it benefits them).

This situation could lead to massive distrust that paralyzes economic and social behavior. It won't, because we have no choice but to deal with each other to survive, and so eventually we will come to terms. But we will take much longer to come to those terms—and they will cost us more—than if we had some reason to have confidence in management and its information in the first place, if we had some reason to trust them.

But a society of self-interest makes trust difficult if not impossible. Recall that I criticized Rawls by arguing that his grounding of the original position in self-interest limited the caring society he was trying to create. The same problem is at work here, although to a much greater degree. A society of self-interest will lead people to have concern for the welfare of others only to the extent that it benefits them. That means that each of us not only will try to maximize our self-interest but, as a direct function of that process, will wind up spending an inordinate amount of time on self-protection. We cannot rely on anybody else— we must watch out for ourselves. This is the ethic of self-reliance brought to its logical conclusion. And it is an ethic that cannot sustain trust. Because it cannot sustain trust, it creates relationships of mutual suspicion and self-protection. It makes it far more difficult to have meaningful and rich interactions with other people, at least those outside our immediate families and close circles of friends (and we may be forgiven for being wary even in these relationships).

Try another example. We don't have to limit ourselves to economic transactions. Think about how you would go about establishing personal relationships in such a society. Say, for example, that you've met a woman (or man) in whom you have some romantic interest. As I suggested in Chapter Three, this very context immediately begins to remove us from the realm of rationality. In the society of self-interest, though, you will work to make your reason overcome your emotions. My guess is that, whatever the social ethic, you will initially be rather cautious. After all, the more you expose your interest in her (at least without her doing the same), the more vulnerable you make yourself to her. And she's got the same problem. Neither of you has any particular reason to trust one another initially. So you will be reluctant to reveal any more than you have to to get the relationship started, which may lead to a stalemate in which the relationship will never begin.

While I suggested that this might be a problem in almost any society, think about how much more of a problem it will be in a society governed by self-interest. The ethic is to take care of yourself and not worry about others. The more vulnerable you are in such a society—the more you have revealed of your interest in this context—the more subject you are to being manipulated and taken advantage of by others for their benefit. You have to protect yourself; you cannot be too exposed. The possibilities of a stalemate increase dramatically, because the chances of real communication are diminished.

The chances of real communication are diminished because you have no reason to trust anybody else. And you know that if you do trust—and trust wrongly—there will be no social help for you at all. Instead of blaming the perfidious actor who has betrayed your trust, we'll blame you. "Too bad," we'll say, " you were stupid to trust X in the first place. Don't do it again." Chances are, you won't.

Societies breed the types of people they idealize. And the types of people they idealize depend on what it is that the society values. It is also those social values that provide the possibility of trust. As the philosopher Annette Baier has pointed out, trust can flourish only in an environment of shared values. Those values can be as transcendent as the worship of a particular vision of God in a particular way, or as down to earth as the love of two parents for a child and their common interest in her welfare.[10]

A society that expresses its central value as the importance of the self will idealize those who best look out for themselves. Those are the people we'll want to emulate. But if self-interest is our central value—if the pursuit of self-interest is the tie that binds us—then what are the possibilities for trust? All that we will be able to trust in is that each of us will pursue his own interests. This ethic, as I illustrated above, cannot sustain widespread trust (and even limits the possibility of interpersonal trust).

My point here is not to suggest that trust ought to be the basis of all emotional and commercial relationships. We cannot know everyone with whom we deal well enough to structure our relationships with them solely on the basis of trust. My point is simply to demonstrate the way in which the absence of trust can impede communication between individuals and can remove a very powerful lubricant from social and personal relationships. If trust is of diminished importance in a society, because of formal reliance on contract or process, for example, people will limit their communications with others to the minimum necessary to engage in transactions. They will tend to spend their energies monitoring their communications with others to avoid exposing themselves to manipulation or abuse. By contrast, if trust is a preeminent value, people will be less hesitant to engage in meaningful communication, facilitating commercial as well as emotional interaction. If communicating with others is part of living a good life, trust is necessary to permit that communication to occur.[11] Without such communications, our relationships will be impoverished, both materially and personally. I will never sell you my car. We will never establish a relationship.

On one hand, people in a society based on an ethic of self-interest and self-reliance will have a great deal of difficulty forming and fostering trust, whether at a social or an interpersonal level. A society that acknowledges the reality of vulnerability, on the other hand, will go a long way toward ensuring that trust is both possible and widespread. For what is a relationship based on trust but one in which one person makes herself vulnerable to another? It may be as complete and pervasive as the deep and abiding trust that is necessary to ensure a good marriage, or as episodic as the trust in our mutual good faith that leads to our agreement for you to buy my car.

When you adopt an attitude of trust toward another person or institution (our government, for example), you are volunteering to make yourself vulnerable to that person or institution. Of course this is not the only way you can become vulnerable, as the examples we have seen make clear. A child is vulnerable to his parents (and pretty much everybody else), regardless of whether he trusts them. And we are vulnerable to our government and economic institutions as well, simply by virtue of living in a society in which they are dominant. If we do not trust them, we can, as the child can eventually—and probably will—rebel. But this is hardly an ideal solution.

It would be much better, I think, if we could trust our society and our institutions, if we could trust our fellow citizens. But what I have said so far should make it clear that in a society governed by self-interest, such trust would be irrational. How can we ever really trust somebody we know is out only for himself? We may face certain ineradicable vulnerabilities—the complexity of society guarantees that. But we will not make ourselves any more vulnerable than we have to. We will not trust.

Trust has important social dimensions. It may be that a society based on self-interest can be as stable as one based on trust. You know what to expect and can adjust your behavior accordingly. You will be neither surprised nor disillusioned when people and institutions take advantage of you, for that is what you expect. The self-interested society may even be somewhat more stable than a trusting society, because it will have protected itself from the destabilizing disappointments that come with betrayed trust.

But a society of self-interest would be a bleak society. It would be a society in which our constant attitude was one of suspicion and self-protection. It would be a society in which close human relationships rarely flourished, and easily came apart. It would be a society without a common purpose, for the perpetuation of our individual self-interest hardly is a common purpose, and it therefore would be a society that would find it hard to maintain our loyalty. It is the society that we are becoming.

Trust is far more likely to flourish in a society whose members openly acknowledge their interdependencies and vulnerabilities and build their ethic of fairness around this realization. It is not enough simply to acknowledge vulnerability, if we continue to justify taking advantage of it. We must understand that it is only fair that we take others' vulnerabilities into account in structuring our institutions, our laws, and our relationships. Only if we change both our perspective on and our attitudes toward vulnerability are we likely to develop a level of trust that is sufficient to continue to bind our society as we head toward the future.

A Change in Attitude

What do we do with all this? How do we change our society to create true fairness and the trust that is so dependent on it? I have neither the space nor the expertise to offer a detailed list of social programs that will incorporate the ideas I have set forth in this book. For those of you who like concrete proposals, this will come as a disappointment.

That's not really my point, at least in this project. I have tried to address a set of attitudes, of ways of thinking about the world, that are deeply ingrained in American social thought and action. In doing so, my goal has been to show how these ideas—meritorious as some of them are—are based on a misperception of reality and a denial of our deepest intuitions. It's not that we have to throw these ideas out, at least not completely. Rather, we have to adjust them, both to reflect the realities of the world in which we live and to permit our deeper moral impulses to flourish.

What I am suggesting is a change in attitude. If we make this change— if we approach social, political, and economic issues, as well as our relations with others in our daily lives, as if we were trying to create a society we would like for our children—the rest, I think, will follow. We will hesitate before blaming the poor for their condition and before withdrawing important means of support. We will work to see that our schools—all our schools—are adequately funded and staffed. We will perhaps come up with loan programs to help the disadvantaged start their own businesses, to help the Lamberts get on their feet. We will stop the hypocrisy of providing corporate welfare at the same time that we withdraw welfare from the poor. We will examine the tax breaks available to wealthy Americans in a new light, understanding that they compound the selfishness surplus. Our courts will look at the parties before them as individuals in particular contexts and loosen their reliance on formal autonomy.

We will not change overnight. Nor will we choose to change everything. We may decide, for example, that capital gains tax relief really does result in the creation of new jobs. We may find better ways of helping the poor than with simple welfare checks—providing education, job training, and low-cost loans, for example. We may focus our current efforts at making higher education affordable on those, like the Lamberts, who truly need the aid and not on those who could pay for college if they put off buying a new Mercedes.

But even if we retain some of our current benefits for the advantaged and modify the aid we provide for the vulnerable, we will do so with a new attitude. We will provide these benefits because we think they best help those who need it. We will understand that our advantages are undeserved in a real sense and work to help those who lack them. We will acknowledge the possibility of autonomy for the vulnerable by seeking their input in structuring programs of help. And we will come to understand that we all are in this together—that at bottom we all are vulnerable.

We can start by changing our minds—by changing the ways we think about these issues. We can start by understanding that fairness is all about vulnerability. If we do, we will breed trust. We will breed social cohesion. We will build community.

Notes

Chapter One

1. Ralph Henry Gabriel, *The Course of American Democratic Thought*, 3d ed., with Robert H. Walker (New York: Greenwood Press, 1986), p. 12.

2. Ibid., p. 19.

3. Ibid., pp. 45–46.

4. Thomas J. Wertenbaker, *The Puritan Oligarchy: The Founding of American Civilization* (New York: Scribner, 1947). Wertenbaker in fact argues that the individualism that formed the centerpiece of the theology was itself a primary factor in destroying the cohesiveness and order of the Puritan community.

5. Bernard Bailyn, *The Ideological Origins of the American Revolution* (Cambridge: Harvard University Press, Belknap Press, 1967).

6. Edward Pessen, *The Log Cabin Myth: The Social Backgrounds of the Presidents* (New Haven: Yale University Press, 1984), pp. 7, 8.

7. Quoted in ibid., p. 18.

8. Ibid.

9. Ibid., p. 68.

10. Ibid., p. 25.

11. Ibid., p. 54.

12. Michael Kelly, "The President's Past," *New York Times Magazine*, July 31, 1994, pp. 20, 24.

13. The *New Republic* opined in 1983 that only 59 percent of the Forbes 400 "seem really to have built their fortunes from scratch." "The TRB Fifty-Nine," *New Republic*, October 24, 1983, p. 4. My own check of the 1995 Forbes 400 leads me to much the same conclusion.

14. Robert N. Bellah et al., *Habits of the Heart* (Berkeley: University of California Press, 1985), p. 84.

15. Ibid., p. 82.

16. U.S. Department of Commerce, Bureau of the Census, *Statistical Abstract of the United States*, no. 1076 (Washington, D.C., 1996).

17. Mary Swander, "A Farmer's Tale," *USA Today*, March 21, 1995, p. 9A.

18. U.S. Department of Commerce, Bureau of the Census, *Consolidated Federal*

211

Funds Report, Fiscal Year 1995 (Washington, D.C.: U.S. Government Printing Office).

19. U.S. Department of Commerce, Bureau of the Census, *Statistical Abstract of the United States: 1996*, no. 528 (Washington, D.C., 1996).

20. Charles M. Sennott, "The $150 Billion Welfare Recipients: U.S. Corporations," *Boston Globe*, July 7, 1996, p. 1.

21. Stephen Moore and Dean Stansel, *Ending Corporate Welfare as We Know It*, Policy Analysis no. 225 (Washington, D.C.: Cato Institute, 1995), p. 3.

22. "Cutting Fat by Committee," *Atlanta Journal-Constitution*, March 19, 1996, p. 14A.

23. Sennott, "$150 Billion Welfare Recipients," p. 1.

24. John Case, "The Origins of Entrepreneurship," *INC.*, June 1989, p. 51.

25. Ibid, p. 52.

26. Vernon E. Jordan, Jr., "Affirmative Action Works: Thomas Proves It," *Wall Street Journal*, August 20, 1991, p. A14.

27. Derek Bok, *The State of the Nation: Government and the Quest for a Better Society* (Cambridge: Harvard University Press, 1996), p. 204.

28. Albert Szymanski, *Class Structure: A Critical Perspective* (New York: Praeger Special Studies, 1983), p. 280. See also Richard D. Kahlenberg, *The Remedy: Class, Race, and Affirmative Action* (New York: Basic Books, a New Republic Book, 1996), p. 90.

29. Upton Sinclair, *The Jungle* (1905; reprint, New York: Albert & Charles Boni, 1928).

30. Wirthlin Quorum survey, conducted from December 1, 1995, to December 3, 1995.

31. "Financial Success and the American Dream," conducted by the Roper Center on behalf of Shearson Lehman Brothers, in May 1992.

32. ABC News poll, conducted from April 30, 1996, to May 6, 1996; *Washington Post* poll, conducted from July 20, 1995, to September 28, 1995; Wirthlin Quorum survey, conducted from December 1, 1995, to December 3, 1995.

33. Wirthlin Quorum survey, conducted from December 1, 1995, to December 3, 1995.

34. *The New Political Landscape* (Times Mirror Center for the People and the Press, 1994), p. 143.

35. James Kluegel and Eliot R. Smith, *Beliefs about Inequality: Americans' Views of What Is and What Ought to Be* (Hawthorne, N.Y.: De Gruyter, 1986), pp. 45–46, 48.

36. John E. Schwartz and Thomas J. Volgy, *The Forgotten Americans* (New York: Norton, 1992), p. 3.

37. Ibid., pp. 4, 50–51.

38. For various reasons, such as illness and layoff, some of these people did not actually work full time during the year of measurement. Refining the numbers, Schwartz and Volgy note that 5.9 million American workers who did work full time, with households of 18 million people, lived at income levels that denied them self-sufficiency. *Forgotten Americans*, pp. 64–65.

39. "Financial Success and the American Dream," conducted by the Roper

Center for Shearson Lehman Brothers. See also the ABC News poll conducted from April 30, 1996, to May 6, 1996 (American Dream still possible), and the *Washington Post* poll conducted from July 20, 1995, to September 28, 1995. Interestingly, according to the Roper/Shearson Lehman poll, the respondents, who had median savings of $5,000 and 56 percent of whom believed they were halfway or more along the road to realizing their American Dream, said they and their families needed $36,000 per year before taxes—quite close to the median—to live in "reasonable comfort."

40. Ed Gillespie and Bob Schellhas, eds., *Contract with America: The Bold Plan by Rep. Newt Gingrich, Rep. Dick Armey and the House Republicans to Change the Nation* (New York: Random House, 1994), p. 4.

41. Ibid., p. 5.

42. Information is taken and derived from *Statistical Abstract of the United States: 1996*, no. 528; *Consolidated Federal Funds Report, Fiscal Year 1995*, p. 12.

43. Bellah et al, *Habits of the Heart*, p. 198.

Chapter Two

1. Richard Cohen, "Mondale's Vindication," *Washington Post*, October 30, 1987, p. A25; see also Richard Cohen, "The Myth Merchant," *Washington Post*, November 8, 1984, p. A27.

2. The poll was conducted from December 9, 1995, to December 11, 1995.

3. Another *New York Times* poll revealed overwhelmingly negative attitudes among Americans toward welfare at the same time that it found virtually equal support for increasing aid to children. Jason DeParle, "The Nation: Despising Welfare, Pitying Its Young," *New York Times*, December 18, 1994, sec. 4, p. 5.

4. Sixty-three percent of respondents to a 1997 CBS News poll (conducted from January 30 to February 1) believed that most welfare recipients really do not want to work. Sixty-seven percent of respondents to a 1995 *New York Times*/CBS News poll (conducted from February 22 to February 25) agreed with this belief, as did 63 percent of respondents to a 1994 *New York Times*/CBS News poll (conducted from January 15 to January 17) and 58 percent of respondents to another 1994 *New York Times*/CBS News poll (conducted from December 6 to December 9). Seventy-six percent of respondents to a 1995 *New York Times*/CBS News poll (conducted from December 9 to December 11) believed that jobs were available for welfare recipients who really wanted to work. Further, 52 percent of respondents to a 1995 Public Agenda Foundation survey (conducted from December 8 to December 17) believed that welfare recipients are lazier than other Americans.

5. The ABC News/*Washington Post* poll was conducted from August 1, 1996, to August 5, 1996. The poll involved 1,514 adult respondents who were asked whether they supported the Welfare Reform Bill. For the decline in approval of government care for the poor, see *The New Political Landscape* (Times Mirror Center for the People and the Press, 1994), p. 32.

6. *New Political Landscape*, p. 4.

7. Ibid., p. 33.

8. On the general existence of American ambivalence toward the poor, see

Leonard Beeghley, *The Structure of Social Stratification in the U.S.* (Boston: Allyn and Bacon, 1996), p. 82.

9. Seventy-one percent of respondents to a 1995 *New York Times*/CBS News poll, conducted from December 9 to December 11, answered that jobs available for welfare recipients generally did not pay enough to support a family. At least before passage of the 1996 Welfare Reform Bill, a majority of Americans appeared to support providing benefits for those who are willing to work. *New York Times*/CBS News poll conducted from December 6, 1994, to December 9, 1994. Perhaps most interesting (and consistent with my point in the text), 78 percent of respondents to a 1994 Cable News Network/*USA Today* poll, conducted by The Gallup Organization from April 16 to April 18, said they thought that separate benefits should be provided for children, even if their parents did not work.

10. I suspect this emotional mechanism partly underlies William Julius Wilson's and Theda Skocpol's belief that broad-based social programs that benefit people beyond the poor have much greater political support and ultimate viability. See William Julius Wilson, *The Truly Disadvantaged: The Inner City, the Underclass, and Public Policy* (Chicago: University of Chicago Press, 1987), and Theda Skocpol, "Targeting within Universalism: Politically Viable Policies to Combat Poverty in the United States," in *The Urban Underclass*, ed. Christopher Jencks and Paul E. Peterson (Washington, D.C.: Brookings Institution, 1991), p. 411.

11. The story of the Lamberts is told in John E. Schwartz and Thomas J. Volgy, *The Forgotten Americans* (New York: Norton, 1992), especially in Chapter 2, from which this description is taken.

12. Ibid., pp. 19, 20.

13. David M. Gordon, *Fat and Mean: The Corporate Squeeze of Working Americans and the Myth of Managerial "Downsizing"* (New York: Free Press, Martin Kessler Books, 1996), p. 100.

14. Ibid., p. 99.

15. During a colloquium on this book I was asked whether people like the Lamberts (and clearly, by extension, welfare recipients) ought simply to stop having children if they cannot afford them. Reasons this is a bad idea include the practical and ethical problems posed by a government or even ethical policy that discourages childbearing by the poor or working poor. See Christopher Jencks and Kathryn Edin, "Do Poor Women Have a Right to Bear Children?" *American Prospect* (Winter 1995): 43–52, for a discussion of these issues as well as the potential efficacy of such a policy. Moreover, whereas a prospective recantation of the American ethic I discuss in Chapter Ten might lead people to forgo having children, it would have no effect on those people who, relying on the promise of rewards for hard work, have already chosen to have children.

16. Data are summarized in Gordon, *Fat and Mean*, p. 126. See Roberta Spalter-Roth et al., *Welfare That Works: The Working Lives of AFDC Recipients* (Washington, D.C.: Institute for Women's Policy Studies, 1995).

17. Paul E. Peterson, "The Urban Underclass and the Poverty Paradox," in Jencks and Peterson, *Urban Underclass*, p. 15.

18. Figures were provided by the U.S. Department of Health and Human Services and the House Ways and Means Committee and are reported in Herbert

Sample, "Battle Shapes Up on GOP's Plan to Overhaul Welfare," *Sacramento Bee*, December 30, 1994, p. A1.

19. According to Schwartz and Volgy (*Forgotten Americans*, p. 61), the Lamberts and others like them appear to know that something is wrong with the myth. It is interesting that the polling data reported in Chapter One suggest that the myth remains so widespread, since more than 10 percent of the full-time workforce in 1990 faced a similar predicament.

20. James R. Kluegel and Eliot R. Smith, *Beliefs about Inequality: Americans' Views of What Is and What Ought to Be* (Hawthorne, N.Y.: De Gruyter, 1986), p. 78.

21. Data provided by Schwartz and Volgy suggest that the Lamberts' children will have limited chances as well. The evidence shows that students attending schools in lower-income areas are significantly more likely to attend weaker schools and to show less academic achievement than students raised in more solidly middle-class neighborhoods. Schwartz and Volgy, *Forgotten Americans*, pp. 49, 50. See also the discussion of the relationship between "poor" schools and the ability of their students to escape from poverty in Susan E. Mayer, "How Much Does a High School's Racial and Socioeconomic Mix Affect Graduation and Teenage Fertility Rates?" in Jencks and Peterson, *Urban Underclass*, p. 321.

22. Public Agenda Foundation, What Americans Want from Welfare Reform Survey. The survey was conducted by the Public Agenda Foundation from December 8, 1995, to December 17, 1995. The survey involved one thousand adult respondents who were asked whether they thought welfare recipients were more or less likely to have suffered bad luck in their lives.

23. Roper Center for Public Opinion Research, "Thinking about Welfare: The View from New York," *Public Perspective* 6, no. 2 (1995): 35.

24. Skocpol, "Targeting within Universalism," p. 414.

25. Kluegel and Smith, *Beliefs about Inequality*, p. 80.

26. Ibid., p. 24, discussing the work of R. E. Lane. It is also striking, and in this context corroborative of this theory, to note historical explanations, drawing on similar psychological phenomena, for poor whites' support of the antebellum southern aristocracy and the institution of slavery. On blaming the poor generally, see John Dalphin, *The Persistence of Social Inequality in America* (Cambridge, Mass.: Schenkman Books, 1987), pp. 87–90, and Joe R. Feagin, *Subordinating the Poor: Welfare and American Beliefs* (Englewood Cliffs, N.J.: Prentice-Hall, 1975), chap. 4.

27. Peterson, "Urban Underclass," p. 10.

28. I know this is a dramatic overstatement, increasingly belied by advances in health practices and medical care. I also know that it includes within it elderly who have accumulated means during their period of productivity to continue to support themselves. But it is generally true even as it stands, and the success of social security in diminishing poverty among the elderly is a widely accepted fact.

29. Philip E. Kaplan, "Which Is Worse: Stairs into Public Buildings or Federal Laws That Force Sensitivity?" *Arkansas Lawyer* 27 (1993): 39.

30. An example of such a society might be one that has achieved a state of mechanical solidarity. See Emile Durkheim, *The Division of Labor in Society*, trans. W. D. Halls (New York: Free Press, 1984).

31. Take, as an example, Manhattan. The residents of that island have no capac-

ity for food production and no internal source of the raw materials necessary for industrial production (including the land for extensive manufacturing facilities). Leaving aside the interdependencies created among themselves to sustain urban life, they are clearly dependent on others beyond their island in a way that creates significant vulnerabilities.

32. Of course modern society has also made possible enormous advances in a wide range of life's concerns. Modern medicine, communications, transportation, education, food production, and the like have improved our lives in many ways at the same time that they have multiplied dependencies and increased vulnerabilities. My point is not that we should necessarily reject, Luddite-like, any or all of these advances. Rather, it is that we need to acknowledge more frankly the proliferation of vulnerabilities as their underside. We also need to recognize that the benefits from these improvements are not evenly shared.

33. Anyone who denies the immutability of religious vulnerabilities need only recall the treatment of those who were "part Jewish" or of Jewish heritage in Nazi Germany.

34. Robert E. Goodin, *Protecting the Vulnerable: A Reanalysis of Our Social Responsibilities* (Chicago: University of Chicago Press, 1985), p. 192. See, generally, Adam Smith, *The Theory of Moral Sentiments*, ed. D. D. Raphael and A. L. Macfie (Oxford: Oxford University Press, 1976; reprint., Indianapolis: Liberty Fund, 1982), pt. II, sec. ii, chap. 3, discussing the role of the virtue of benevolence in contributing to the overall happiness of society.

35. Anthony Lewis, "Abroad at Home: Is Reality Dawning?" *New York Times*, July 31, 1995, p. A13.

36. Of course I rely on far more than law to protect me in each of these circumstances. The interest of those who provide goods and services in the profitability of their businesses is a powerful inducement. I also feel confidence as a result of repeat dealings with persons and institutions in circumstances that have served me well. Cf. Niklas Luhmann, *Trust and Power* (Chichester: Wiley, 1979), for an analysis of the function of trust in society and ways in which it develops. Law, however, does provide a minimal threshold of social protection. One only has to look at the pre-regulatory state of food production (e.g., Upton Sinclair, *The Jungle* [1905; reprint, New York: Albert & Charles Boni, 1928]) or securities regulation (e.g., Joel Seligman, *The Transformation of Wall Street* [Boston: Houghton Mifflin, 1982]) to realize this. In addition to the sanction it provides, law provides societal norms as to appropriate behavior. I have explored some of these arguments in my essays "Trust. Contract. Process," in *Progressive Corporate Law*, ed. Lawrence E. Mitchell (Boulder, Colo.: Westview Press, 1995), and Lawrence E. Mitchell, "Trust and the Overlapping Consensus," *Columbia Law Review* 94 (1994): 1918.

37. Some forms of minority status, that of sexual orientation, for example, remain unprotected, presumably because we have not yet achieved consensus on their legitimacy as vulnerabilities we are obligated to ameliorate.

38. By this I mean something like what Hannah Arendt described as man's lack of freedom because of his failure to recognize his subjection to necessity. Arendt, *The Human Condition* (Chicago: University of Chicago Press, 1958). Ernest Becker

similarly provides a psychologically based explanation for social inequalities and ritual grounded in the human denial of death, a concept that may be similar to the denial of vulnerability I am describing. Becker, *Escape from Evil* (New York: Free Press, 1975). See also Becker, *The Denial of Death* (New York: Free Press, 1973).

39. Kluegel and Smith, *Beliefs about Inequality*, pp. 22, 23.

40. Ibid., pp. 62, 64, 68.

41. See, e.g., Peter T. Kilborn, "How a Work Force Responds When Equal Rights Is a Goal," *New York Times*, March 12, 1991, p. A1; Susan Faludi, *Backlash: The Undeclared War against American Women* (New York: Crown, 1991).

42. Katherine S. Newman, *Declining Fortunes: The Withering of the American Dream* (New York: Basic Books, 1993), p. 24.

43. Ibid., pp. 28, 29.

44. Ibid., p. 44.

45. Ibid., p. 130.

46. Marc Cooper, "Montana's Mother of All Militias," *The Nation*, May 22, 1995, p. 716.

47. Valerie Alvord, "Terror in the Heartland: Bombing in Oklahoma City," *San Diego Union-Tribune*, May 1, 1995, p. A1 (quoting defense lawyer Peter Vance).

48. "Federal Critics Won't Back Violence," *Rocky Mountain News*, May 12, 1995, p. 51A.

49. See Mack Tanner, "Extreme Prejudice: How the Media Misrepresent the Militia Movement," *Reason*, July 1, 1995, which presents a sympathetic account of the militia movement in which a variety of fears are identified as motivating factors.

50. Cooper, "Montana's Mother," p. 716.

51. *The Points of Light Initiative: Community Service as National Policy* (Washington, D.C.: U.S. Government Printing Office, 1989).

Chapter Three

1. See *Meinhard v. Salmon*, 164 N.E. 545, 546 (N.Y. 1928), holding that partners in a business venture each owe the other fiduciary obligations because they enter into the relationship "for better or for worse."

2. Of course, there are marriages of convenience in which this assertion is not true. What I describe in the text I believe is our ideal model of marriage, and it is on that ideal that I shall focus.

3. Not all courts do this. Some jurisdictions treat the status of marriage in formation and, more frequently, dissolution, as contexts in which the bonds of trust and dependency have not yet been formed (or have been broken). I think this is wrong but will not examine the reasons here. Rather, I think the reasons will be made clear through my discussion of the cases.

4. Gail Frommer Brod, "Premarital Agreements and Gender Justice," *Yale Journal of Law and Feminism* 6 (1994): 248–49.

5. *DeLorean v. DeLorean*, 511 A.2d 1257, 1259 (N.J. Super. 1986).

6. Ibid., p. 1259.

7. Ibid.

8. Lynn A. Baker and Robert E. Emery, "When Every Relationship Is Above Average? Perceptions and Expectations of Divorce at the Time of Marriage," *Law and Human Behavior* 17 (1993): 439, 443, 447.

9. Brod, "Premarital Agreements," pp. 244–46.

10. Robin Gaby Fisher and Bev McCarron, "DeLorean," *Newark Star Ledger*, December 10, 1995, p. 1, sec. 1.

11. *Williams v. Williams*, 617 So. 2d 1029, 1030 (1992).

12. Mrs. Donahue's son also owned a small number of shares left to him by his father.

13. *Donahue v. Rodd Electrotype Company of New England*, 328 N.E. 2d 505 (Mass. 1975). Technically, the corporation was obligated only to repurchase the same proportion of her shares as it had Harry's.

14. *Ingle v. Glamore Motor Sales, Inc.*, 535 N.E. 2d 1311 (N.Y. 1989).

15. *Gallagher v. Lambert*, 549 N.E.2d 136 (N.Y. 1989). The facts surrounding Gallagher's firing were not established in litigation, but under the procedural posture of the case the court was required to accept them as he alleged them.

16. Alan Wolfe, *Whose Keeper? Social Science and Moral Obligation* (Berkeley: University of California Press, 1989).

17. According to a 1995 Korn/Ferry survey, more than 93 percent of the directors of major corporations are men, 7 percent are women, and 2 percent are black. Ralph D. Ward, *21st Century Board* (New York: Wiley, 1997), p. 155. See also Conference Board, *Membership and Organization of Corporate Boards*, Research Report no. 940 (New York, 1990). According to the federal Glass Ceiling Commission, 97 percent of senior managers of Fortune 500 firms are white men.

Chapter Four

1. This is controversial terminology. The controversy derives from the insights of critical, and especially feminist, scholars who argue that all law is public and that relegating certain kinds of laws, especially those governing personal relationships, to a "private" sphere devalues them and removes the subjection of weaker parties from public concern.

2. John E. Nowak and Ronald D. Rotunda, *Constitutional Law* (St. Paul: West, 1991), p. 528.

3. See, e.g., *In re Gault*, 387 U.S. 1, 26 (1967); *Bolling v. Sharpe*, 347 U.S. 497, 499 (1954); *Snyder v. Massachusetts*, 291 U.S. 97, 116 (1934).

4. I recognize that a branch of due process law dealing with what is commonly called "substantive due process" exists. See, e.g., *DeShaney v. Winnebago County Department of Social Services*, 489 U.S. 189 (1989). Analytically, however, this material is more closely related to equal protection analysis.

5. 416 U.S. 134 (1974).

6. These autonomy concerns are not unlimited. Theoretically, the concern for human autonomy could lead to required processes for every government interference with personal liberty and even a delegitimation of any government restrictions at all. Jerry L. Mashaw, Richard A. Merrill, and Peter M. Shane, *Administrative Law: The American Public Law System: Cases and Materials* (St. Paul: West, 1992), p. 272.

Although this may be true theoretically, and a danger inherent in an administrative approach to due process based on natural rights, these risks do not belie the fact that, regardless of the manner in which due process standards are applied, they find their philosophical origins in the importance of human autonomy.

7. 397 U.S. 254 (1970).

8. These facts are reported in *Kelly v. Wyman*, 294 F. Supp. 893, 899–900 (S.D.N.Y. 1968).

9. *Goldberg*, 397 U.S. at 264–65.

10. Ibid., pp. 268–69 n.7. See also Jerry L. Mashaw, "Organizing Adjudication: Reflections on the Prospects for Artisans in the Age of Robots," *UCLA Law Review* 39 (1992): 1055.

11. *Matthews v. Eldridge*, 424 U.S. 319 (1976).

12. Ibid., p. 350.

13. Ibid., p. 342.

14. Ibid., p. 334, citing *Cafeteria Workers v. McElroy*, 367 U.S. 886, 895 (1961).

15. While life and liberty are also covered by the due process clause, it is generally obvious when these are at issue. Moreover, in the criminal context in which they are most likely to arise, the full panoply of procedural protections for the defendant is generally not disputed.

16. *Cleveland Board of Education v. Loudermill*, 470 U.S. 532 (1985), holding that the employee was entitled to some pretermination opportunity to respond but a hearing only after termination and that a nine-month delay between termination and hearing was constitutionally permissible.

17. 430 U.S. 651 (1977).

18. Laurence H. Tribe, *American Constitutional Law*, 2d ed. (Mineola, N.Y.: Foundation Press, 1988), pp. 1436–37.

19. John Hart Ely, *Democracy and Distrust* (Cambridge: Harvard University Press, 1980), pp. 82–85.

20. Tribe, *American Constitutional Law*, pp. 1437–38. Equal autonomy appears, albeit in a more limited way, in Ely's theory, which sees the fundamental constitutional values as guaranteeing an equal opportunity for all citizens to participate in the political process. See, generally, Ely, *Democracy and Distrust*, chap. 4.

21. Tribe, *American Constitutional Law*, p. 1465.

22. *Nordlinger v. Hahn*, 505 U.S. 1 (1992).

23. Equal protection analysis contains three levels of review: rationality review, which is the most deferential; strict scrutiny review, which is not deferential; and heightened scrutiny review, which is moderately deferential, applying to classifications that, while not technically "suspect," are at least somewhat suspicious. See, generally, Nowak and Rotunda, *Constitutional Law*, § 14.3.

24. *Loving v. Virginia*, 388 U.S. 1 (1967).

25. Tribe, *American Constitutional Law*, pp. 1439.

26. Ibid., p. 1438.

27. Ibid., p. 1439 n.21.

28. Bruce A. Ackerman, "Beyond Carolene Products," *Harvard Law Review* 98 (1985): 719. Ackerman recognizes, as an important qualification to this, that minorities may not be denied the right to participate in the political process.

29. A discussion of political obligation generally, although relevant to this chapter in particular, is beyond the scope of this book.

30. See *City of Cleburne, Texas v. Cleburne Living Center, Inc.*, 473 U.S. 432, 440–43 (1985).

31. See, generally, Ely, *Democracy and Distrust*.

32. *United States v. Carolene Products* 304 U.S. 144, 152–53 n.4 (1938).

33. I think that it goes without saying that legislation that discriminated against Democrats or Republicans as such would be constitutionally impermissible.

34. *Davis v. Bandemer*, 478 U.S. 109 (1986).

35. There is also a historical and legal basis for the centrality of race to equal protection analysis in that the Fourteenth Amendment was a direct result of the Civil War and the conditions of slavery preceding it, as well as the fact that it was considered for passage roughly contemporaneously with the Thirteenth Amendment (prohibiting slavery) and the Fifteenth Amendment (ensuring voting rights regardless of race).

36. Donald E. Lively and Stephen Plass, "Equal Protection: The Jurisprudence of Denial and Evasion," *American University Law Review* 40 (1991): 1307, 1339–40, report this argument and are highly critical of it.

37. Tribe, *American Constitutional Law*, p. 1454; see also § 16–12.

38. For a general discussion, see *Cleburne*, 473 U.S. at 440. For a more detailed analysis, see *Loving v. Virginia*, 388 U.S. 1, 11 (1967) (discussing race); *Graham v. Richardson*, 403 U.S. 365, 372 (1971) (dealing with alienage); *Hirabayashi v. United States*, 320 U.S. 81, 100 (1943) (discussing national origin). Discrimination on the basis of alienage is permissible in certain circumstances. *Foley v. Connelie*, 435 U.S. 291 (1978).

39. *Craig v. Boren*, 429 U.S. 190, 197 (1976).

40. *United States v. Virginia*, 116 S. Ct. 2264, 2275 (1996).

41. Christine A. Littleton, "Reconstructing Sexual Equality," *California Law Review* 75 (1987): 1279–337.

42. 417 U.S. 484, 496–97 n.20 (1974).

43. *Romer v. Evans*, 116 S. Ct. 1620 (1996).

44. For a discussion of the way in which legal invalidation of discrimination helped lead to a significant public ethic of nondiscrimination, see Alexander M. Bickel, *The Least Dangerous Branch* (New Haven: Yale University Press, 1986).

45. In *Cleburne* the Court nonetheless struck down a zoning ordinance under rationality review in which the only conceivable reason for the legislation was to exclude mentally retarded persons from living in the area.

46. 42 U.S.C. § 12112(a) (1990).

47. 42 U.S.C. § 12112(b)(5)(A) (1990).

48. 42 U.S.C. § 12101(a)(9).

49. Not every instance of disability leads to a substantive result—that is, to employer-provided special facilities. The act instead provides the employer with an exception if she can prove that providing the requested facilities would cause her an "undue hardship." 42 U.S.C. § 12112(b)(5)(B).

50. 42 U.S.C. § 12101(a)(7). While the language of "discrete and insular mi-

nority" obviously is meant to invoke the highest classification of equal protection analysis, this legislative pronouncement is not binding upon the federal judiciary for constitutional purposes.

51. The act defines as a disability "(A) a physical or mental impairment that substantially limits one or more of the major life activities of such individual; (B) a record of such an impairment; or (C) being regarded as having such an impairment." 42 U.S.C. § 12102(2). This has been interpreted to include those who suffer from physical, mental, or psychological disorders or cosmetic disfigurement. R. Bales, "Libertarianism, Environmentalism, and Utilitarianism: An Examination of the Theoretical Frameworks for Enforcing Title I of the Americans with Disabilities Act," *Detroit College of Law Review* 1993: 1163–1220.

52. Patrick L. Vaccaro and Margaret R. Bryant, "Looking Back on the First Year of the Americans with Disabilities Act," *Legal Management* 13 (January–February 1994): 12.

Chapter Five

1. There are, of course, other political philosophies that are pursued in our intellectual debates. I will not discuss those on the libertarian side of the spectrum because what I have to say about liberalism applies, *a fortiori*, to libertarian approaches. Nor will I discuss philosophies on the communist side of the spectrum. My goal here is to develop a conception of fairness that is consistent with liberal philosophy and, in fact, must underlie it. Therefore, although I lean strongly toward communitarian goals, I see little point in critiquing philosophical approaches that I assume are not in play.

2. I shall be fairly inclusive in my understanding of liberal theory. In particular, I include the earlier ideas of Richard Posner, which, although they tend toward libertarianism, are ultimately based on a utilitarianism that may defensibly be described as liberal.

3. John Rawls, *A Theory of Justice* (Cambridge: Harvard University Press, Belknap Press, 1971), p. 98; see also John Rawls, *Political Liberalism* (New York: Columbia University Press, 1993), p. 7 n.5 (acknowledging the interpretive difficulties raised by the fact that the least advantaged members are designated "by description and not by a rigid designator"). See also Tom L. Beauchamp, "Distributive Justice and Difference Principle," in *John Rawls' Theory of Social Justice: An Introduction*, ed. H. Gene Blocker and Elizabeth H. Smith (Athens: Ohio University Press, 1980), pp. 132, 152–53; Thomas W. Pogge, *Realizing Rawls* (Ithaca: Cornell University Press, 1989), pp. 118–19, 203–4 (in each case discussing the difficulties in understanding Rawls's definition of the least advantaged group).

4. In describing the worst off as the poorest, I am taking some liberties with Rawls's work. He doesn't clearly identify those he believes to be the worst off.

5. Oddly, in light of the importance of fairness to his theory, Rawls never defines what he means by fairness but instead leaves it implicit as equal autonomy. He also never explores why fairness is important but leaves its importance assumed. Indeed, in arguing for a theory of justice as fairness, Rawls seems to be suggesting

the prior importance of fairness to justice and therefore that fairness is a more fundamental concern than justice. This makes the absence of a careful discussion of fairness itself all the more surprising.

6. Rawls, *Theory of Justice*, pp. 513–20, 142–45. See also John Rawls, "Justice as Fairness," *Philosophical Review* 67 (1958): 164–94. Rawls's notion of autonomy is complex, and my textual description is necessarily oversimplified given the nature of this book. I think that for present purposes, however, it is sufficient.

7. This in fact is his principle of fair play, which I discuss in more detail in note 10.

8. Rawls, *Theory of Justice*, p. 92.

9. Ibid., p. 546.

10. Rawls's starting point of autonomy also dooms his attempt to ground our motivation to fairness in a Humean account of sympathy. To acknowledge the constraint of the principle of fair play (which is a variant of fairness in real-world application in contrast to its presence in the original position), Rawls appears to argue, is to recognize the humanity of others. If I accept and acknowledge the burdens of the principle, I have necessarily recognized you as a person with interests and desires much like my own. Conversely, to deny the principle is to deny your equal humanity. "In the same way that, failing a special explanation, the criterion for the recognition of suffering is helping one who suffers, acknowledging the duty of fair play is a necessary part of the criterion for recognizing another as a person with similar interests and feelings as oneself." Rawls, "Justice as Fairness," p. 182. In short, sympathetic identification with others breeds fairness.

But this presents an internal contradiction in Rawls's theory, as Michael Sandel has clearly demonstrated, for Rawls's principles (and especially the difference principle) depend on communal understanding although his baseline is autonomy. As Sandel puts it, "What the bounds between persons confine is less the reach of our sentiments . . . than the reach of our understanding, of our cognitive access to others." *Liberalism and the Limits of Justice* (Cambridge: Cambridge University Press, 1982), p. 172. Because of the stark separation of the Rawlsian self, it cannot even have the understanding necessary to motivate the development of the shared ends necessary for the development of Rawls's principles of justice. So if sympathy (or something like it) is the motivating force, Rawls's moral anthropology must be wrong. If it is not, then the motivation to fairness is unclear. In the same way that Rawlsian people are unable to understand others, Rawls fails to perceive the necessary grounding in vulnerability that motivates the difference principle and, at bottom, our concern with fairness.

11. Although he claims not to be attempting to develop a comprehensive political theory.

12. Ronald Dworkin, "Will Clinton's Plan Be Fair?" *New York Review of Books*, January 13, 1994, pp. 20–25.

13. I recognize that this statement is not self-evident and that there are circumstances under which treating people equally would require a different distribution of pie. See, generally, Lani Guinier, "Groups, Representation, and Race-Conscious Districting: A Case of the Emperor's Clothes," *Texas Law Review* 71 (1993): 1589.

Dworkin makes a distinction between treating people equally and treating them as equals. To the extent that circumstances require some deviation from strict equality, he seems to account for this in his distinction between ambitions and circumstances, a distinction I will take up shortly.

14. Dworkin's argument is laid out in a series of articles, especially "What Is Equality? Part 1: Equality of Welfare," *Philosophy & Public Affairs* 10 (Summer 1981): 185–246; "What Is Equality? Part 2: Equality of Resources," *Philosophy & Public Affairs* 10 (Summer 1981): 283–345; "What Is Equality? Part 3: The Place of Liberty," *Iowa Law Review* 73 (1987): 1–54; and "What Is Equality? Part 4: Political Equality," *University of San Francisco Law Review* 22 (1987): 1–30.

15. There are limits to this, of course. Libertarian theories such as Robert Nozick's emphasize both the legitimacy of the way in which one acquires property and prohibits certain methods of acquisition, such as fraud and theft. Nozick, *Anarchy, State, and Utopia* (New York: Basic Books, 1974).

16. Dworkin spends no time on good brute luck. The real problem he addresses is compensating those who are disadvantaged, not disgorging from those who just get lucky.

17. Although he does not acknowledge it, this converts Dworkin's argument for equality of resources into an argument for equal opportunity, at least in part. This is because equalizing resources gives each person an equal opportunity to alter the effects of luck. Moreover, the failure to avail oneself of that opportunity resigns one to the consequences of one's choice. This observation is striking in light of the pains Dworkin takes to distinguish his theory from one of equal opportunity.

18. Dworkin is not unmindful that some types of brute luck are genetic or congenital. To solve this problem, he posits a hypothetical insurance market in which rates are established on the basis of what people would have paid to insure against such luck had they had the opportunity to do so.

19. I should note as an aside that, to argue this, Dworkin seems to collapse his distinction between welfare equality and resource equality. He now includes one's occupation in the bundle of resources to be equalized, so as to introduce a metric of choice between work and leisure, career satisfaction and dissatisfaction. Although he sidesteps the issue, it is hard to see how this avoids introducing a welfare component into what purports to be an argument purely about equal resources.

20. Of course, this assumes that the prodigy finds fulfillment in pursuing a career as a pianist and would rather do that than, say, be a professional tennis player but chooses the life of a pianist because it is all he feels he can do.

21. In making this argument, Dworkin tries very hard to distinguish his theory from what he describes as "starting-gate" theories of equal resources—that is, theories that provide equal resources as an initial matter but let laissez-faire market activities determine allocations thereafter. But such diachronic equality is possible only if there were equality of life span, with an ultimate reckoning up, so Dworkin's theory is, in practice, a starting-gate theory. Moreover, that there is not equality of life span is, of course, a matter of luck.

22. That Dworkin is centrally concerned with facilitating autonomy and free choice as the goals of equality (which is justice which is fairness) is made even

clearer by his later arguments. Dworkin shores up his choice of resource equality by demonstrating its integral relationship with a theory of liberty and the centrality of choice to both.

23. Richard A. Posner, "The Ethical and Political Basis of the Efficiency Norm in Common Law Adjudication," *Hofstra Law Review* 8 (1980): 487; Richard A. Posner, "Utilitarianism, Economics, and Legal Theory," *Journal of Legal Studies* 8 (1979): 103.

24. Posner, "Utilitarianism," p. 128.

25. Ibid.

26. Rawls, of course, would argue that Posner's theory does not fit with our considered intuitions and so would not in fact be the result of a fair process of social contracting. That may be so. But it does not refute the theoretical grounding of Posner's theory in one of consent, and that is all that is relevant for my purposes.

27. In this Posner is quite different from Rawls, whose entire project is to articulate a coherent theory to serve as an alternative to utilitarianism.

28. Posner, "Ethical and Political Basis of the Efficiency Norm," p. 487.

29. Ibid., pp. 489–90.

30. Ibid., pp. 490, 497.

31. Ibid., p. 492.

32. Dworkin has disputed this point but for reasons that are here unimportant. Ronald Dworkin, "Is Wealth a Value?" *Journal of Legal Studies* 9 (1980): 191–226.

33. Rawls's answer, although grounded in Kantian respect for personhood, is, as I have suggested, flawed by the self-interest in which his principles are grounded.

Chapter Six

1. Gay Block and Malka Drucker, *Rescuers: Portraits of Moral Courage in the Holocaust* (New York: Holmes & Meier, 1992), pp. 43–44.

2. Ibid., p. 198.

3. Will Kymlicka, *Contemporary Political Philosophy: An Introduction* (Oxford: Clarendon Press, 1990), pp. 50–55.

4. Brian Barry, *Theories of Justice* (Berkeley: University of California Press, 1989), p. 289.

5. Theodore Dreiser, *Sister Carrie* (New York: Library of America, 1987), pp. 8–9.

6. See Curtis L. Taylor, " ' Let It Go'; Genovese Case's Reopening Rankles," *Newsday*, July 23, 1995, p. A3 (providing a brief description of Genovese case).

7. One could fairly argue that compelling him to go to school is itself an interference with his autonomous choice. That is true, and so by isolating his choice to stay up late I am somewhat artificially limiting the discussion. The alternative would be to play out his series of choices to a point that may leave him uneducated and unemployable. It is this potential result that provides one of the reasons for the legal compulsion for him to attend school (and my insistence that he do so).

8. Gilligan is not so crude as to make the stark claim that I have implied in the text, that women's psychological development is inevitably different from that of men. Rather, she argues that looking at the psychological development of women

suggests different conclusions than the self-consciously Kantian analysis of Kohlberg and Jean Piaget and that men (as well as women) arguably can be conditioned
to consider moral problems differently given a particular environment and context.
See, generally, Carol Gilligan, *In a Different Voice: Psychological Theory and Women's
Development* (Cambridge: Harvard University Press, 1982).

9. Joel Feinberg, "Legal Paternalism," in *Paternalism*, ed. Rolf Sartorius (Minneapolis: University of Minnesota Press, 1983), pp. 3, 13.

10. Adam Smith, *The Theory of Moral Sentiments*, ed. D. D. Raphael and A. L.
Macfie (Oxford: Oxford University Press, 1976; reprint, Indianapolis: Liberty Fund,
1982), pt. I, sec. iii, chap. 1. Iris Murdoch, writing from a different philosophical
perspective, notes a similar phenomenon. *The Sovereignty of Good* (New York:
Schocken Books, 1971), p. 73.

11. The importance of perceiving relationships between ourselves and others to
our identification with, and willingness to cooperate with them, has been noted in
the context of modern game theory. See, e.g., Robert Sugden, "Thinking as a
Team: Towards an Explanation of Nonselfish Behavior," in *Altruism*, ed. Ellen
Frankel Paul, Fred D. Miller, Jr., and Jeffrey Paul (Cambridge: Cambridge University Press, 1993), pp. 69, 89 (players will cooperate to the extent that they recognize
one another as members of a team but will refuse to cooperate if they see each other
as different). See, generally, K. G. Binmore, *Playing Fair: Game Theory and the Social
Contract* (Cambridge: MIT Press, 1994).

12. Dirk Johnson, "Terror in Oklahoma," *New York Times*, April 25, 1995,
p. A20.

13. This is the essential point of Robert Goodin's argument deriving responsibility from vulnerability. See Robert E. Goodin, *Protecting the Vulnerable: A Reanalysis of Our Social Responsibilities* (Chicago: University of Chicago Press, 1985), pp. 4–
5, 36–37.

14. Here Goodin's distinction between the individual's responsibility to aid the
vulnerable and a collective responsibility to do so is instructive. Ibid., p. 138.

15. Mary Ann Glendon, *Rights Talk: The Impoverishment of Political Discourse*
(New York: Free Press, 1991), pp. 14, 73.

16. Philip E. Kaplan, "Which Is Worse: Stairs into Public Buildings or Federal
Laws That Force Sensitivity?" *Arkansas Lawyer* 27 (1993): 38–39.

17. Todd S. Purdum, "Terror in Oklahoma: The President," *New York Times*,
April 25, 1995, p. A19. Of course dehumanizing rhetoric is not the exclusive province of conservatives. Louis Farrakhan has called Judaism a "gutter religion," and
in a well-known incident a close aide called Jews the "bloodsuckers of the black
nation" who "crucified Jesus in a Kangaroo Court." Steven A. Holmes, "Farrakhan
Is Warned over Aide's Invective," *New York Times*, January 25, 1994, p. A12. In fact,
I suspect that we all, to some degree, engage in this practice from time to time.

18. See, e.g., transcripts of the Rush Limbaugh show for August 25, 1993, November 12, 1993, March 10, 1994, June 30, 1994, January 8, 1996, January 18, 1996,
January 25, 1996, and July 8, 1996, available on Nexis.

19. David Hume, *A Treatise of Human Nature*, ed. Ernest C. Mossner (London:
Penguin Books, 1969), bk. II, pt. I, sec. XI.

Chapter Seven

1. It is possible that you won't divide the resources equally but rather will fight over their distribution. If you prefer fighting to equality, then I concede that my story doesn't make a lot of sense.

2. Claude S. Fischer et al., *Inequality by Design: Cracking the Bell Curve Myth* (Princeton: Princeton University Press, 1996), p. 108.

3. I know perfectly well that you can take issue with my claim of irreversibility here. But I think that it is reasonably clear that only a major social upheaval will reverse our current reliance on government, and the failure of the Gingrich revolution provides some evidence that we are not ready to engage in that revolution. Nor, I suspect, are we ready to cast to the vagaries of others' good will the unfortunate and needy among us; in essence, we are not ready to adopt Posner's society, no matter how philosophically appealing some might find it. So, without engaging in more extended debate, I stand by my statement in the text, confident that, upon realistic and self-conscious reflection, most of you will agree.

4. For a discussion of the New Bedford rape case and whether bystanders may be held liable for failing to intervene, see Daniel B. Yeager, "A Radical Community of Aid: A Rejoinder to Opponents of Affirmative Duties to Help Strangers," *Washington University Law Quarterly* 71 (1993): 1. See also *Commonwealth v. Vieira*, 519 N.E. 2d 1320, 1321–23 (Mass. 1988) (recounting the facts in the New Bedford case).

5. *DeShaney v. Winnebago County Department of Social Services*, 489 U.S. 189 (1989).

6. In *DeShaney*, the Court did not address the argument of whether the state had violated its own statutes regarding "inherent rights" and the protection of abused or neglected children. 489 U.S. at 195 n. 2. The child's lawyer failed to raise that argument in the lower courts or in the petition for certiorari. Ibid. It is reasonable to infer from the lawyer's failure to raise this issue in the lower courts that it had little chance of success.

7. Rawls does describe the representative persons in the original position as heads of families. *A Theory of Justice* (Cambridge: Harvard University Press, Belknap Press, 1971), p. 128. This does not, however, address my question because he describes such a person's concern for his dependents as grounded in that representative person's interest, *not* the interests of his descendants. My question is designed to address the concerns of descendants directly as a separate matter.

8. Emotions are not universally absent from liberal theory. In Chapter Six we saw that two philosophers, Joel Feinberg and Brian Barry, have asked questions that were clearly prompted by the emotional instincts we discussed, and other liberal philosophers, including Rawls, have done the same. In general, however, they have not completely followed through on the implications of this realization. But see Robert E. Goodin, *Protecting the Vulnerable: A Reanalysis of Our Social Responsibilities* (Chicago: University of Chicago Press, 1985), who has, as I have, grounded an appreciation of vulnerability and a duty to help in our relationships with those closest to us, including our children.

9. U.S. Bureau of the Census, *Statistical Abstract of the United States* (Washington, D.C.: U.S. Government Printing Office, 1995), p. 470.

10. Children of well-to-do parents have distinct starting point advantages and you might expect to be successful enough that you would be willing to expose your children to the risk that you will fail in order to provide them with advantages if you succeed. My argument is not that you would definitely not make this choice; it is, rather, that if you are deciding on behalf of those vulnerable to you, you will do so more cautiously than if you are deciding solely for yourself.

Chapter Eight

1. 198 U.S. 45 (1905).

2. For a description of the difficult working conditions of New York bakers at the turn of the century, see Dorothee Schneider, "The German Bakers of New York City: Between Ethnic Particularism and Working-Class Consciousness," in *The Politics of Immigrant Workers: Labor Activism and Migration in the World Economy since 1830*, ed. Camille Guerin-Gonzales and Carl Strikwerd (New York: Holmes & Meier, 1993), pp. 49–69.

3. Fairly late in my writing I came across the thoughtful and, to my mind, compelling response to Charles A. Murray and Richard J. Herrnstein's *The Bell Curve: Intelligence and Class Structure in American Life* (New York: Free Press, 1994) by a group of sociologists at the University of California at Berkeley: Claude S. Fischer et al., *Inequality by Design: Cracking the Bell Curve Myth* (Princeton: Princeton University Press, 1996). Chapters 6 and 7 of that book detail many of the ways in which our social, political, and economic structures create precisely the intrinsic advantages and disadvantages that I have been at pains to illustrate.

4. Substantial evidence to support this point is provided in Albert Szymanski, *Class Structure: A Critical Perspective* (New York: Praeger Special Studies, 1983). See, generally, John Westergaard, *Who Gets What? The Hardening of Class Inequality in the Late Twentieth Century* (Oxford: Polity, 1995). Szymanksi provides considerable data showing the increasing impermeability of class lines in the United States, and in *Inequality by Design* (especially Chapter 5) Fischer et al. demonstrate the importance of starting position to the ultimate success of Americans.

5. Szymanski, *Class Structure*.

6. It is worth noting that economists find an increase of 5 to 15 percent in annual earnings associated with each additional year of formal schooling. *Economic Report of the President* (Washington, D.C.: U.S. Government Printing Office, 1996), p. 196.

7. Data come from the Population and Demographics subdirectory of the Directories and Reference Materials database on Westlaw.

8. Fischer et al., *Inequality by Design*, p. 132 (most recent data).

9. Prior to accepting the personal loan from former senator Bob Dole, Speaker Gingrich rejected the notion of paying the fine from his own pocket. See Robert Novak, "Newt Rejects Paying Fine from Own Pocket," *Chicago Sun-Times*, March 23, 1997, p. 39; John E. Yang, "Gingrich Pays Part of Penalty, Speaker

Sets $150,000 Limit on Borrowing from Dole," *Washington Post*, May 16, 1997, p. A1.

10. Fischer et al., *Inequality by Design*, clearly confirm this in their data.

11. Alexander M. Bickel, *The Least Dangerous Branch* (New Haven: Yale University Press, 1986), pp. 245–47.

12. See Lenore Walker, *The Battered Woman* (New York: Harper & Row, 1979); Richard A. Rosen, "On Self-Defense, Imminence, and Women Who Kill Their Batterers," *North Carolina Law Review* 71 (1993): 371.

13. *Katz v. Oak Industries, Inc.*, 508 A. 2d 873 (Del. Ch. 1986).

14. To be fair to Dworkin, in his world of equal resources, the Jimmys of the world would be less likely to exist—resource equality would improve the conditions of his choosing, so that the choice not to attend college would more appropriately be seen as an autonomous choice. Of course we are not likely to reach such a state of resource equality any time soon, and even if we did, I continue to have problems with Dworkin's focus on autonomy as I discussed in Chapters Five and Six. Rawls acknowledges the degree to which circumstances help to determine matters such as ambition and effort. John Rawls, *A Theory of Justice* (Cambridge: Harvard University Press, Belknap Press, 1971), pp. 301, 312.

15. Naomi R. Cahn, "The Looseness of Legal Language: The Reasonable Woman Standard in Theory and in Practice," *Cornell Law Review* 77 (1992): 1398.

16. For a discussion of these policies, see Chapter 7 of Fischer et al., *Inequality by Design*.

17. Ibid., pp. 126–28.

18. The fate of the former Soviet Union—the favorite poster child of those who make the incentives argument—is not a good counterexample. That society was not really a society that gave primacy to fairness as I understand it; it was a society in which socialism was enforced by a totalitarian government on a historically repressed population. The source of the ethic I am advocating would, I hope, be the American people themselves, and my project has been both to reveal the existence of the ethic and to suggest some ways of recapturing it.

19. I draw loosely for this point on G. A. Cohen, "Where the Action Is: On the Site of Distributive Justice," *Philosophy & Public Affairs* 26, no. 1 (1997): 3–30.

20. Posner, I think, is honest enough to have recognized this reality. His good society does have one unique common end, and his freedoms are geared toward the choice of the means for achieving it.

Chapter Nine

1. See the analogous statement by John Hart Ely, *Democracy and Distrust* (Cambridge: Harvard University Press, 1980), p. 79.

2. Some people, such as professional athletes, may be forced to play particular games to sustain themselves, but this competition is grounded in their choice to make a livelihood of their sport (assuming they have autonomously chosen to do so under good conditions of choice), with its rules and institutional structure.

3. John Rawls, "Justice as Fairness," *Philosophical Review* 67 (1958): 179.

4. While it is true that Rawls describes a hypothetical choice, not actual choice, in modeling justice as fairness, this seems to share the flaw of games in general in abstracting too greatly from reality. Imagine the bewildered response of a homeless person in Washington, D.C., when asked to acknowledge the principles of hypothetical choice in the original position.

5. John W. Chapman, "Justice and Fairness," in *Nomos VI: Justice*, ed. Carl J. Freidrich and John W. Chapman (New York: Atherton Books, 1963), p. 147.

6. Again, this is untrue in the context of tournament play. But as with a professional athlete, the tournament player chooses to enter the tournament, which in some relevant ways is structured as a metagame.

7. For a description of cooperative games, see the introduction to Jon Elster, ed., *Rational Choice* (New York: NYU Press, 1986), p. 8. I am also mindful that feminist psychology has suggested that girls often tend more than boys to play cooperative games. Carol Gilligan, *In a Different Voice: Psychological Theory and Women's Development* (Cambridge: Harvard University Press, 1982); Jean Piaget, *The Moral Judgment of the Child*, trans. Marjorie Gabain (New York: Free Press, 1966). While I will argue that the game theoretic approach to cooperative games does not provide an exception to my argument, the feminist view of cooperative games does. This is because of the common assumptions and the ethic of care that feminist psychology shares with my analysis in Chapters Five, Six, and Seven.

8. This is not to disregard the reality that the participants themselves want to win.

9. I assume this is our central goal for discussion purposes. It is beyond my task here to evaluate this claim.

10. Except, that is, in Posner's society.

11. This, of course, doesn't mean that there won't be inequalities, or that individual players will not be unhappy with the result. It simply means that, given the relative positions of the parties, they cannot change the result without disadvantaging others. This, in turn, requires them to justify their right to disadvantage others. It is at least in part on this basis that Rawls criticizes Braithwaite in a trenchant passage: "To each according to his threat advantage is hardly the principle of fairness." Rawls, "Justice as Fairness," p. 177 n.12.

12. See the discussion of this in Brian Barry, *Theories of Justice* (Berkeley: University of California Press, 1989).

13. R. B. Braithwaite, *Theory of Games as a Tool for the Moral Philosopher* (Cambridge: Cambridge University Press, 1955).

Chapter Ten

1. Lani Guinier, "Groups, Representation, and Race-Conscious Districting: A Case of the Emperor's Clothes," *Texas Law Review* 71 (1993): 1589.

2. My phrasing here should seem somewhat peculiar. If, as I have argued, we do not deserve our advantages—if there is something illegitimate about them—then we ought not to question giving them up. But I am trying to be practical. Our system has effectively defined these advantages as property rights, and so any redis-

tribution will indeed be seen as giving something up. In talking about it this way, I am in no way conceding the arguably implicit point that we are entitled to our advantages.

3. Kathleen A. Hughes, "Remember the Time 'Don't Fence Me In' Applied to Cowboys?" *Wall Street Journal*, March 17, 1997, p. 1. For an academic study of the gated community phenomenon supporting my point in the text, see also Edward J. Blakely and Mary Gail Snyder, *Fortress America: Gated and Walled Communities in the United States* (Cambridge: Lincoln Institute of Land Policy, 1995).

4. Dale Maharidge, "Walled Off," *Mother Jones* (November/December 1994), p. 26.

5. Robert Axelrod, *The Evolution of Cooperation* (New York: Basic Books, 1984).

6. Many of our laws, like those of contract, really do originate in custom, as legal scholars have widely observed.

7. Otto Keck develops an example structurally similar to that in the text in game theoretic terms in "The Information Dilemma: Private Information as a Cause of Transaction Failure in Markets, Regulation, Hierarchy and Politics," *Journal of Conflict Resolution* 31 (March 1987): 139–63. He demonstrates that self-interest is often better served by solving information dilemmas through cooperation rather than competition.

8. This phenomenon is one that generally is recognized in the economics literature. See, generally, Richard A. Brealey and Stuart C. Myers, *Principles of Corporate Finance*, 3d ed. (New York: McGraw-Hill, 1988), pp. 12–14. The phenomenon has been specifically analyzed in the automobile market. George Akerlof, "The Market for 'Lemons ': Quality Uncertainty and the Market Mechanism," *Quarterly Journal of Economics* 84 (August 1970): 488–500.

9. Of course there would still be the need for defense and foreign relations, which require the coordinating abilities of a central government.

10. Annette Baier, "Trust and Antitrust," *Ethics* 96 (1986): 231, 253–54.

11. It also appears to be the case that for persons with an individualistic orientation communication is necessary to permit trust to develop. Morton Deutsch, "Trust and Suspicion," *Journal of Conflict Resolution* 2 (1958): 265–75.

Bibliography

Books and Journal Articles

Ackerman, Bruce A. "Beyond Carolene Products." *Harvard Law Review* 98 (1985): 713–46.

Akerlof, George. "The Market for 'Lemons': Quality Uncertainty and the Market Mechanism." *Quarterly Journal of Economics* 84 (August 1970): 488–500.

American Law Institute. *Principles of Corporate Governance: Analysis and Recommendations*, vol. 1. St. Paul: American Law Institute, 1994.

Aquinas, Thomas. *The "Summa Theologica" of St. Thomas Aquinas.* Translated by Fathers of the English Dominican Province. London: Burns, Oates & Washburne, 1922.

Arendt, Hannah. *The Human Condition.* Chicago: University of Chicago Press, 1958.

Aristotle. *Nicomachean Ethics.* Translated by Terence Irwin. Indianapolis: Hackett, 1985.

———. *The Complete Works of Aristotle.* Edited by Jonathan Barnes. Vol. 2, *Politics.* Bollingen Series no. 71. Princeton: Princeton University Press, 1984.

———. *The Rhetoric of Aristotle.* Translated by Lane Cooper. New York: D. Appleton, 1932.

Arneson, Richard. "Liberalism, Distributive Subjectivism, and Equal Opportunity for Welfare." *Philosophy & Public Affairs* 19 (Spring 1990): 158–94.

Axelrod, Robert. *The Evolution of Cooperation.* New York: Basic Books, 1984.

Badwhar, Neera Kapur. "Altruism versus Self-Interest: Sometimes a False Dichotomy." In *Altruism,* edited by Ellen Frankel Paul, Fred D. Miller, and Jeffrey Paul, pp. 90–117. Cambridge: Cambridge University Press, 1993.

Baier, Annette. *Moral Prejudices.* Cambridge: Harvard University Press, 1994.

———. *A Progress of Sentiments: Reflections on Hume's Treatise.* Cambridge: Harvard University Press, 1991.

———. "Sustaining Trust." In *Tanner Lectures on Human Values,* vol. 13, edited by Grethe B. Peterson, pp. 136–74. Salt Lake City: University of Utah Press, 1992.

———. "Trust and Antitrust." *Ethics* 96 (January 1986): 231–60.

———. "Trust and Its Vulnerabilities." In *Tanner Lectures on Human Values,* vol. 13, edited by Grethe B. Peterson, pp. 107–36. Salt Lake City: University of Utah Press, 1992.

Bailyn, Bernard. *The Ideological Origins of the American Revolution*. Cambridge: Harvard University Press, Belknap Press, 1967.

Baker, Lynn A., and Robert E. Emery. "When Every Relationship Is Above Average? Perceptions and Expectations of Divorce at the Time of Marriage." *Law and Human Behavior* 17 (1993): 439–50.

Bales, R. "Libertarianism, Environmentalism, and Utilitarianism: An Examination of the Theoretical Frameworks for Enforcing Title I of the Americans with Disabilities Act." *Detroit College of Law Review* 1993: 1163–1220.

Barber, Bernard. *The Logic and Limits of Trust*. New Brunswick, N.J.: Rutgers University Press, 1983.

Barry, Brian. *Theories of Justice*. Berkeley: University of California Press, 1989.

Bateson, Patrick. "The Biological Evolution of Trust." In *Trust: Making and Breaking Cooperative Relations*, edited by Diego Gambetta, pp. 14–30. New York: Basil Blackwell, 1988.

Beauchamp, Tom L. "Distributive Justice and the Difference Principle." In *John Rawls' Theory of Social Justice: An Introduction*, edited by H. Gene Blocker and Elizabeth H. Smith, pp. 132–61. Athens: Ohio University Press, 1980.

Becker, Ernest. *The Denial of Death*. New York: Free Press, 1973.

———. *Escape from Evil*. New York: Free Press, 1975.

Becker, Lawrence C. *Reciprocity*. Chicago: University of Chicago Press, 1990.

Beeghley, Leonard. *The Structure of Social Stratification in the U.S.* Boston: Allyn & Bacon, 1996.

Bellah, Robert N., et al. *Habits of the Heart*. Berkeley: University of California Press, 1985.

Bennett, William J. *The Book of Virtues: A Treasury of Great Moral Stories*. New York: Simon & Schuster, 1993.

Berlin, Isaiah. *Two Concepts of Liberty*. Oxford: Clarendon Press, 1958.

Bickel, Alexander M. *The Least Dangerous Branch*. New Haven: Yale University Press, 1986.

Binmore, K. G. *Playing Fair: Game Theory and the Social Contract*. Cambridge: MIT Press, 1994.

Blakely, Edward J., and Mary Gail Snyder. *Fortress America: Gated and Walled Communities in the United States*. Cambridge, Mass.: Lincoln Institute of Land Policy, 1995.

Block, Gay, and Malka Drucker. *Rescuers: Portraits of Moral Courage in the Holocaust*. New York: Holmes & Meier, 1992.

Blum, Larry. "Deceiving, Hurting, and Using." In *Philosophy and Personal Relations: An Anglo-French Study*, edited by Alan Montefiore, pp. 34–61. Montreal: McGill-Queen's University Press, 1973.

Bobbio, Norberto. *Thomas Hobbes and the Natural Law Tradition*. Translated by Daniela Gobetti. Chicago: University of Chicago Press, 1993.

Bok, Derek. *The State of the Nation: Government and the Quest for a Better Society*. Cambridge: Harvard University Press, 1996.

Bok, Sissela. *Lying: Moral Choice in Public and Private Life.* New York: Pantheon Books, 1978.

Bork, Robert. "The Constitution, Original Intent, and Economic Rights." *San Diego Law Review* 23 (1986): 823–32.

Braithwaite, R. B. *Theory of Games as a Tool for the Moral Philosopher.* Cambridge: Cambridge University Press, 1955.

Brealey, Richard A., and Stewart C. Myers. *Principles of Corporate Finance.* 3d ed. New York: McGraw-Hill, 1988.

Brod, Gail Frommer. "Premarital Agreements and Gender Justice." *Yale Journal of Law and Feminism* 6 (1994): 229–95.

Brosnan, Donald F. "Virtue Ethics in a Perfectionist Theory of Law and Justice." *Cardozo Law Review* 11 (1989): 335–425.

Brook, J. A. "How to Treat Persons as Persons." In *Philosophy and Personal Relations: An Anglo-French Study*, edited by Alan Montefiore, pp. 62–82. Montreal: McGill-Queen's University Press, 1973.

Brown, Roger. *Social Psychology: The Second Edition.* New York: Free Press, 1986.

Cahn, Edmond. *The Sense of Injustice.* Bloomington: Indiana University Press, 1964.

Cahn, Naomi. "The Looseness of Legal Language: The Reasonable Woman Standard in Theory and in Practice." *Cornell Law Review* 77 (1992): 1398–1446.

Chapman, John W. "Justice and Fairness." In *Nomos VI: Justice*, edited by Carl J. Friedrich and John W. Chapman, pp. 147–69. New York: Atherton Books, 1963.

Cheit, Ross E. "Competing Models of Fair Representation: The Perfunctory Processing Cases." *Boston College Law Review* 24 (1982): 1–44.

Clark, Julia Penny. "The Duty of Fair Representation: A Theoretical Structure." *Texas Law Review* 51 (1973): 1119–78.

Coase, Ronald H. "The Problem of Social Cost." *Journal of Law and Economics* 3 (1960): 1–44.

Cohen, G. A. "Equality of What? On Welfare, Goods, and Capabilities." In *The Quality of Life*, edited by Martha C. Nussbaum and Amartya Sen, pp. 9–29. Oxford: Clarendon Press, 1993.

———. "On the Currency of Egalitarian Justice." *Ethics* 99 (July 1989): 906–44.

———. "Where the Action Is: On the Site of Distributive Justice." *Philosophy & Public Affairs* 26, no. 1 (1997): 3–30.

Coleman, Jules L. "The Normative Basis of Economic Analysis: A Critical Review of Richard Posner's 'The Economics of Justice.' " *Stanford Law Review* 34 (1982): 1105–31.

Corcoran, Kevin J. "The Relationship of Interpersonal Trust to Self-Disclosure When Confidentiality Is Assured." *Journal of Psychology* 122 (March 1988): 193–95.

Cox, Archibald. "The Duty of Fair Representation." *Villanova Law Review* 2 (1957): 151–77.

Dalphin, John. *The Persistence of Inequality in America.* Cambridge, Mass.: Schenkman Books, 1987.

Dasgupta, Partha. "Trust as Commodity." In *Trust: Making and Breaking Coopera-*

tive Relations, edited by Diego Gambetta, pp. 49–72. New York: Basil Blackwell, 1988.

Dash, Leon. *Rosa Lee: A Mother and Her Family in Urban America*. New York: Basic Books, 1996.

Deutsch, Morton, "Trust and Suspicion." *Journal of Conflict Resolution* 2 (1958): 265–79.

Dreiser, Theodore. *Sister Carrie*. New York: Library of America, 1987.

Dunn, John. "Trust and Political Agency." In *Interpreting Political Responsibility*, pp. 26–44. Princeton: Princeton University Press, 1990.

Durkheim, Emile. *The Division of Labor in Society*. Translated by W. D. Halls. New York: Free Press, 1984.

Dworkin, Gerald. "Paternalism." In *Paternalism*, edited by Rolf Sartorius, pp. 19–34. Minneapolis: University of Minnesota Press, 1983.

———. "Paternalism: Some Second Thoughts." In *Paternalism*, edited by Rolf Sartorius, pp. 105–11. Minneapolis: University of Minnesota Press, 1983.

Dworkin, Ronald. "Is Wealth a Value?" *Journal of Legal Studies* 9 (1980): 191–226.

———. "Liberalism." In *Public and Private Morality*, edited by Stuart Hampshire, pp. 113–43. Cambridge: Cambridge University Press, 1978.

———. *Life's Dominion*. New York: Knopf, 1993.

———. "What Is Equality? Part 1: Equality of Welfare." *Philosophy & Public Affairs* 10 (Summer 1981): 185–246.

———. "What Is Equality? Part 2: Equality of Resources." *Philosophy & Public Affairs* 10 (Summer 1981): 283–345.

———. "What Is Equality? Part 3: The Place of Liberty." *Iowa Law Review* 73 (1987): 1–54.

———. "What Is Equality? Part 4: Political Equality." *University of San Francisco Law Review* 22 (1987): 1–30.

———. "Will Clinton's Plan Be Fair?" *New York Review of Books*, January 13, 1994, pp. 20–25.

Elshtain, Jean Bethke. *Public Man, Private Woman: Women in Social and Political Thought*. Princeton: Princeton University Press, 1981.

Elster, Jon. *Nuts and Bolts for the Social Sciences*. Cambridge: Cambridge University Press, 1989.

———, ed. *Rational Choice*. New York: NYU Press, 1986.

Ely, John Hart. *Democracy and Distrust*. Cambridge: Harvard University Press, 1980.

Fallon, Richard H., Jr. "Two Senses of Autonomy." *Stanford Law Review* 46 (1994): 875–905.

Faludi, Susan. *Backlash: The Undeclared War against American Women*. New York: Crown, 1991.

Feagin, Joe R. *Subordinating the Poor: Welfare and American Beliefs*. Englewood Cliffs, N.J.: Prentice-Hall, 1975.

Feinberg, Joel. *Doing and Deserving*. Princeton: Princeton University Press, 1970.

———. "Legal Paternalism." In *Paternalism*, edited by Rolf Sartorius, pp. 3–18. Minneapolis: University of Minnesota Press, 1983.

———. "Noncoercive Exploitation." In *Paternalism*, edited by Rolf Sartorius, 201–35. Minneapolis: University of Minnesota Press, 1983.

Feinman, Jay M. "The Significance of Contract Theory." *University of Cincinnati Law Review* 58 (1990): 1283–318.

Finkin, Matthew W. "The Limits of Majority Rule in Collective Bargaining." *Minnesota Law Review* 64 (1980): 183–274.

Finnis, John. *Natural Law and Natural Rights*. Oxford: Clarendon Press, 1980.

Fischer, Claude S., et al. *Inequality by Design: Cracking the Bell Curve Myth*. Princeton: Princeton University Press, 1996.

Flaherty, Neva S. "Determining Standards for a Union's Duty of Fair Representation: The Case for Ordinary Negligence." *Cornell Law Review* 65 (1980): 634–58.

Fogelman, Eva. *Conscience and Courage: Rescuers of Jews during the Holocaust*. New York: Doubleday, 1994.

Frank, Robert. *Passions within Reason: The Strategic Role of the Emotions*. New York: Norton, 1988.

French, Peter. *Collective and Corporate Responsibility*. New York: Columbia University Press, 1984.

Fried, Charles. *Contract as Promise: A Theory of Contractual Obligation*. Cambridge: Harvard University Press, 1981.

Friedman, Lawrence M. *The Republic of Choice: Law, Authority, and Culture*. Cambridge: Harvard University Press, 1990.

Fukuyama, Francis. *Trust: The Social Virtues and the Creation of Prosperity*. New York: Free Press, 1995.

Fuller, Lon L. *The Morality of Law*. New Haven: Yale University Press, 1964.

———. "Two Principles of Human Association." In *Nomos XI: Voluntary Associations*, edited by J. Roland Pennock and John W. Chapman, pp. 3–23. New York: Atherton Press, 1969.

Gabriel, Ralph Henry. *The Course of American Democratic Thought*, 3d ed., with Robert H. Walker. New York: Greenwood Press, 1986.

Galston, Miriam. "Taking Aristotle Seriously: Republican-Oriented Legal Theory and the Moral Foundation of Deliberative Democracy." *California Law Review* 82 (1994): 331–99.

Galston, William A. *Liberal Purposes: Goods, Virtues, and Diversity in the Liberal State*. Cambridge: Cambridge University Press, 1991.

Gambetta, Diego. "Mafia: The Price of Distrust." In *Trust: Making and Breaking Cooperative Relations*, edited by Diego Gambetta, pp. 158–75. New York: Basil Blackwell, 1988.

Gardbaum, Stephen A. "Law, Politics, and the Claims of Community." *Michigan Law Review* 90 (1992): 685–760.

Gilligan, Carol. *In a Different Voice: Psychological Theory and Women's Development*. Cambridge: Harvard University Press, 1982.

Glendon, Mary Ann. *Rights Talk: The Impoverishment of Political Discourse*. New York: Free Press, 1991.

Goldberg, Michael J. "The Duty of Fair Representation: What the Courts Do in Fact." *Buffalo Law Review* 34 (1985): 89–171.

Good, David. "Individuals, Interpersonal Relations, and Trust." In *Trust: Making and Breaking Cooperative Relations*, edited by Diego Gambetta, pp. 31–48. New York: Basil Blackwell, 1988.

Goodin, Robert E. *Protecting the Vulnerable: A Reanalysis of Our Social Responsibilities.* Chicago: University of Chicago Press, 1985.

Gordon, David M. *Fat and Mean: The Corporate Squeeze of Working Americans and the Myth of Managerial "Downsizing."* New York: Free Press, Martin Kessler Books, 1996.

Grice, Paul. *Studies in the Way of Words.* Cambridge: Harvard University Press, 1989.

Guinier, Lani. "Groups, Representation, and Race-Conscious Districting: A Case of the Emperor's Clothes." *Texas Law Review* 71 (1993): 1589–1641.

Hallett, Garth L. *Christian Neighbor-Love: An Assessment of Six Rival Versions.* Washington, D.C.: Georgetown University Press, 1989.

Harper, Michael C., and Ira C. Lupu. "Fair Representation as Equal Protection." *Harvard Law Review* 98 (1985): 1212–83.

Hart, H.L.A. "Are There Any Natural Rights?" *Philosophical Review* 64 (1955): 175–91.

———. *The Concept of Law.* Oxford: Clarendon Press, 1961.

Held, Virginia. *Rights and Goods: Justifying Social Action.* Chicago: University of Chicago Press, 1989.

Hill, Thomas E., Jr. "The Importance of Autonomy." In *Women and Moral Theory*, edited by Eva Feder Kittay and Diana T. Meyers, pp. 129–38. Totowa, N.J.: Rowman & Littlefield, 1987.

Hirschman, Nancy J. *Rethinking Obligation: A Feminist Method for Political Theory.* Ithaca: Cornell University Press, 1992.

Hobbes, Thomas. *Leviathan.* Edited by Herbert W. Schneider. Indianapolis: Bobbs-Merrill, 1958.

Holmes, Oliver Wendell. "The Path of Law." *Harvard Law Review* 10 (1897): 457–77.

Hughes, M. W. "Our Concern with Others." In *Philosophy and Personal Relations: An Anglo-French Study*, edited by Alan Montefiore, pp. 83–112. Montreal: McGill-Queen's University Press, 1973.

Hume, David. *A Treatise of Human Nature.* Edited by Ernest C. Mossner. London: Penguin Books, 1969.

Irwin, T. H. "The Structure of Aristotelian Happiness." *Ethics* 101 (January 1991): 382–91.

Jencks, Christoper, and Kathryn Edin. "Do Poor Women Have a Right to Bear Children?" *American Prospect*, Winter 1995, pp. 43–52.

Jencks, Christopher, and Paul E. Peterson, eds. *The Urban Underclass.* Washington, D.C.: Brookings Institution, 1991.

Jencks, Christopher, et al. *Inequality: A Reassessment of the Effect of Family and Schooling in America.* New York: Basic Books, 1972.

Kahlenberg, Richard D. *The Remedy: Class, Race, and Affirmative Action.* New York: Basic Books, a New Republic Book, 1996.

Kahn, Jr., Peter H., and Elliot Turiel. "Children's Conceptions of Trust in the Context of Social Expectations." *Merrill-Palmer Quarterly* 34 (October 1988): 403–19.

Kant, Immanuel. *Critique of Practical Reason.* 3d ed. Translated by Lewis White Beck. New York: Macmillan, 1993.

———. *Foundations of the Metaphysics of Morals.* Translated by Lewis Beck White. New York: Macmillan, 1989.

———. *The Metaphysics of Morals.* Translated by Mary Gregor. Cambridge: Cambridge University Press, 1991.

Kaplan, Philip E. "Which Is Worse: Stairs into Public Buildings or Federal Laws That Force Sensitivity?" *Arkansas Lawyer* 27 (1993): 38–40.

Kavka, Gregory, S. *Hobbesian Moral and Political Theory.* Princeton: Princeton University Press, 1986.

Keck, Otto. "The Information Dilemma: Private Information as a Cause of Transaction Failure in Markets, Regulation, Hierarchy and Politics." *Journal of Conflict Resolution* 31 (March 1987): 139–63.

Keeton, W. Page, et al. *Prosser and Keeton on the Law of Torts.* 5th ed. St. Paul: West, 1984.

Kennedy, Duncan. "Distributive and Paternalistic Motives in Contract and Tort Law, with Special Reference to Compulsory Terms and Unequal Bargaining Power." *Maryland Law Review* 41 (1982): 563–658.

———. "Form and Substance in Private Law Adjudication." *Harvard Law Review* 89 (1976): 1685–1778.

Killilea, Alfred G. "Death and Democratic Theory: The Political Benefits of Vulnerability." *Midwest Quarterly* 25 (Spring 1984): 283–97.

King, Jonathan B. "Prisoner's Paradoxes." *Journal of Business Ethics* 7 (July 1988): 475–87.

Klare, Karl E. "The Quest for Industrial Democracy and the Struggle against Racism: Perspectives from Labor Law and Civil Rights Law." *Oregon Law Review* 61 (1982): 157–200.

Klosko, George. "Presumptive Benefit, Fairness, and Political Obligation." *Philosophy & Public Affairs* 16 (Summer 1987): 241–59.

———. "The Principle of Fairness and Political Obligation." *Ethics* 97 (January 1987): 353–62.

Kluegel, James R., and Eliot R. Smith. *Beliefs about Inequality: Americans' Views of What Is and What Ought To Be.* Hawthorne, N.Y.: De Gruyter, 1986.

Kohlberg, Lawrence. *The Philosophy of Moral Development.* San Francisco: Harper & Row, 1981.

Kosman, L. A. "Being Properly Affected: Virtues and Feelings in Aristotle's Ethics." In *Essays on Aristotle's Ethics*, edited by A. O. Rorty, pp. 103–16. Berkeley: University of California Press, 1980.

Kraut, Richard. *Aristotle on the Human Good.* Princeton: Princeton University Press, 1989.

Kymlicka, Will. *Contemporary Political Philosophy: An Introduction.* Oxford: Clarendon Press, 1990.

———. *Liberalism, Community, and Culture.* Oxford: Clarendon Press, 1989.

Leffler, Fredric C. "Piercing the Duty of Fair Representation: The Dichotomy between Negotiations and Grievance Handling." *University of Illinois Law Forum* 1979: 35–65.

Lichtenberg, Judith. "The Right, the All Right, and the Good." *Yale Law Journal* 92 (1983): 544–63.

Limbaugh, Rush H. *The Way Things Ought to Be.* New York: Pocket Books, 1992.

Lipset, Seymour Martin, and Reinhard Bendix. *Social Mobility in Industrial Society.* Berkeley: University of California Press, 1959.

Littleton, Christine A. "Reconstructing Sexual Equality." *California Law Review* 75 (1987): 1279–337.

Lively, Donald E., and Stephen Plass. "Equal Protection: The Jurisprudence of Denial and Evasion." *American University Law Review* 40 (1991): 1307–55.

Luban, David. "Freedom and Constraint in Legal Ethics: Some Mid-Course Corrections to Lawyers and Justice." *Maryland Law Review* 49 (1990): 424–62.

———. *Lawyers and Justice: An Ethical Study.* Princeton: Princeton University Press, 1988.

———. "The Quality of Justice," *Denver University Law Review* 66 (1989): 381–417.

Luhmann, Niklas. "Familiarity, Confidence, Trust: Problems and Alternatives." In *Trust: Making and Breaking Cooperative Relations*, edited by Diego Gambetta, pp. 94–107. New York: Basil Blackwell, 1988.

———. *Trust and Power.* Chichester: Wiley, 1979.

MacCallum, Gerald C., Jr. "Negative and Positive Freedom." In *Philosophy, Politics, and Society*, no. 4, edited by Peter Laslett, W. G. Runciman, and Quentin Skinner, pp. 174–93. Oxford: Basil Blackwell, 1972.

MacIntyre, Alasdair. *After Virtue: A Study in Moral Theory.* 2d ed. Notre Dame, Ind.: University of Notre Dame Press, 1984.

———. *Whose Justice? Which Rationality?* Notre Dame, Ind.: University of Notre Dame Press, 1988.

MacNeil, Ian R. *The New Social Contract: An Inquiry into Modern Contractual Relations.* New Haven: Yale University Press, 1980.

Margalit, Avishai. *The Decent Society.* Translated by Naomi Goldblum. Cambridge: Harvard University Press, 1996.

Marx, Karl. *Capital.* Edited by Frederick Engels. Translated by Samuel Moore and Edward Aveling. New York: International Publishers, 1967.

Mashaw, Jerry L. "Organizing Adjudication: Reflections on the Prospects for Artisans in the Age of Robots." *UCLA Law Review* 39 (1992): 1055–64.

Mashaw, Jerry L., Richard A. Merrill, and Peter M. Shane. *Administrative Law: The American Public Law System: Cases and Materials.* St. Paul: West, 1992.

Mayer, Susan E. "How Much Does a High School's Racial and Socioeconomic Mix Affect Graduation and Teenage Fertility Rates?" In *The Urban Underclass*, edited by Christoper Jencks and Paul E. Peterson. Washington, D.C.: Brookings Institution, 1991.

McClennen, Edward F. "Constitutional Choice: Rawls vs. Harsanyi." In *Philosophy in Economics*, vol. 16, edited by Joseph C. Pitt, pp. 93–109. University of Western Ontario Series in the Philosophy of Science. Dordrecht, Holland: D. Reidel, 1981.

McLeod, Jane D., and Ronald C. Kessler. "Socioeconomic Status Differences in

Vulnerability to Undesirable Life Events." *Journal of Health & Social Behavior* 31 (June 1990): 162–72.

Mill, John Stuart, *On Liberty*. Edited by David Spitz. New York: Norton, 1975.

Mitchell, Lawrence E. "The Death of Fiduciary Duty in Close Corporations." *University of Pennsylvania Law Review* 138 (1990): 1675–731.

———. "Fairness and Trust in Corporate Law." *Duke Law Journal* 43 (1993): 425–91.

———. "Trust and the Overlapping Consensus." *Columbia Law Review* 94 (1994): 1918–35.

———. "Trust. Contract. Process." In *Progressive Corporate Law*, edited by Lawrence E. Mitchell, pp. 185–217. Boulder, Colo.: Westview Press, 1995.

Moore, Stephen, and Dean Stansel. *Ending Corporate Welfare as We Know It*. Policy Analysis no. 225. Washington, D.C.: Cato Institute, 1995.

Murdoch, Iris. *The Sovereignty of Good*. New York: Schocken Books, 1971.

Newman, Katherine S. *Declining Fortunes: The Withering of the American Dream*. New York: Basic Books, 1993.

Nowak, John E. and Ronald D. Rotunda. *Constitutional Law*. St. Paul: West, 1991.

Nozick, Robert, *Anarchy, State, and Utopia*. New York: Basic Books, 1974.

O'Malley, William J. "Atticus Finch and the Family." *America*, May 11, 1991, pp. 509–11.

Outka, Gene H. *Agape: An Ethical Analysis*. New Haven: Yale University Press, 1972.

Palmer, John L., Timothy Smeeding, and Barbara Boyle Torrey, eds. *The Vulnerable*. Washington, D.C.: Urban Institute Press, 1988.

Pessen, Edward. *The Log Cabin Myth: The Social Backgrounds of the Presidents*. New Haven: Yale University Press, 1984.

Piaget, Jean. *The Moral Judgment of the Child*. Translated by Marjorie Gabain. New York: Free Press, 1966.

Pogge, Thomas W. *Realizing Rawls*. Ithaca: Cornell University Press, 1989.

Posner, Richard A. *The Economic Analysis of Law*. 4th ed. Boston: Little, Brown, 1992.

———. *The Economics of Justice*. Cambridge: Harvard University Press, 1981.

———. "The Ethical and Political Basis of the Efficiency Norm in Common Law Adjudication." *Hofstra Law Review* 8 (1980) 487–507.

———. *The Problems of Jurisprudence*. Cambridge: Harvard University Press, 1990.

———. "Utilitarianism, Economics, and Legal Theory." *Journal of Legal Studies* 8 (1979): 103–40.

Rakowski, Eric. *Equal Justice*. Oxford: Clarendon, 1991.

Rawls, John. "Fairness to Goodness." *Philosophical Review* 84 (1975): 536–54.

———. "Justice as Fairness." *Philosophical Review* 67 (1958) 164–94.

———. "Justice as Fairness: Political Not Metaphysical." *Philosophy & Public Affairs* 14 (Summer 1985): 223–51.

———. "Legal Obligation and the Duty of Fair Play." *Law and Philosophy: A Symposium*, edited by Sidney Hook, pp. 3–18. New York Institute of Philosophy no. 6. New York: NYU Press, 1964.

———. *Political Liberalism*. New York: Columbia University Press, 1993.

———. *A Theory of Justice*. Cambridge: Harvard University Press, Belknap Press, 1971.

Regan, Donald H. "Paternalism, Freedom, Identity, and Commitment." In *Paternalism*, edited by Rolf Sartorius, pp. 113–38. Minneapolis: University of Minnesota Press, 1983.

Roemer, John. "The Mismarriage of Bargaining Theory and Distributive Justice." *Ethics* 97 (October 1986): 88–110.

Rosen, Richard A. "On Self-Defense, Imminence, and Women Who Kill Their Batterers. *North Carolina Law Review* 71 (1993): 371.

Rosenfeld, Michel. "Contract and Justice: The Relation between Classical Contract Law and Social Contract Theory." *Iowa Law Review* 70 (1985): 769–900.

Ross, W. D. *The Right and the Good*. Oxford: Clarendon Press, 1930.

Rotter, J. B. "Interpersonal Trust, Trustworthiness and Gullibility." *American Psychologist* 35 (January 1980): 1–7.

Sandel, Michael J. *Liberalism and the Limits of Justice*. Cambridge: Cambridge University Press, 1982.

Scanlon, T. M. "The Significance of Choice." In *Tanner Lectures on Human Values*, vol. 8, edited by Sterling M. McMurrin, pp. 149–216. Salt Lake City: University of Utah Press, 1988.

Schneider, Dorothee. "The German Bakers of New York City: Between Ethnic Particularism and Working-Class Consciousness." In *The Politics of Immigrant Workers: Labor Activism and Migration in the World Economy since 1830*, edited by Camille Guerin-Gonzales and Carl Strikwerd, pp. 46–69. New York: Holmes & Meier, 1993.

Schwartz, Barry. *The Battle for Human Nature: Science, Morality, and Modern Life*. New York: Norton, 1986.

Schwartz, John E., and Thomas J. Volgy. *The Forgotten Americans*. New York: Norton, 1992.

Seligman, Joel. *The Transformation of Wall Street*. Boston: Houghton Mifflin, 1982.

Skocpol, Theda. "Targeting within Universalism: Politically Viable Policies to Combat Poverty in the United States." In *The Urban Underclass*, edited by Christopher Jencks and Paul Peterson, pp. 411–36. Washington, D.C.: Brookings Institution, 1991.

Sen, Amartya. "Equality of What?" In *Tanner Lectures on Human Values*, vol. 1, edited by Sterling M. McMurrin, pp. 195–220. Salt Lake City: University of Utah Press, 1980.

———. *Inequality Reexamined*. Cambridge: Harvard University Press, 1992.

———. "Well-Being, Agency and Freedom: The Dewey Lectures 1984." *Journal of Philosophy* 82 (April 1985): 169–221.

Simmons, A. John. "The Principle of Fair Play." *Philosophy & Public Affairs* 8 (Summer 1979): 307–37.

Sinclair, Upton. *The Jungle*. 1905. Reprint, New York: Albert & Charles Boni, 1928.

Slote, Michael. *Beyond Optimizing: A Study of Rational Choice*. Cambridge: Harvard University Press, 1989.

———. *Common-Sense Morality and Consequentialism*. London: Routledge, 1985.

Smith, Adam. *The Theory of Moral Sentiments.* Edited by D. D. Raphael and A. L. Macfie. Oxford: Oxford University Press, 1976. Reprint, Indianapolis: Liberty Fund, 1982.

Spalter-Roth, Roberta, et al. *Welfare That Works: The Working Lives of AFDC Recipients.* Washington, D.C.: Institute for Women's Policy Studies, 1995.

Steel, Jennifer L. "Interpersonal Correlates of Trust and Self-Disclosure." *Psychological Reports* 68 (June 1991 pt. 2): 1319–20.

Sugden, Robert. "Thinking as a Team: Towards an Explanation of Nonselfish Behavior." In *Altruism,* edited by Ellen Frankel Paul, Fred D. Miller, Jr., and Jeffrey Paul, pp. 69–89. Cambridge: Cambridge University Press, 1993.

Summers, Clyde W. "Effective Remedies for Employment Rights: Preliminary Guidelines and Proposals." *University of Pennsylvania Law Review* 141 (1992): 457–546.

———. "Individual Rights in Collective Agreements and Arbitration." *New York University Law Review* 37 (1962): 362–410.

Szymanski, Albert. *Class Structure: A Critical Perspective.* New York: Praeger Special Studies, 1983.

Taylor, Charles. *Sources of the Self: The Making of the Modern Identity.* Cambridge: Harvard University Press, 1989.

Tourangeau, Roger, Kenneth A. Rasiniski, and Roy D'Andrade. "Attitude Structure and Belief Accessibility." *Journal of Experimental Psychology* 27 (1991): 48–75.

Tribe, Laurence H. *American Constitutional Law.* 2d ed. Mineola, N.Y.: Foundation Press, 1988.

———. "The Puzzling Persistence of Process-Based Constitutional Theories." *Yale Law Journal* 89 (1980): 1063–80.

Tronto, Joan. "Beyond Gender Difference to a Theory of Care." *Signs* 12 (Summer 1987): 644–54.

Tuttle, Robert W. "The Fiduciary's Fiduciary: Legal Ethics in Fiduciary Representation." *Illinois Law Review* (1994): 889–954.

Unger, Roberto Mangabeira. *The Critical Legal Studies Movement.* Cambridge: Harvard University Press, 1986.

———. *Knowledge and Politics.* New York: Free Press, 1975.

Vaccaro, Patrick L., and Margaret R. Bryant. "Looking Back on the First Year of the Americans with Disabilities Act." *Legal Management* 13 (January-February 1994): 12.

VanderVelde, Lea S. "A Fair Process Model for the Union's Fair Representation Duty." *Minnesota Law Review* 67 (1983): 1079–1164.

Walker, Lenore. *The Battered Woman.* New York: Harper & Row, 1979.

Walzer, Michael. *Spheres of Justice: A Defense of Pluralism and Equality.* New York: Basic Books, 1983.

Ward, Ralph D. *21st Century Board.* New York: Wiley, 1997.

Wattenberg, Ben J. *Values Matter Most: How Republicans or Democrats or a Third Party Can Win and Renew the American Way of Life.* New York: Free Press, 1995.

Wechsler, Herbert. "Toward Neutral Principles of Constitutional Law." *Harvard Law Review* 73 (1959): 1–20.

West, Robin. "Jurisprudence and Gender." *University of Chicago Law Review* 55 (1988): 1–72.

———. "Toward an Abolitionist Interpretation of the Fourteenth Amendment." *West Virginia Law Review* 94 (1991): 111–55.

Wertenbaker, Thomas J. *The Puritan Oligarchy: The Founding of American Civilization.* New York: Scribner, 1947.

Westen, Peter. "The Empty Idea of Equality." *Harvard Law Review* 95 (1982): 537–96.

Westergaard, John. *Who Gets What? The Hardening of Class Inequality in the Late Twentieth Century.* Oxford: Polity, 1995.

Williams, Bernard. *Moral Luck: Philosophical Papers, 1973–1980.* Cambridge: Cambridge University Press, 1981.

Williamson, Oliver. "Calculativeness, Trust, and Economic Organization." *Journal of Law and Economics* 36 (1993): 453–86.

Wilson, James Q. *The Moral Sense.* New York: Free Press, 1993.

Wilson, John R. S. "In One Another's Power." *Ethics* 88 (July 1978): 299–315.

Wilson, William Julius. *The Truly Disadvantaged: The Inner City, the Underclass, and Public Policy.* Chicago: University of Chicago Press, 1987.

Wolfe, Alan. *Whose Keeper? Social Science and Moral Obligation.* Berkeley: University of California Press, 1989.

Wolgast, Elizabeth H. *Ethics of an Artificial Person: Lost Responsibility in Professions and Organizations.* Stanford: Stanford University Press, 1992.

———. *The Grammar of Justice.* Ithaca: Cornell University Press, 1987.

———. "Public Reason." *Columbia Law Review* 94 (1994): 1936–49.

Wright, Robert. *The Moral Animal: The New Science of Evolutionary Psychology.* New York: Pantheon Books, 1994.

Yeager, Daniel B. "A Radical Community of Aid: A Rejoinder to Opponents of Affirmative Duties to Help Strangers." *Washington University Law Quarterly* 71 (1993): 1–58.

Cases

Abbey v. Montedison S.P.A., 539 N.Y.S.2d 862 (Sup. Ct. 1989).

Arnett v. Kennedy, 461 U.S. 134 (1974).

Barton Brands, Ltd. v. National Labor Relations Board, 529 F.2d 793 (7th Cir. 1976).

Bolling v. Sharpe, 347 U.S. 497 (1954).

Bowers v. Hardwick, 478 U.S. 186 (1986).

Christian v. Christian, 365 N.E.2d 849 (N.Y. 1977).

Cleveland Board of Education v. Loudermill, 470 U.S. 532 (1985).

City of Cleburne, Texas v. Cleburne Living Center, Inc., 473 U.S. 432 (1985).

Conley v. Gibson, 355 U.S. 41 (1957).

Commonwealth v. Vieira, 519 N.E. 2d 1320 (Mass. 1988).

Coppage v. Kansas, 236 U.S. 1 (1915).

Craig v. Boren, 429 U.S. 190 (1976).

Cruzan v. Director Missouri Department of Health, 497 U.S. 261 (1990).

Davis v. Bandemer, 478 U.S. 109 (1986).

DeLorean v. DeLorean, 511 A.2d 1257 (N.J. Super. 1986).

Del Vecchio v. Del Vecchio, 143 So. 2d. 17 (Fla. 1962).

DeShaney v. Winnebago County Department of Social Services, 489 U.S. 189 (1989).

Doe v. Bolton, 410 U.S. 179 (1973).

Dominick v. Dominick, 463 N.E.2d 564 (Mass. App. 1984).

Donahue v. Rodd Electrotype Company of New England, 328 N.E. 2d 505 (1975).

Eisenstadt v. Baird, 405 U.S. 438 (1972).

Fleming v. Fleming, 406 N.E.2d 879 (Ill. App. Ct. 1980).

Foley v. Connelie, 435 U.S. 291 (1978).

Ford Motor Co. v. Huffman, 345 U.S. 330 (1953).

Gallagher v. Lambert, 549 N.E.2d 136 (N.Y. 1989).

In re *Gault*, 387 U.S. 1 (1967).

Geddes v. Anaconda Copper Mining Co., 245 F. 225 (9th Cir. 1917), *rev'd*, 254 U.S. 590 (1921).

Geduldig v. Aiello, 417 U.S. 484 (1974).

Goldberg v. Kelly, 397 U.S. 254 (1970).

Graham v. Richardson, 403 U.S. 365 (1971).

Hanson v. Denckla, 357 U.S. 235 (1958).

Hines v. Anchor Motor Freight, Inc., 424 U.S. 554 (1976).

Hirabayashi v. United States, 320 U.S. 81 (1943).

Humphrey v. Moore, 375 U.S. 335 (1964).

Ingle v. Glamore Motor Sales, Inc., 535 N.E. 2d 1311 (N.Y. 1989).

Ingraham v. Wright, 430 U.S. 651 (1977).

International Shoe Co. v. Washington, 326 U.S. 310 (1945).

Joseph v. Shell Oil Co., 482 A.2d 335 (Del. Ch. 1984).

Katz v. Oak Industries, Inc., 508 A. 2d 873 (Del. Ch. 1986).

Keeton v. Hustler Magazine, 465 U.S. 770 (1984).

Kelly v. Wyman, 294 F. Supp. 893 (S.D.N.Y. 1968).

Knoll v. Knoll, 671 P.2d 718 (Or. App. 1983).

Levine v. Levine, 436 N.E.2d 476 (N.Y. 1982).

Lochner v. New York, 198 U.S. 45 (1905).

Loving v. Virginia, 388 U.S. 1, 11 (1967)

Marciano v. Nakash, 535 A.2d 400 (Del. 1987).

In re *Marriage of Manzo*, 659 P.2d 669 (Colo. 1983).

In re *Marriage of Carlson*, 428 N.E.2d 1005 (Ill. App. Ct. 1981).

Matter of Estate of Crawford, 730 P.2d 675 (Wash. 1986).

Matter of Estate of Lesbock, 618 P.2d 683 (Colo.Ct. App. 1980).

Matter of Quinlan, 355 A.2d. 647 (N.J. 1976).

Matthews v. Eldridge, 424 U.S. 319 (1976).

Nordlinger v. Hahn, 505 U.S. 1 (1992).

Oberly v. Kirby, 592 A.2d 445 (Del. 1991).

Olmstead v. United States, 277 U.S. 438 (1928).

Pepper v. Litton, 308 U.S. 295 (1939).

Perkins v. Benguet Mining Co., 342 U.S. 437 (1952).

Planned Parenthood of Southeastern Pennsylvania v. Casey, 112 S. Ct. 2791 (1992).

Posner v. Posner, 233 So. 2d 381 (Fla. 1970).

Posner v. Posner, 257 So.2d 530 (Fla. 1972).
Romer v. Evans, 116 S. Ct. 1620 (1996).
Rush v. Savchuk, 444 U.S. 320 (1980).
Ryken v. Ryken, 461 N.W.2d 122 (S.D. 1990).
Shaffer v. Heitner, 433 U.S. 186 (1977).
Snyder v. Massachusetts, 291 U.S. 97 (1934).
Sogg v. Nevada State Bank, 832 P.2d 781 (Nev. 1992).
Stanley v. Georgia, 394 U.S. 557 (1969).
Steele v. Louisville & Nashville Railroad Co., 323 U.S. 192 (1944).
Syres v. Oil Workers Local 23, 350 U.S. 892 (1955).
Twin-Lick Oil Co. v. Marbury, 91 U.S. 587 (1875).
United States v. Carolene Products Co., 304 U.S. 144 (1938).
United States v. Virginia, 116 S. Ct. 2264 (1996).
Vaca v. Sipes, 386 U.S. 171 (1967).
Wallace Corp. v. National Labor Relations Board, 323 U.S. 248 (1944).
Williams v. Walker-Thomas Furniture Co., 350 F.2d 445 (D.C. Cir. 1965).
Williams v. Williams, 617 So. 2d 1029 (1992).
World-Wide Volkswagen Corp. v. Woodson, 444 U.S. 286 (1980).
Zablocki v. Redhail, 434 U.S. 374 (1978).
Zimmie v. Zimmie, 464 N.E.2d 142 (Ohio 1984).

Index

245

test of, 58–59
See also Unfairness
Fair play (Rawls), 185
Fault, 171n
Feinberg, Joel, 130–31
Fiduciary law, 58–59
Fischer, Claude, 165–66
Foreseeability concept, 179, 203
Formalism, 159
Freedom
in early American thought, 15–16
freedom of contract ideal, 59
under law, 52–53
in liberal notion of autonomy, 91
Rawls's condition of liberal, 100
See also Liberty
Fukuyama, Francis, 13
Fuller, Lon, 200

Gabriel, Ralph, 12, 13
Gallagher v. Lambert (1989), 68–69
Galston, William, 53, 91
Games
fairness in, 185–86
game theory, 191–93
Game theory, 191–93
See also Cooperation; Prisoner's dilemma
Geduldig v. Aiello (1974), 86
Gender, 86–87
Genovese, Kitty, 146
Gilligan, Carol, 128
Gingrich, Newt, 27, 167–68
Glendon, Mary Ann, 135
Goldberg v. Kelly (1970), 77–78, 87
Gordon, David, 33
Guinier, Lani, 194

Hart, H. L. A., 14
Hobbes, Thomas, 52
Homosexuality, 87
Hume, David, 125, 133–34

Incentives, 181–82
Independence
ideal of individual, 16–17
in liberal theory, 140–44
See also Autonomy; Dependence; Freedom; Self-reliance
Individual, the
in Kant's categorical imperative, 90

in liberal ideal, 90–91
in Rawls's original position, 96–97
Individualism
American ideal of, 12–17
with autonomy, 135
ethic of, 14–15
in liberal theory, 139–40, 144–49
myth of, 17–27, 29, 50–51
values of, 93
Inequality
of difference principle (Rawls), 97–99
as social condition, 41–43
in society, 181
Ingle v. Glamore Motor Sales, Inc. (1989), 66–68
Ingraham v. Wright (1977), 81–82
Institutions
based on autonomy, 134–35
lack of focus on vulnerabilities, 5
masking of vulnerabilities by, 44–46
Intuition
effect of liberal theory on, 132
in Rawls's social democracy theory, 119
testing, 120–22

Jackson, Andrew, 17
Jeffrey, Christina, 168
Jordan, Vernon, 22
Justice
distinct from fairness (Rawls), 186–87
due process social, 75–76

Kahlenberg, Richard, 164–65
Kaldor-Hicks efficiency, 113–14
Kant, Immanuel, 16, 50, 90
Kluegel, John, 25–26, 35
Kohlberg, Lawrence, 128
Kymlicka, Will, 53

Law
American belief in fundamental, 12–13
autonomy in some laws, 5, 50–53, 76–88
concealed in mutual dependency, 44–45
of corporations, 64–72
equal protection under, 82–88
fairness ideal in, 55–58
of fiduciary obligation, 55–64
function in society of, 52–53
with ideal of fairness, 56
in ideal of individualism, 12–13